Just the Facts, Ma'am

FIRST EDITION

Just the Facts, Ma'am:

The Authorized Biography of

Jack Webb

Creator of
Dragnet, Adam-12, and Emergency

by
Daniel Moyer and Eugene Alvarez

Writers Direct, Kaua'i, Hawaii

Just the Facts, Ma'am:
The Authorized Biography of Jack Webb
by Daniel Moyer and Eugene Alvarez

Published by:
Writers Direct
An Imprint of Titlewaves Publishing
Book Division of H&S Publishing
1351 Kuhio Highway Kapaa, Kaua'i, HI 96746 USA

Copyright © 1999 by Daniel Moyer and Eugene Alvarez
First Printing, 1999
Printed in the United States of America

Titlewaves and H&S Publishing's Cataloging-in-Publication Data
Moyer, Daniel and Alvarez, Eugene
Just the Facts, Ma'am: The Authorized Biography of Jack Webb / by Daniel Moyer and Eugene Alvarez
p.   cm.
Includes Index, Glossary, Chronology, Research Notes, and Bibliography
1. Webb, Jack, 1920-1982.
2. Motion pictures actors and actresses–United States–biography
3. Motion pictures producers and directors-United States–biography
I. Moyer, Daniel and Alvarez, Eugene,   II. Title.
LC-class.Sxx   1999
791.43'028'092-dc21   LC-card pending
ISBN: 1-57077-714-4

For additional copies of this book or quantity orders for special events or organizations, please contact:

TITLEWAVES / WRITERS DIRECT
H&S Publishing, Book Division
1351 Kuhio Highway • Kapaa, HI 96746

800-835-0583
808-822-7449 808-822-2312 fax
Email: hspub@hshawaii.com

Publisher's Dedication

The publisher wishes to dedicate this work to all those in law enforcement, entertainment, and military professions who are committed to improving people's lives. We know that your life's work is often challenging and we acknowledge and appreciate how much you give of yourselves so that others may benefit.

We would like to give special recognition to all those unknown heroes and heroines behind the scenes of notoriety who do so much good, though anonymous, work. We take this moment to sing your praise, so that you know that your service does not go unsung. And we take this moment to applaud you, so that you know that your contribution does not go unnoticed.

In keeping with Jack Webb's spirit of supporting law enforcement, this authorized biography was published and first released at the 6th Annual Los Angeles Police Department Historical Society's Jack Webb Awards on October 22, 1999 at the Beverly Hilton Hotel in Beverly Hills, California. Now everyone can keep a hard copy of "Just the Facts, Ma'am."

C O N T E N T S

Chapter   Page

CONTENTS

PREFACE & ACKNOWLEDGMENTS

Jack Webb was an entertainment giant, whose *Dragnet* and other creations have been known worldwide for nearly five decades. As a part of television's "Golden Years," his productions were in competition with *I Love Lucy*, *The Arthur Godfrey Show*, *All In The Family* and *Gunsmoke*. Most everyone over the age of forty will recognize *Dragnet's* famous four musical notes, and Webb's monotone, "My name's Friday! — I'm A Cop." Such "Dragnetese" as, "Just The Facts, Ma'am," remains a part of American pop culture today.

Many standard works concerning radio, motion pictures, and television were used for this biography that chronicled Webb's work; yet information conflicts were found. Another valuable source was *TV Guide*. However, other than for Mr. Webb, no attempt was made to list completely every film or broadcast in which Jack's associates and friends appeared.

In telling this story of Mr. Webb's life, the authors are grateful to the many persons who assisted us with this work. Among those recognized are Jack's school friends, and the men he served with in the World War II U. S. Army Air Corps. Had it not been for their recollections and respect for Jack, much of his early life and military experience would be lost. Those who knew Webb in radio, television, and motion pictures offered insight regarding Jack's personality and his projects, as did Stacy Webb, Jean Miles, Jackie Loughery, and Opal Webb.

Special recognition is extended to Messrs. Bob Forward and Herman S. Saunders, who intimately knew and worked with Jack. Both of these successful and talented gentlemen devoted much of their time to reading this work, offering suggestions and significant corrections and additions to the manuscript. Retired Detective Sergeant Dick Kalk of the Los Angeles Police Department, and the Director of its Historical Society, deserves special mention for offering his expertise and LAPD historical assistance. We are further indebted to the wise direction afforded us by Attorney Thomas H. Greenwald and the encouragement of our publisher, notably Rob Sanford. Firelands Photography arranged the reproduction of photographs.

Equally deserving of our gratitude are the courteous and assisting persons acknowledged below. All of them have fascinating stories to tell regarding Jack, in addition to their professional and personal lives. Professional and other titles have been omitted in this truly diverse group to avoid any error or omission. Our fervent and sincere gratitude are extended to all.

Ken Ackerman, Mr. & Mrs. Charles B. Anderson, Jim Armamino, Dan Aykroyd, Marion Fitzsimmons [Barnes], Harry Bartell, Walter Bagley, Dick Belding, Mel Bishop, Dorothy Randles [Blaine], Eddie Brandt's Saturday Matinee, Lisa Webb [Breen], Pierce Brooks, Michael Burns, Frank Comstock, Dan Cooke, Nicole Covert, Maggie Crumrine, Martin Fentress, Ella Fitzgerald, Bob Forward, Jay Fox, Mary Galliger, Al Gentry, Joe Gilmore, Hal Graham, Tom Greenwald, Joseph C. Holmes, Dick Kalk, Roy Knight, Clem Koselke, Lloyd Lavine, Bob Leeds, Janet Leigh, Lenore Levine, Marco Lopez, Charles A. Love, Margaret MacGregor, Henry McAnn, Richard Mample, Billy May, Jean Miles, Mr. & Mrs. Donald T. Miller, Jim Moore, Judy Moyer, Jerry Nailor, Mr. & Mrs. Harold Nottke, William O'Connell, Dave Paulsen, Harry Reder, Ann Rodgers, Ronald F. Rodgers, Jane Gibson [Rowe], Herman S. & Kae Saunders, Carl Sberna, Joe Schlecter, Jackie Loughery [Webb] Schwietzer, Ken Sealy, Frank Sinatra, Jr., Mr. & Mrs. Gus Stamos, George Stevens, Jr., John C. Stevens III, Bobby Troup, Julie London [Webb] Troup, Dick "Moe" Turner, Douglas L. Waide, Mr. & Mrs. Ed Walker, Len Wayland, Opal Webb, Stacy Webb, Peggy Webber, Lloyd W. Whitlow, Fred Yanari.

It is regrettable that Stacy Webb was denied the opportunity to assist completing her father's biography. However, many of her Mark VII Limited collection photographs are used in this work, and we have included a prologue first written by Stacy — we dedicate this book in memory of her. The authors accept full responsibility for any errors, whether of omission or commission, which are ours alone.

Daniel Moyer
Eugene Alvarez

Filming *Dragnet 1966* at Parker Center.

Courtesy of Jack Webb Archives

PROLOGUE

By Stacy Webb

Jack Webb achieved fame as a film and television actor, producer, and director who created the most popular crime drama of its time. His fast-paced and long-running *Dragnet* set standards and formats that influence television and motion picture films today.

Until *Dragnet,* police and detective stories mostly concerned commercial, glamorized characters, about whom real-life officers frequently laughed. However, Webb's contribution to police work was that his stories addressed the daily trials and tribulations of an actual large city department, from whose records he used true-to-life accounts. Authenticity was paramount, and Webb scrutinized every *Dragnet* program. In some episodes controversial subjects for the post World War II era and the 1950's were approached, which became commonplace in later years.

Jack insisted there must be some humor in each story to dramatize the in-the-trenches lifestyle of police officers that he wanted to convey. That humor was accomplished at times by episode content, and "Sergeant Joe Friday's" associates and partners, notably officers "Frank Smith" and "Bill Gannon." The Webb formula also encouraged audiences to believe the persons portrayed in his productions were genuine and that their stories appear true.

Jack was a film pioneer whose style and methods were copied by his colleagues, and taught in university cinema classes. His quest for realism and perfection is near legendary. Whenever possible, Webb filmed on a precise location. The Los Angeles City Hall and Parker Center were a major part of *Dragnet.* If necessary, for accuracy Webb resorted to set scale City Hall and Parker Center interiors, offered by his creative Set Decorator, John Sturtevant. If for any reason the sets did not reproduce an accurate image, Jack ordered his staff to reconstruct them.

Webb's attention for film accuracy included dispatching a production team to the Parris Island, South Carolina, Marine Corps Recruit Depot to record voice and training sounds, and to photograph military barracks which were meticulously recreated for *The D.I.* He otherwise demanded that 1920's cigar bands be duplicated when a smoking scene was filmed for *Pete Kelly's Blues*, and his fanatical attention to detail carried over into his personal life, too. For his Encino, California, home Jack desired a kidney shaped swimming pool, but somehow the contractor misunderstood his instructions and installed a rectangular Olympic-sized pool. Webb ordered the beautiful pool to be completely removed, and a kidney-shaped one constructed to his specifications — exact to the inch.

Jack Webb's life was his work. He was demanding on the set, but he did not ask any crew or staff members to perform tasks he would not do himself. He hired and was surrounded by excellent talent, and his Mark

VII Limited employees were well paid. Loyalty was another important trait practiced in his professional life. Actress Peggy Webber found that, "Jack was the most loyal person in show business. He said that whatever he did we were going to be a part of it. He was always true to his people." This was evident over the years in his numerous productions, as he continued employing familiar actors and film crews in his diverse shows. Yet, new talent was afforded the chance to perform, too.

My sincere gratitude is extended to my dear friend and associate Dan Moyer, who was the driving force behind this book. Dan, and the recollections and cooperation of many persons in Jack's life have significantly contributed to this work, and I am grateful to each and every one of them. Gene Alvarez joined us as a writer and contributed additional research. The three of us offer this authorized and authentic true-to-life story of my wonderful dad — Jack Webb.

Stacy Webb (1996)

A light moment on the set of *Dragnet 1967* with Chief of Detectives, Thad Brown(l), Jack Webb, and Inspector Ed Walker (r)

Courtesy of Jack Webb Archives

"We were unbelievably poor."

Who was Jack Webb? What are the real-life facts of this "Just the Facts, Ma'am" man? Did he live both a charmed and haunted life? For all the detective work he portrayed, why was he unable to uncover his biological father's identity? Did his absent, unknown dad contribute to both his childhood poverty and his obsession for focusing on the facts and authenticity in film making?

What drove the creative mind of this man who pioneered many filming techniques (including "teleprompter" dialogue use, close-up shots, and vehicle "Tow Shots") that revolutionized the industry and are taught in university cinema classes today? What pulled at the heartstrings of the man whose first wife was the famous singer/actress Julie London and third wife was the first Miss USA, Jackie Loughery? What was it about Jack Webb that made him one of the most popular male television actors through the 1950's, appearing on the covers of *Time, TV Guide*, and other magazines?

What of Jack's spirit can be found in his portrayal of police, government, and paramedics in *Dragnet, Adam-12, Emergency*, and others – portrayals so authentic that many episodes are still used today for training purposes? What was it about this man's achievements, both personal and professional, that compelled the Television Academy Of Arts And Sciences to give a "Lifetime Achievement Award" to him and induct him into their exclusive Hall Of Fame in 1993? And why does the Los Angeles Police Department Historical Society hold an event every year in his honor called the Jack Webb Awards to recognize outstanding community and business leaders in law enforcement and children's issues?

We discovered the answers to these questions and more in writing his biography. We are happy to share these discoveries with you in pictures and text, in true Jack Webb style, to give you the facts so you, too, can discover the truth behind this fascinating and complex man's mind, heart, and spirit.

Jack Randolph Webb was born in Santa Monica, California, on April 2, 1920. His mother joked that the baby narrowly missed the "day of fools" by only hours, but in later years her only child demonstrated to the world, that if there was ever a true-to-life Horatio Alger — it was Jack Webb.

When Jack was born into the prosperous "Roaring Twenties," World War I had recently ended and Americans boasted, "My God, how the money rolls in!" The decade is alternately recalled as one of Prohibition, "boot-leg" liquor, alarming crime, jazz music, "flappers," and Ku Klux Klan lynchings. Sports, national, and other luminaries of the day included such celebrities as Bobby Jones, Babe Ruth, Jack Dempsey, George Gershwin, and Charles A. Lindbergh. With the ratification of the 19th Amendment to the U.S. Constitution in 1920, women were guaranteed the right to vote. The 1929 Wall Street Crash and an ensuing Depression ended "The Jazz Age." President Franklin D. Roosevelt's "New Deal" affected everyone's life in the 1930's under the shadow of a growing nationalism in Asia and Europe that would produce World War II. The

American economy would not rebound until the 1940's. This socio-economic climate was the environment of Jack Webb's childhood.

Significantly, radio in the 1920's and 1930's became a necessary household appliance rather than a mere novelty item. Radio pioneer David Sarnoff by then had envisioned a broadcasting industry with stations serving a "radio music box" to be sold on the commercial market to a nation of potential users. The Radio Corporation of America (RCA) was formed in 1919, and on November 22, 1920, Pittsburgh station KDKA became the first commercially licensed station to go on the air. Five hundred stations were operating by 1922 and, in 1930, approximately 13.7 million sets were entertaining and enlightening people in the United States. The medium brought the World Series and international events into thousands of homes, chronicled the Depression, and the onset of World War II. However, for two destitute women and a sickly boy living amidst poverty in a run-down Los Angeles inner city neighborhood, their personal survival and future was a greater concern.

As an only child, Jack's childhood typically would have been profusely recorded; however, such was not the case. Several aspects of his infancy and his childhood are at best unclear. For example, he listed his birthplace as Santa Monica, California; yet Los Angeles Unified School District records state that Jack was born in Ocean Park, California, a part of Santa Monica.

Little is known about Jack's father. Webb's former wife, Jackie Loughery recalled that Webb's Uncle Frank Smith mentioned a Samuel Chester Webb, who may have been a Jewish trumpet player in a San Francisco jazz band, but records were not discovered to confirm this relation. School mates Gus Stamos and Roy Knight remember Jack telling them that his father may have been part American Indian and part Jewish, but that his mother — who Webb mostly resembled — and his grandmother

Jack's early home: The St. Regis Apartments at 237 South Flower St. located in the shadow of the Los Angeles City Hall, a future Dragnet icon.

Cosmopolitan Magazine —
Courtesy of Jack Webb Archives

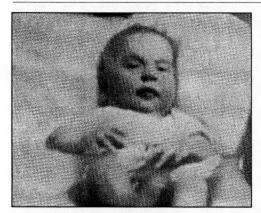

Webb stated, "This first baby picture of me made no wire service."

Courtesy of Jack Webb Archives

were not of the Jewish faith. Jack did not openly practice Judaism or any other religious doctrine, but his love for God was evident in his many motion picture and television films. Others record that Webb's mother and father were briefly married or were wed for only two years. One undocumented story is that his father may have been a sailor living in San Pedro. However, we know that Samuel Webb was never seen by Jack, Roy, or Gus who observed, "His father is a very dark cloud."

Having an unknown father haunted Jack his entire life. He usually avoided the subject, but in a 1959 interview he identified his father as an "Egyptologist" for the Smithsonian Institute, who possibly served as an officer in World War I. Classmate Charles Anderson visited Washington, D. C. in 1939 and inquired of Webb's father at the Smithsonian at Jack's request. No records were discovered regarding a "Captain [Samuel Chester] Webb" and Anderson reported that "Jack was a little disappointed when I couldn't find out anything." In all likelihood, Jack Webb fabricated the 1959 Smithsonian story to protect his fame, as he may have been an illegitimately-conceived child. "I never knew my father," Jack recalled, and "he never got in touch with me." No photographs of Samuel Webb were in the household as the boy grew up.

Jack's mother, Margaret "Maggie" Smith-Webb, was a destitute Idaho-born Irish-Catholic woman, whose father is believed to have been a surveyor for the Santa Fe Railroad. She once confided to a friend that she married Samuel in San Pedro, California, but there is no proof if the remark is true. Moreover, Los Angeles school records list her as "Margaret Spencer," suggesting another brief marriage or creating additional suspicion regarding Jack's legitimate birth. Strangely, no birth certificate was discovered in Los Angeles County or California state records. Apparently, Jack was born in a private residence, a common occurrence in the United States until the end of World War II.

Within two years of Jack's birth, Margaret, now penniless and abandoned, was joined by her mother Emma ("Gram") to help raise the child. Records also suggest that Margaret (or the three of them) briefly lived in various San Francisco apartments in 1920 and 1921 after leaving Santa Monica. Nevertheless, they quickly exited the Bay City for Los Angeles, where the women rented a single room in the stucco St. Regis Apartments at Third and 237 South Flower

Streets. Jack recalled the neighborhood as a part of Los Angeles' Bunker Hill area, which was so socially and economically depressed that many considered the area "too poor to steal in." Ironically, the St. Regis Apartments were in the shadow of the Los Angeles City Hall, an icon identified in later years with Webb and his most memorable creation — *Dragnet*.

Jack confided during his adult life to several persons that he spent some time in and out of juvenile halls and foster homes between the ages of two and eight. However, his home for 17 years was mostly Apartment 339, a third-floor single rear room facing an area littered with garbage cans and trash. From the refuse, the destitute boy scavenged what was, according to Jack, "a million dollars worth of property," including a lamp shade, a red pennant, a chalk Kewpie doll minus one leg, a mah-jong game, and discarded magazines that he read voraciously.

Grandmother Emma S. Smith mostly raised the child, as "Maggie" (Jack seldom called her "mother" or "mom") was in and out of the boy's life due to her work schedule or problems with alcohol. Some suggest, though without proof, that "Gram" was a musician and possessed a law degree. In any case, "Gram" had a passion for words, taught Jack to read, and cultivated his love for reading. The boy's first reader was a Morton's salt box. His grandmother later encouraged young Jack to read newspapers and explain to her what he had read. The child became a frequent library patron and the works of Mark Twain and Robert Louis Stevenson were among his favorite early books.

Jack was fascinated when he witnessed Henry Clive paint several Los Angeles library murals, an event which prompted the two women in his life to encourage the boy's curiosity in acting and art. "Gram" supplied Jack every tool of the trade that she could afford, so he always had paintbrushes, crayons, and drawing paper to facilitate his budding creativity. The small family income was derived from the two women working in cafeterias and department stores. "Gram" later managed downtown Los Angeles rooming and apartment houses on Third and Flower, and Eighth and San Pedro Streets.

As an asthmatic child, Jack was frequently carried by the two women up to their third floor apartment. "Maggie" and "Gram" would often sit up with the boy at night to burn asthmatic powders to help him breathe more easily. Webb almost died of asthma repeatedly at four, six, and eleven years of age. Double pneumonia left him with bronchitis. Climbing the Flower Street hill was a physical challenge for him, even "painfully tough for a Model T [automobile] or the iceman's horse," as he would later recall. However, by age 10, Webb climbed the hill alone and by age 18, most of his asthma was gone. As an adult who occasionally had twinges of asthma, Jack never forgot the "terribly painful memories of the many attacks I had years ago."

The boy was frequently at home alone. As an asthmatic, he could not keep pace with the neighborhood's healthy kids. Considering the vicinity where he lived, Jack could have easily joined a street gang. Webb recalled that if he had become a gang member, he would have been in fights much of the time: "I am still not quite sure what kept me out of trouble," since "we lived in a cheap neighborhood." His Buster Brown-styled haircut labeled him a "sissy" and he was possibly considered a "mama's boy" with noticeably large ears. Webb

Cosmopolitan Magazine —
Courtesy of Jack Webb Archives

The St. Regis' back alley which Jack called "my backyard."

later recalled that his famous modified crew haircut may have been a rebellious statement "against the long bangs I had as a boy."

Jack Webb never forgot that his family lived on relief in Los Angeles and were "unbelievably poor." From his childhood, he remembered "the sacks labeled 'BEANS' and the sacks labeled 'RICE,' and the day-old bread the county gave out." He received wilted carrots and beets in brown paper bags doled out by relief agencies and patched his shoe soles with folded covers of *National Geographic* magazines. "When we were lucky enough to have a cake [block] of ice on a hot day, my grandmother wrapped it in newspapers to make it last longer." Newspapers were also used for insulation to keep "Gram" warm at night. Welfare clothing included blue denim work shirts and overalls donated by the county for the destitute. Webb recalled, "It seemed to me they had the same stigma as a striped suit in a prison yard. I hated to be seen in those county clothes." Jack and his friends often traded the garments for more stylish wear at a five-to-one-ratio in second-hand clothing stores.

Webb's childhood and teen years included relatives, friends, and persons whose character or names were later used in his television and motion picture productions. One St. Regis Apartments tenant who impressed the boy was an itinerant musician who played jazz records on a windup victrola phonograph machine and loaned Jack his cornet to play. "I couldn't play, but I used to hold the cornet and wish that I could make the sounds that came out of that victrola."

When the musician vacated the apartments, he presented the boy Bix Beiderbecke's *At The Jazz Band Ball* recording, which Jack treasured his entire life. Beiderbecke (1903-1931) surely inspired Webb later to create on radio, television, and film *Pete Kelly's Blues*, whose story centered on a cornet-playing jazz musician. Beiderbecke is also credited as the inspiration for the 1950 movie *Young Man With A Horn*. Still another character in *Pete Kelly's Blues* was derived from a St. Regis Apartments bootlegger, who Jack remembered as "large as a bear," and wore a heavy coat that fell to his ankles. The huge horse blanket coat was worn all year to hide and sell pint bottles of illegal liquor in the neighborhood.

Classmate "Chuck" Anderson recalled that Jack used Chuck's father's name in one *Dragnet* episode for a character who was deaf and dumb, and blinked his eyes to answer questions from his hospital bed. Classmate Marion Fitzsimmons' name was used for a mean and nasty landlady in one of Jack's scripts.

Jack was fascinated with motion pictures, so "Gram" and "Maggie" gave the lad movie money to keep him off the streets. The first film he recalled starred John Gilbert and Renee Adoree in *The Big Parade*. The 1925 production was a superb World War I story known for its realistic battle scenes. Another later cinema Webb especially remembered was Frank Capra's 1936 Oscar award winning *Mr. Deeds Goes To Town*, starring Gary Cooper and Jean Arthur.

As the youth matured, he improved his talent for acting, poetry and art. "Chuck" Anderson recalled that teacher Cora McGomrey "was a good dramatics coach," who was impressed with Jack; the two "really went for each other." Artists he admired included N. C. Wyeth and Norman Rockwell.

Jack and his friend Sam Ettingoff created a comic strip entitled "Clark Collins." Their work was submitted to a syndicate, but was never seriously considered. Webb also forwarded his drawings to Walt Disney, who later joked, "I'm glad you became an actor instead of a cartoonist." Disney's comment recognized the adult Webb's impact on the entertainment industry and the competition that Jack may have represented to Disney had Webb pursued animation. The two men would later become close friends.

Whether as cartoonist, actor, or producer, Jack Webb would live with the mystery of his father's identity. Perhaps his obsession for realism was an outer reflection of his inner search for the father he was never to know. Jack's curiosity for the facts of his true identity carried over into his school years when he created the heritage he either preferred or was never given. From his childhood, Jack himself was faced with the question "Who really is Jack Webb?".

"No, Ma'am, I'm Jewish and Irish."

Jack was enrolled at the Fremont Avenue Grade School from 1926 to 1932 and attended Central Junior High School until February 1935. However, an earthquake damaged Central on March 10, 1933, resulting in shorter class days and the utilization of Belmont High School, from which Webb graduated in 1938.

At Fremont, the boy acquired a degree of self-esteem and confidence, excelling in poetry and art. When a sixth grade teacher read tales about the adventures of medieval knights to his students from *Otto Of The Silverhand*, Jack drew story pictures on the chalkboard of characters portrayed in the book. For his high school yearbook, he drew a picture of knights on horses and he regularly headed any list of student art honors. His classmates believed that he would one day become a professional artist — his childhood profession of choice.

In grade and junior high schools, young Jack demonstrated a propensity to entertain students, earning for him their respect and contributing to his blossoming self-esteem. He seemed to take pleasure in carrying a cornet about the school, as he had a love for music all of his life. Yet, Jack was forever frustrated that he could not play even one instrument, especially the trumpet or the cornet. Years later Webb admitted, "The only instrument I can play is a small comb with tissue paper around it, and the neighbors are not overwhelmed with the sound." Jack was, never-

Artwork from the Belmont Campanile Yearbook, 1936

Donated by Gus Stamos —
Courtesy of Jack Webb Archives

23

WO-PEEN AS HE DANCED THE RAIN-DANCE
in the Lecture-Room of the Los Angeles Library.
Sketched from Life by Jack Webb

WO-PEEN as he danced "The Rain Dance" in the lecture room of the Los Angeles Library, sketched from life by Jack Webb

Donated by Jane Gibson (Rowe) —

Courtesy of Jack Webb Archives

theless, involved in numerous musical projects. By the time he graduated from high school, he possessed an impressive collection of mostly jazz recordings.

Webb met Roy Knight in 1933. Both were energetic and creative boys, who were inseparable school mates and brothers in friendship for years. Roy recalled, "Jack was someone you could really call a friend — a really good friend." Along with Gus Stamos, the boys entertained their classmates by memorizing jokes performed on radio programs and repeating them as their own the next day at school. Their comic routine could have an entire class laughing, as did Webb's imitation of radio comic Joe Penner. In the 1930's, Penner made "Ya' wanna buy a duck?" a household phrase. Jack also wrote and served as an art editor and illustrator for *The Central Idea* school newspaper.

By the time Webb entered junior high school, he was a polite young man, though on at least one occasion, he was called before the Vice-Principal. During a fire drill, the children were ordered outside and told to stand under some trees until the all-clear bell was heard. The students were not permitted to move or talk, but Jack was unfortunately standing in the middle of an anthill. Jack recalled, "I squirmed and grunted and tried to stand still; but the ants crawled higher and higher, and I finally let out a yell and began slapping my pants." According to Jack, the Vice-Principal, initially not very understanding of Jack's outburst, "dressed me down for breaking the rule," until he heard Webb's explanation. In later years, Jack laughed when the Vice-Principal lectured him, "I should have known you'd go places. You had ants in your pants even then."

Webb was a well-groomed young man who wore his dark hair combed back in junior high school. He preferred dressing in black baggy trousers, white shirts, and a fuzzy black sweater. Junior high school classmate Marion

A sketch from classmate Gus Stamos' yearbook, 1937.

Courtesy of Jack Webb Archives

Fitzsimmons recalled that Jack "was a very unusual looking child, and that on one occasion, an insensitive teacher inquired of his nationality, asking if Webb was Japanese or Chinese? He politely replied, 'No, Ma'am, I'm Jewish and Irish.'" The clipped, soldierly and youthful matter-of-fact reply became a trademark of Webb in his celebrity years.

Twelve-year-old Jack appeared in his first motion picture while a student at Central Junior High. That chance event occurred in 1932, when several hundred of the smaller students were selected as "extras" for the filming of a New York school yard scene in *Three On A Match*. If one looks closely, Jack appears during the opening minutes of the film. The children were promised $7.00 each for their participation, but received only $3.00 and ice cream. Several rising film legends in the movie included Humphrey Bogart, Bette Davis, and Joan Blondell. One professional child actor was Sidney Miller, who later acted in *Dragnet*.

Webb and Dorothy Randles received an American Legion award presented to a boy and a girl from each junior high school class. The honor recognized "Overall achievement and qualities of character, courage, and companionship." His poetry earned more honors and a special recognition. Jack was the most productive poet in the Central Junior High School graduation program. He, classmate Jane Gibson, and others compiled a book of student poems called *The Rain Dance And Other Poems* for which Jack sketched an American Indian. A sampling of his work included, *"The Human Plan," "Roy Andrews Dragon Hunter," "A Memory," "Relativity," "Pain And Pleasure," "A Storm,"* and *"The Rain-Dance Of Wo-Peen."*

Young Jack's sensitivity to any criticism of being part Jewish was prophetic, as revealed in a touching junior high school poem he composed regarding a childhood female friend.

Maybe 'Tis So

Pretty Anna May Malone
Has a heart as hard as stone.
Every year since we were eight
She has been my best playmate.

I half loved that Irish kid
Till she said just what she did.
Said her love for me was through
'Cause she heard I'm half a Jew.

She's no reason to feel high tone
Cause her dad kissed the blarney stone.
I don't think I should know it all
'Cause my dad had a wailing wall.

Time will show you, Anna May,
The big mistake you made today.
It's the truth I'm half a Jew,
But that's the half that cared for you.

Jack Webb (1933)

Some of Jack's classmates observed that his mother "Maggie" was neglecting him by the time he graduated from Central Junior High School on January 31, 1935. Despite his increasing achievements, the boy remained sensitive to his life of poverty and was embarrassed whenever his mother visited his school. He seldom spoke with his classmates about the St. Regis Apartments or his home life of which he had little, as "Maggie" and "Gram" were usually at work. One Sunday afternoon when classmate Marion Fitzsimmons was out for a walk, she happened to see Jack sitting inside a first floor window of the St. Regis Apartments. Unaware that this was his residence, she waved and noticed that Jack dropped his head and did not reply. She sensed that something must be wrong as his behavior was out of character. Her curiosity would remain unsatisfied for one more day.

"A well-favoured man is the gift of fortune."

At school the next day, Jack explained to Marion, "I don't live there. I was just visiting." In some ways, Jack preferred being at school to being at home. He would especially prefer high school.

When Jack entered Belmont High School at 1575 West Second Street in February 1935, the nation remained mired in the terrible Depression. The school campus was located in a mixed ethnic section of Los Angeles where one might expect numerous socio-economic problems. However, baring the usual exceptions, such difficulties seemed not to exist. The pupils were mostly unconcerned about race, religion, national origin, wealth, or poverty. Instead, students were judged by how well they associated with one another and performed in class. Most of the children were enrolled in college preparatory courses and admired their teachers, who in turn "expected a lot from us, as did our families." Belmont's dress code often required males to wear ties to school and always for assemblies.

High school graduation picture, 1938.

Donated by Dorothy Randles (Blaine) —
Courtesy of Jack Webb Archives

In high school, Jack noticed the contrast in the lifestyles of the "haves" and the "have-nots," and recalled, "I guess that was when I decided I wasn't going to be poor all my life." Any remaining inferiority feelings were overcome at Belmont where Webb's leadership and pleasant personality asserted itself. Moreover, Jack never ceased being an over-achiever. He approached everything he did intensely. The teenager had a way of gathering friends about him and he brought out the best of student talents in high school plays that he directed and wrote. Although "Maggie" and "Gram" were proud of their boy

Belmont Knights High School
Principal Benshimol (center)
featuring Gus Stamos
(2nd row, 2nd from right)
with Jack (far right 2nd row)

Donated by Marion Fitzsimmons (Barnes) —
Courtesy of Jack Webb Archives

in every way, the three saw less of one another during Jack's high school days.

Jack was a well-groomed and neat person who kept things in their place throughout his life. This characteristic may have come from his having to stay organized in their small apartment, where there was little surplus space. Perhaps being an only child reared by two women contributed to his neatness.

Jack's favorite sweater was his "Knights" high school sweater and in high school, he began wearing red socks, associated with him in later years. This preference was born from his friend and classmate Willy Shulack, who wore red socks and argued that red was a "neutral color which went with everything." Jack may have also accepted Willy's logic for his rebellious adolescence.

Jack's high school grades were average, though he excelled as a student playwright, actor, mimic, emcee, announcer, and poet. As a talented cartoonist, he drew and wrote for school yearbooks, At age 16, Jack painted an impressive Katherine Hepburn portrait, which is in the possession of his widow, Mrs.

Opal Webb. His musical record collection grew to over 300 discs, which Webb could not afford at retail price. He may have had connections with radio disc jockeys who sold discarded promotional recordings for pocket change. "Jack The Bell-Boy" was one of his favorite radio disc jockeys that Jack listened to each day.

In high school, Webb attempted to master a musical instrument once more. One evening he briefly experimented with the string bass, when playing with a schoolmate's band at a gig for the deaf! The boys played the same song repeatedly and joked about the stunt. They did not realize that many in the room read lips and were insulted, so the band was never invited to perform again. Jack's musical obstacle was that he never understood "the beat." His musical zenith was as a stand-in performer with "Chuck" Anderson's band. They performed for an Italian wedding reception, whose contract stated that seven people must appear on the stage. Jack volunteered to substitute for an absent stringed bass musician, even though he could not play any instrument or could not so much as count time. Jack played on the second and fourth beat as the band played on the first and third. A drunk from the audience walked up to Webb and said, "I'm a bass player, and that sure sounds good." Jack, aware of his pitiful lack of musicianship and never lacking for a quip replied, "Yeah, man! I do that all the time!"

As high school Student Body President, Jack stated that if he ever had a "big head" as Belmont's president, "I would call it a favor if someone could give me a punch in the nose!"

Yearbook donated by Gus Stamos — Courtesy of Jack Webb Archives

Webb belonged to the school's most prestigious student organization, the Belmont Knights. His other memberships included participation in the Belmont Squires, the exclusive Hi-Y Club, a Boys' Service Club, and the Ephebians Club. The *Los Angeles Times* carried a group picture of the distinguished scholars being inducted into the Ephebian Honor Society on December 22, 1937.

However, Jack was not a saint. He played practical jokes and indulged in

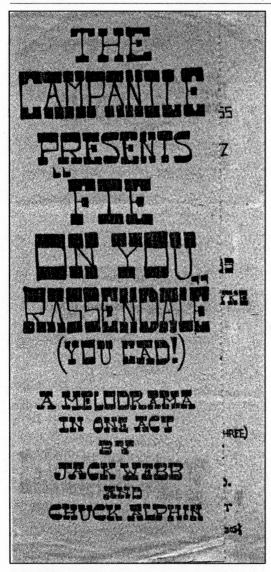

THE CAMPANILE PRESENTS "PIE ON YOU, RASSENDALE (YOU CAD!)" A MELODRAMA IN ONE ACT BY JACK WEBB AND CHUCK ALPHIN

Program for the play _Rassendale_ was printed on paper towels

Donated by Charles Anderson —
Courtesy of Jack Webb Archives

Halloween pranks. He and Gus coated trolley car tracks with grease and positioned themselves nonchalantly on a street corner until a trolley began its climb up-hill. The car would sit on the greased track and spin its wheels, as the operator became enraged. The two boys watched the helpless car and tried not to laugh, as the car attendant realized that he had been tricked.

By the time that Webb was in high school, he preferred visiting other people's homes, rather than spending time in his own apartment at Third and Flowers Streets. Jack and Roy passed much of their time on weekends visiting the Public Library and shooting free pool at the YMCA. Attending movies was a favorite entertainment, and the two boys frequently visited the Paramount Theater on Third and Broadway Streets. Once, Willy Shulack, "Chuck" Anderson, and Webb absconded with some wine produced by Willy's father. On another occasion, Jack stole a traffic stop sign. He also "borrowed" from a studio lot an aircraft propeller used on the set during the 1927 filming of _Wings_ to add to his film memorabilia. The motion picture is significant for its remarkable combat air scenes and was the first film to win an Academy Award as the Best Picture 1927-1928.

Across the street from Belmont High School was a malt

shop where the students gathered to play pinball machines, smoke cigarettes, and snack, because the school cafeteria food was too expensive for the poorer pupils to afford. Principal A. L. Benshimol was concerned about students leaving the school grounds, because Belmont was technically a closed campus. Gus Stamos and Webb saw a solution to keeping everyone on campus while reducing food prices by campaigning for and receiving the addition of a campus malt shop. No sign was posted at the gathering place, but the cafe was popularly known as "Webb's Malt Shop." Jack worked there with Gus and Baylor Maynard daily. Malts on campus sold for the low price of ten cents. Webb's influence to acquire the malt shop did not go unnoticed, as he was considered for the office of the Belmont High School Student Body President.

Upon the insistence of his friends Roy Knight and Sam Ettingoff, Webb entered the election, asking, "Who me? I've never won anything in my life!" Roy reasoned, "You're a commercial art major and all you need is some election posters and you can paint them yourself." Jack did so, but he believed that he had little chance of defeating Bob Brown and Lee Clark, two of Belmont's most popular athletes. Webb enjoyed, but only attended, sporting events. He had as little talent for athletics as he did for playing musical instruments. Several friends recalled that Jack was not athletic, "had little coordination," and "threw a ball like a girl."

Principal Benshimol forewarned Jack that if elected, not to count on having scores of shows and being a "jazzy" class president. Webb was informed, "I'll block you at every turn." The stern warning damaged the boy's zeal – Jack cried walking all the way home from school that day. Jack and Mr. Benshimol later became and remained good friends until the principal's early death. Webb, years later as the head of a large entertainment company, recalled how Benshimol had hurt him and that Jack must never make such mistakes with his own employees and friends.

The three candidates wagered that the one having the least number of votes would purchase a one pound layer cake. The runner-up would buy a quart of ice cream and the two losers would witness the winner enjoy his feast and not share it with the other two. Webb recalled:

> I ran against Bob Brown, captain of the high school football team, and as I recall, I got some 1,900 out of 2,400 votes. If I live to be a hundred, make a million dollars, and win an Academy Award, I will never be as proud as I was after that victory. Not because I won the election, with the principal against me, but only because my fellow students cared enough to give me their confidence. I was a nobody. But I was wanted and I was needed and it gave a sickly, insecure boy a new slant on life.

Following his victory, Webb generously shared the cake and ice cream with his new-found friends, a gesture that was characteristic of his generosity in later years. For example, Jack often accepted the blame when things went wrong during film production, was generous with staff salary raises and gifts, and was concerned about his cast and their children. He performed numerous favors that often went unnoticed or were later forgotten by some people. Regarding Jack's image, one person said, "The guy acts like he's afraid someone will discover he has a heart."

Jack stated that if he ever had "a big head" as Belmont's class president, "I would call it a favor if someone would give me a punch in the nose." That was an unlikely event, as Webb was a capable and popular student body leader. His mutual admiration for Belmont's students appeared in a compassionate article that he wrote for the school yearbook. The teen searched for a suitable and appropriate message, having considered the many themes commonly found in yearbooks. "But when I sat down and started to compose the message, I found that all of the subjects were taught to me by you — the student body. So this message is written by you, you who showed me the magnificent warmth of friendship which I know, and you know, I will carry with me forever."

Radio competed with art as Jack's first love. He derived much of what he learned about radio mechanics from disassembling old sets purchased from a Goodwill Industries store. He learned his initial announcing and disc jockey skills at Belmont's radio station, BHS. Jack quickly became an excellent announcer and ad lib artist, blessed with a distinctive and friendly sounding deep voice — once likened to a foghorn. At times he emceed for bands and with his private record collection, Webb worked as an event disc jockey at night. He always carried a note pad in his pocket to jot down the best jokes he heard on the Jack Benny, Fred Allen, and Bob Hope radio shows. He also listened to mysteries including *Chandu The Magician* and *The Eno Crime Clues*. He later speculated that his boyhood attraction to police and crime programs may have planted the seed that eventually produced *Dragnet*.

Jack participated in and produced many high school theater productions, including *Pennies From Heaven*, for which he requested and received studio permission to perform the 1936 motion picture as a school play. He also produced *Monsieur Beaucaire*, which was taken from a Booth Tarkington story in 1938. Classmate Dorothy Randles recalled that his productions were "way above high school level."

Rassendale was another Webb production, for which he used a program printed on paper towels. The school janitor furnished the towels and the printing shop produced the programs. Webb, who never lacked for imagination or innovation, reasoned the paper towel technique would reduce paper costs and provide the audience with ready-made tissues for tears they might shed. He also appeared in and helped direct *Journey's End*, which was the Belmont senior class play. "Jack Of All Trades" Webb additionally emceed several variety shows to raise money for Belmont team equipment and football uniforms.

Webb exaggerated when he recalled, "I was twenty-one before I smoked a cigarette, took a drink or learned all about girls." He spoke of Anna May Malone in his grade school poem and he dated several girls in junior and senior high school. One was Roberta Sadler. The teen was a most attractive and "heavily endowed" classmate, who Webb intensely admired. The two had a stormy relationship and broke up many times. He and Roy frequently walked Margaret MacGregor and Marion Fitzsimmons home from school. Margaret

Front page of L.A. Times December 22, 1937. Five of the six members of the senior class of Belmont High School who were selected Ephebia. Fred Yanari(left rear)**, William Betcher.** Front l. to r.: **Jerry Reynolds, Dorothy Randles and Jack Webb**

Donated by Dorothy Randles (Blaine) —
Courtesy of Jack Webb Archives

and Jack became long time sweethearts. The young lady saw Webb as "a genius at a young age," but she was bored when he sat through a movie several times to study if the scenes were edited correctly, with no visual errors. On one occasion, Webb viewed a picture multiple times to detect if Bette Davis' cigarette was the same length in each scene of the film. No detail was so small to escape his critical eyes.

Margaret recalled that Jack occasionally wondered about his father and that he was embarrassed of his home. Once, he embarrassed her while visiting her home. That gaffe resulted when Jack visited Margaret's house with his black and white Boston Bulldog that "had a black spot across its chest that looked like a bra." In jest, he ordered the dog to roll over and "show us what the girls in Hollywood do." The dog indifferently spread it legs in canine abandon without humility. Margaret recalled years later, "I was so embarrassed, I pretended that I didn't hear him."

Jack could draw most anything. At age 13, he sent juvenile love notes with characters sketched at the bottom of the page to Margaret. He also drew pictures for her. One of his pictures was signed, "To The Most Beautiful Girl In The World." Margaret was impressed, though she noticed that several other names below the drawing had been erased. She considered the incident humorous and sophisticated, since "at that age most guys wouldn't admit they liked you." When Jack assisted Chuck's sister with several plays for her private girls school, he was also popular with the young ladies there.

Through the efforts of his high school art teacher, Lola Holton, Jack was offered an art scholarship to the University of Southern California. Webb's dream was to attend the university, but out of financial necessity, he declined the opportunity. Instead, he became a breadwinner in the household. Jack washed dishes in the high school cafeteria and clerked in a plumbing supply store during the summer months, which eased the family financial burden during the Depression. At other times, he collected discarded light bulbs to sell at junkyards. The bulbs were broken open for the filaments. A dozen filaments would earn him about one dollar. Jack also became handy mechanically while learning how to repair items around the apartment. He explained, "As a kid, I was poor, and poor kids learn to use their hands. They have to make everything themselves, or chisel to get it. I never was much good at chiseling, so …"

The boy's 1938 graduation photograph caption read, "JACK WEBB — A well-favoured man is the gift of fortune." Several of his poems were placed in a Belmont High School time capsule and for the senior class will he wrote, "I, Jack Webb, leave my inflated ego to some other taker-off of Joe Penner." He might have included one of his favorite life tenets: "You're never out when you're knocked down. You're out when you don't get up!" Although he did not have the money to attend college following graduation, Jack listed his ambition as studying film directing and radio announcing at a Los Angeles Junior College or the University of Southern California. He wrote in one school yearbook that he wanted to write, direct, and star in a movie. The *Campanile* yearbook asked, "Who knows, but there may be a mayor, governor, or president of tomorrow leaving Belmont. Time will tell!" No mention was made of a student who could become a radio, television, and motion picture mogul — who the world would come to know as Jack Webb.

"My heart did not belong to Hart, Schaffner & Marx."

In 1938 the Great Depression persisted, and China and Japan were at war in Asia. Germany's Adolf Hitler was dismantling Europe, as "Maggie," "Gram," and Jack moved from their St. Regis Apartment to Eighth and San Pedro Streets in February. Gus Stamos also shared the two-room residence, which was essentially a rooming house above a commercial storage site. However, the family was beginning to disintegrate since "Gram" began losing her sight as early as 1936 and "Maggie" became engaged to a local barber in

Jack and Gus Stamos at Big Bear, California

Donated by Gus Stamos —
Courtesy of Jack Webb Archives

1938. Jack was eighteen and paying more attention to girls, but he had yet to commit himself to a career in art or radio, his two favorite fields.

Jack's fascination with jazz did not wane after high school. He enjoyed listening to his records every morning to begin the new day. Though his favorite singer was Ella Fitzgerald whom he later knew and employed, Louie "Satchmo" Armstrong was for Webb "the dean of them all." For extra money, Jack submitted scripts to CBS or NBC in Hollywood or pooled his funds with Gus and schoolmate Harry Reder to visit Catalina Island and listen to the big bands play. Sometimes Jack and his friends remained on the island several days dancing at the Casino and enjoying the music the swing and jazz bands played.

Roy Knight taught Jack how to drive. Jack bought his first car while living on Eighth and San Pedro Streets. The Model T Ford he bought was sitting on blocks and cost Webb $4.50 — requiring fifty cents down, twenty-five cents a week, and a mechanic to get the car in running condition. Not long after the vehicle became roadworthy, the eighteen-year-old Webb rammed a parked car in front of the apartment. The accident required that he work at the aggrieved man's plumbing store until the damage debt was fully paid. After high school, Jack apparently had some interest in automobile racing drivers. He and Roy visited the Ascott Speedway, where Webb collected driver autographs and sketched pictures of the men. Wilbur Shaw was one of his subjects, who later became the President of the famous Indianapolis Motor Speedway.

In October 1938, Jack, Gus, "Gram" and "Maggie" moved to another two-bedroom apartment on 36th Street near Vermont Avenue. Jack then owned a 1936 Oldsmobile convertible, but he discovered his dream machine at a used car lot. A 1936 Cord. Though the Cord was a known "clunker," Webb wanted the prestige of driving a legendary automobile. He committed himself to an outrageous price, and after the purchase papers were completed, Jack and Gus drove the car from Figueroa Boulevard to Exposition Boulevard, where "Maggie's" boy friend lived above the barbershop. However, as the two returned the car to the lot, it literally fell apart. The prestigious Cord lemon was forgotten, and Jack was fortunate to have his 1936 Oldsmobile back.

Webb acquired some experience working in sales for Desmonds Clothing Store, but after high school he, Gus, and Roy found employment at the exclusive Silverwoods Men's Store at Sixth and Broadway Streets. The three first worked in the basement, though Jack was later moved to the top floor to wrap packages for $18.00 a week. He also worked in the alterations department and was not reluctant to buy quality clothing for himself. Once he spent his entire paycheck for a Silverwoods cashmere sweater. Webb recalled that he became a third-rate clothing salesman, which his small commissions confirmed. Later, however, he would emerge as a master salesman in the entertainment field.

Although Jack appreciated fine suits and other clothing, he was never a "clothes horse." His adult wardrobe might consist of four or five suits, a dozen pairs of slacks, and a few comfortable jackets. Some of his *Dragnet* era jackets had one side tailored larger than the other, so that Webb's television and cinema police revolver stayed concealed. ("Policemen have the seams in their coats let out for this reason.") Television wardrobe attendants later appreciated that Jack and his partners generally wore the same clothes, facilitating film editing and garment handling. Webb would subsequently require the use of quality clothing in his productions, as camera close-ups detected the wrinkling of lesser quality clothes.

Expensive jewelry and costly cigarette lighters never impressed Webb, though he later wore an identification bracelet given to him by Julie London, his first wife. He wore a St. Francis medal from "Maggie" around his neck for good luck. The medal had a specially engraved "Star Of David" on the reverse side. One such medal is detected in the closing minutes of the hospital scene in *Dragnet 1966*.

Roy and Jack continued their pranks, though Roy was astonished to hear Jack wish a fellow Silverwoods employee, "Good night, you son-of-a-bitch!" The rude remark was not in Webb's character and Roy later discovered that Jack was joshing the deaf employee. Two other salesmen invited Jack and "Chuck" Anderson to their Hermosa Beach house. The group acted-out their own floor shows. In one skit, Webb used a mop in lieu of a camera, while pretending to be a cameraman interviewing a crowd. In another skit, Webb impersonated a lighthouse.

Early in 1939, Jack, Gus, and "Gram" moved to a Marathon Street Duplex. However, the family soon separated as "Maggie" had married. "Gram" was

In the convertible at Big Bear, California in 1939

Donated by Gus Stamos — Courtesy of Jack Webb Archives

going blind, received a state pension, and was eventually placed in a nursing home. In 1939, Jack was employed at Silverwoods' Wilshire store and was subsequently promoted to assistant manager of the University of Southern California campus store. Jack later recalled that his $35.00 a week "was still just above sea level," and that Silverwoods was a place where he was "only marking time. ... My heart did not belong to Hart, Schaffner & Marx."

At the Wilshire store, Webb first met Dick Turner, whom he nicknamed "Moe." At sixteen, Turner was younger than Jack, though he had already received a tennis scholarship from the University of Southern California. Turner also drew a salary from his part-time job. Dick purchased some of his clothing at Silverwoods, and after several meetings, he and Jack became life-long friends. "You couldn't help but like him; we hit it off great!" Turner recalled. Besides, Turner had a 1937 gloss-black two-door Ford automobile, when Webb no longer even had a car. Jack was even more attracted to what Turner characterized as "fancy looking women and the music of the big bands. So, the two teenage boys and their girlfriends frequently double-dated via Turner's car to Ocean Park, California to listen to such great bands as those of Kay Kyser and Tommy and Jimmy Dorsey.

Jack's writing and acting life was dormant after high school until he was persuaded to perform in a melodrama at the Beverly Boulevard Theater in 1941. Webb played a villain in *The Lighthouse Keeper's Daughter*, whose role included extinguishing the candles when the attractive Keeper's Daughter was nearby. Having previously worked a full day at Silverwoods, Webb said, "I

Jack making a sale at Silverwoods Men's Store where he made up to $35 per week.

Cosmopolitan Magazine —
Courtesy of Jack Webb Archives

didn't have much left for the heroine," and he quit the show. His only other post-high school acting role was in a little theater production of *Hiawatha*, staged by Pasadena's San Marino Hall. Webb played "Hiawatha." Jack also continued his independent disc jockey work. Once, Webb worked as a disc jockey using his record player and amplifier to play his personal music at "Chuck" Anderson's wedding reception in Pasadena. Anderson said that Jack *"was* the entertainment."

On December 7, 1941, when Japanese naval forces attacked Pearl Harbor, Hawaii, drawing the United States into World War II, life in America quickly changed. The patriotic course was for young men to volunteer for military service or contribute in other ways to assist the war effort. The war also created a shortage of cloth for the fine men's wear that Webb sold at Silverwoods. Therefore, after nearly four years of employment with Silverwoods, Roy and Jack left the clothing business. In 1942, they worked the "swing shift" at the Byron Jackson Pump Company where Roy Knight's father found jobs for the young men. Webb labored there as an electric-hacksaw operator for six months making parts for anti-tank guns, but the task had little appeal or adventure for the two young men. The year 1942 had other plans for Jack Webb and his friend.

"I went in with a dream. I came out with a blank page."

Jack could have avoided World War II military duty, since his "draft" or selective service classification was 3-A. This designation was assigned to individuals deferred from military service due to dependent obligations. Webb easily qualified for deferral as the primary support for "Gram," by now legally blind.

Webb, a six-foot tall 165-pound healthy 22-year-old, entertained thoughts of enlisting in the Navy or the Marine Corps. However, he reportedly failed the Navy written test and a bellicose Marine recruiter caused him to shun the Corps. The Army Air Corps was Webb's next choice. Jack's interest in aviation surely came from motion pictures and his reading of the World War I exploits of America's ace Eddie Rickenbacker, French aviator Rene Fonck, and Germany's ace of aces, Baron Manfred von Richthofen, popularly called "The Red Baron" or "The Red Knight."

Wing Inspector Jack Webb

Donated by Al Gentry —
Courtesy of Jack Webb Archives

Before their military induction, Webb and Roy Knight first enrolled in several aircraft engineering courses offered by the University of Southern California to prepare men for enlisting into the Army as "Aviation Cadets." The program was for high school graduates, though applicants with two or more years of college were immediately enrolled in Preflight School. Those in the Aviation Cadet Program were only a small step above the rank of U. S. Army Privates. That small step could prove very slippery for some Cadets.

Jack, Roy Knight, Tommy Thompson, and "Moe" Turner initially enlisted at a U.S. Navy and Air Corps Recruiting Center on Sixth and Main Streets, but Roy reported for active duty two months earlier than Jack. Roy did not hear from Webb again until Preflight School. A large group of enlistees including Jack spent several days at the Center receiving shots and completing enlistment records until they gathered early one January 1943 morning at the Los Angeles Railroad Station. There they boarded an Army troop train and traveled to Fresno in archaic passenger coaches with high interior ceilings appointed with antique chandeliers. The naive and idealistic applicants romanticized about future flying adventures when they would sport the handsome uniforms of Aviation Cadets.

The Fresno base was a fairground that had been recently converted into an Army camp. Any military romanticism disappeared with chants of "You'll Be Sorry" voiced by the veteran Cadets. A 10-day introduction into military service began as the group was housed in new barracks without the creature comforts of civilian life. The Cadets were issued outdated World War I uniforms rather than officers' clothing and were assigned the mundane duties of basic training or boot camp. More medical shots were received, basic administrative records were completed, and Webb was assigned "Army of the United States Serial Number 19-178-356."

Departing Fresno, the Cadets endured a one-week troop-train journey to St. John's (Catholic) University in St. Cloud, Minnesota. There, the College Training Detachment (CTD) program crammed an accelerated and severely abbreviated two years of schooling into approximately four months. The curriculum included math (from basic through calculus), biology, English, history, public speaking, athletics, and military history. Outside the classroom, there was always marching or Close Order Drill. Webb's fellow Cadet Lloyd W. Whitlow observed, "The studies were thrown at us so fast and furious [that] it was like trying to take a drink of water from a fire hose." Further, the men learned they were not yet officially Aviation Cadets. They were classified only as "Aviation Students," requiring the Cadets to perform duties and cleaning chores assigned to lower ranked enlisted men at a lowly pay of $55.00 a month.

Cadet Lloyd W. Whitlow was billeted with Jack at St. John's, as both of their last names began with the letter W. The union proved to be fortunate, since Lloyd excelled in math and physics and Webb in English and other subjects. Lloyd recalled, "We were a good team!" Later, in flight navigation classes, Jack's friend Dick "Moe" Turner tutored Jack in trigonometry and algebra.

The weekdays at St. John's were devoted to studies, but on weekends the Cadets visited the St. Cloud United Services Organization, popularly known as the USO Club. There they enjoyed some respite from military life, and met local or college girls. A city hotel bar was a favorite so-called "pick-up spot" if a Cadet was unsuccessful finding a woman companion at the USO. Though 23 years old, Jack did not devote much time to chasing women. However, he never hesitated to compliment an attractive woman, and women genuinely seemed attracted to him.

For Cadets who rented St. Cloud hotel rooms, pranks were part of an evening's entertainment, especially following several drinks. One stunt involved dropping water-filled condoms out of the hotel windows in a juvenile game called "Bombardier."

While Jack was at St. John's, he received permission to present a weekly variety show in the college or in the St. Cloud high school auditorium on Friday nights. Most of his skits were written in the barracks latrine after taps or "lights out," and Webb included his friends among the writers and performers. However, Jack was always the chief writer, narrator, and star. Friend "Moe" Turner remembers Jack as a "compulsive writer." Many of Webb's acts were patterned after the vaudeville slapstick routines of Olsen & Johnson. For example, "Moe" Turner was programmed to enter the auditorium carrying a small potted plant and shout some name such as, "Is Ann Smith in the audience?" Five, ten, fifteen minutes later Turner re-entered the theater searching for the same person, but with each following appearance the plant grew enormously to eventually become a tree. "The audience was in stitches," according to "Moe."

Army Air Corps Squadron D

Donated by Lloyd Whitlow —
Courtesy of Jack Webb Archives

Jack plagiarized jokes from radio programs to use in his emcee role, but he always gave an excellent performance. He had a good sense of humor and was quick-witted. His humor was never biting or sarcastic, and he never put anyone down. In some productions, Webb was not actually seen announcing until the end of a show. His signature closing was to have all of the house lights turned off, except for one spotlight focused on his hand as he sat at a stage desk writing a letter home. With his unique voice Jack would softly speak "Dear Mother" or "To My Sweetheart" and tell the person to whom he was writing how much he missed them. As all of the auditorium lights were slowly raised, Jack completed the letter and signed it "With Love, Your Son" or "Love, Your Husband." Then the cast received their curtain call and generous applause in an emotional conclusion to an evening of quality, free entertainment. Everyone recalled Jack's shows as "a tremendous success," enjoyed by all.

The variety presentations gave Webb the idea for a production to raise money for the St. Cloud USO Club. Though recruiting actors from the fledgling Cadet Corps was easy, Jack was challenged by the shortage of military orchestra musicians. Ever resourceful, Webb recruited St. John's students and dressed them in regular Army uniforms. The show was called "Flying Blind," and was performed two nights in a St. Cloud auditorium. Part of the money raised was used for a soldier's beer bust at a local club.

The training at St. Cloud had the Cadets making only a few flights with an instructor aboard a small Piper Cub aircraft, but no one "soloed," or flew alone. Lloyd recalled, "Looking back, it was a waste of time and money, but that's the Government!" Moreover, the weeks at St. John's resembled little of genuine Army life, so most of the Cadets enjoyed their residence there.

Webb and Whitlow were ordered to the Santa Ana, California Army Air Base for Aviation Preflight Training (APT) in June 1943. The program combined Officers' Candidate School with learning Morse Code skills, basic schooling on military subjects, and the ever-present Close Order Drill. At Santa Ana, the men were tested to see if they would best qualify as a pilot, navigator or bombardier, and some Cadets were weeded-out of the program at this time. Jack and Lloyd were assigned to the pilot's list. At last, the coveted Aviation Cadet uniforms were issued, and Webb and "Moe" Turner had their uniforms custom altered. Jack wanted to look sharp, as if he were wealthy, but "he never had much in his pockets," as "Moe" Turner recalls of those days. However, the Cadets did not fly at Santa Ana.

For three months, life there was more like the regulation service. The men were assigned to barracks especially for Cadets. Much of the freedom and luxuries enjoyed at St. John's were gone. Students discovered that passes to leave the base were scarce.

When passes were issued, Webb and Whitlow trekked to nearby Los Angeles. On his first pass, Webb searched for any club or gathering where jazz music was played. At this time, Jack met Herman S. "Herm" Saunders, who became another of Webb's lifelong associates and friends. Saunders played piano in the "Swing Wing" Army Air Corps Band, which consisted of enlisted men who were among the best jazz musicians in the United States. Jack frequently visited the transcontinental broadcasts performed weekly by the band from a Santa Ana American Legion Hall, converted into a National Broadcasting Company studio. Many celebrities and entertainment stars visited the facility including singer/actor Bing Crosby and other performers of his stature. In later years, Bing's son Gary acted for Jack.

Visitors were allowed on the post to view the Sunday parades, an important part of the training routine. Webb's squadron twice placed first in parade competition and was rewarded by having their choice of a Primary Flight School to attend. The Squadron was largely composed of Californians who chose the civilian field and facilities of the Tex Rankin Aeronautical Academy, the choice of Jack and Lloyd, at Tulare, California, rather than the nearby Cal Aero at Chino.

Roy Knight arrived at the Academy one month earlier than Jack and was placed in charge of a group of Preflight Cadets. Once when Roy entered Jack's barracks and commanded "attention," all stood rigid except Webb, who remained sitting on his cot perplexed over all of the excitement. After all, Webb had persuaded Roy to join the Air Corps in the first place. Roy was unappreciative of Jack's breach in military courtesy, and asked, "What are you doing, you dirty son-of-a-bitch!" The exchange was taken in good humor and the two men remained close friends.

As members of Class 44-D, Lloyd and Webb lived in a large room assigned to 14 students. The quarters were furnished with seven two-tiered bunks, footlockers, student uniform closets, and a dresser and a chair for each person. At Tulare, Jack received an appointment as a Squadron D Cadet officer and "Wing Inspector," requiring additional responsibility and duties. He was recalled by all of his fellow students as "a hell of a nice guy," humorous, and fun. He did not always take military life seriously. Surprisingly, the gregarious Webb often preferred to be alone and could be very quiet.

Cadet Primary Flight Training was taught in the Stearman PT-17 aircraft, an open cockpit biplane with fixed landing gear. Eight hours of flight training was the normal time allotted before a pilot could solo, with a maximum of 10 hours allowed. Lloyd effortlessly took to flying and soloed in six hours. Webb required an exceptional 15 hours, and then succeeded only because of the patience and support granted him by the civilians, Army officers, and Cadets. "They did all in their power to get him soloed," Lloyd admitted. Webb later passed all of his "Check Rides," including the final test.

Webb and Cadet Lloyd Lavine frequently had breakfast at the

The Spirit of 44-D!

Army Air Corps Squadron D

Donated by Lloyd Whitlow —
Courtesy of Jack Webb Archives

McAlister farm restaurant, adjacent to the Tulare Field and operated by a retired couple. Jack and his friends visited area towns on weekends, and Webb and Doug Waide hitchhiked the several hundred miles from Rankin to Los Angeles to detach themselves from military life. They later made similar but shorter trips to Los Angeles from Taft, California to date women and listen to the big bands play. Though Webb never owned an automobile while he was in the Army, he dreamed of one day driving a Cadillac convertible, a life-goal for him. He told Lloyd Whitlow many times that if he ever "made it big," he would own that Cadillac dream car.

Jack wrote and drew for the *Rank'n File* newspaper and produced a show in the Tulare High School auditorium called *Prop Wash*. As with his St. John's productions, money was raised for a USO Club with funds reserved for a party for the men. This time the event celebrated their completion of the first stage of becoming a pilot and warranted hiring a large swing band, including the appearance of the popular big band singer Anita O'Day. The event became a gala evening of fun and dancing and the night when Jack acquired his nickname — "Lobes." Most of the men had military nicknames and Webb's moniker, of course, concerned his impressive ears. The name was dismissed after Primary School, but Jack's ears later drew the attention of insensitive media reporters and writers during his celebrity days.

After graduating from the Tex Rankin Academy, the Cadets were ordered to Gardner Field. The Basic Flight School, near Taft, California, was on the edge of the San Joaquin Valley and several dozen miles from Tulare. Gardner Field was entirely military and was run by Army officers, with few civilians or frills. The two-man living cubicles were spartan, and Whitlow and Jack remained roommates. While at Gardner Field, Jack suggested to his closest friends that he was uneasy flying and was experiencing some discomfort with heights.

The Gardner Field training was conducted in the BT-13A "Valiant," the basic trainer plane humorously identified by Cadets as the "Vultee Vibrator." The aircraft had fixed landing gear, a low wing, and an enclosed tandem cockpit for a student and instructor. The plane's nickname was derived from the canopy vibrating or shaking as the plane neared stall speed. Lloyd soloed without difficulty, but Webb did not and, after several attempts, "washed-out."

Jack was recalled by some as a "clumsy pilot," who lacked the confidence to fly. "Moe" Turner remembered that Webb was uncomfortable with flying, but Jack's apprehension was camouflaged by his ebullient personality. Jack's post war friend Bob Forward offered that many can perform tasks that others cannot. He recalled that Jack succeeded in most professional endeavors, though not in piloting airplanes. Forward, speaking as a war time Flight Instructor, believed that Webb could have soloed, but not in the allotted time then permitted the Cadets. Turner, who later flew many combat missions and piloted celebrities including Arnold Palmer and Bob Hope, often joked that Jack was afraid to fly and had used his mother "Maggie" as an excuse to leave the Air Corps.

There was no official retribution for a Cadet "washing-out," but Jack was obviously as disappointed as other Cadets who were dismissed from the program. The experience was more disheartening since the rejected men were removed from their Cadet quarters and relocated to a Pool Squadron Barracks. Here, they were reclassified from an "Aviation Cadet" to a "Private" — and then most likely to be enlisted men. All Cadet uniforms were surrendered, and the disqualified were issued standard Army uniforms. Cadet Douglas L. Waide recalled when Webb "washed-out," and described the ensuing circumstances that he observed:

> When Jack washed-out I wanted to say good-bye to him, but his bed was made and his locker was cleaned out. Nothing was there to remind me of him.
>
> The only way in which Cadets knew that someone had washed-out was when all of his gear was suddenly gone and his bed was not slept in. I cannot remember any "goodbyes" or expressions of sympathy or conversation about meeting some time in the future. I believe that Cadets who washed-out were placed into radio operations, gunnery or learned to become an aircraft mechanic. To be washed-out was a very, very traumatic experience.

Cadet Ken Sealy remembered that it was easy to be dismissed from the

One of many memorable performances

Donated by Al Gentry — Courtesy of Jack Webb Archives

school. The smallest mistake could end the ambitions of an aspiring pilot. "Just being airsick, you could 'wash-out.' A lot of us never made it," Sealy recalled.

Lloyd Whitlow and Jack continued to visit occasionally, but Webb, a sensitive person, became despondent and confided in Lloyd that he planned to apply for a Dependency Discharge and be released from military service. Further, Jack was not transferred to a mechanic or gunnery school, but instead became an obscure office clerk. Lloyd recalled:

> I guess it became obvious to the Army [flight instructor] officers that Jack was not cut out to be a pilot. He had all of the makings of a fine officer and would have been an outstanding one. I'm sure that if Jack had requested it he could have gone to Officers' Candidate School. It was a shame that with all of the testing they did at Santa Ana during Classification that it didn't reveal his shortcomings as a pilot. I strongly feel that if Jack had been assigned as a Navigator or Bombardier that he would have had no trouble. This proved that their testing was not 100%.

"Moe" Turner offered that the "Air Corps lost a primary opportunity to commission Jack and to place him in Special Services," a unit responsible for arranging USO tours and providing entertainment for the troops.

Dismissed from flight training, Webb became a "buck private" manning a typewriter in an orderly room at Laughlin Air Force Base in Del Rio, Texas. Roy Knight, now a Flight Instructor at Bergstrom Air Force Base in Austin, visited Jack on weekends. There was little to do in the Del Rio border town. The University of Texas and available women were in Austin. Jack occupied Roy's co-pilot seat, and on one occasion their aircraft lost power, took a nosedive, and nearly crashed into a house. Knight recalled, "We just barely made it," and "our near misfortune scared the wits out of a farmer who was sitting on his porch."

Private Webb applied for and received a hardship discharge to provide for "Maggie" and "Gram" after a little over two years' military service (November 24, 1942 – January 4, 1945) and great disappointment with himself and the Army. Yet, after Webb achieved celebrity status, some misinformed newspaper and magazine reporters printed that he had piloted bombers and downed enemy aircraft in the war. Jack, always the patriot, was particularly hurt when one magazine accused him of faking his war record, which he would have never done. Reluctant to talk about his Army service, Webb replied that his military experience represented "one of the few barren periods of my life. I went in with a dream. I came out with a blank page." He recorded that the only action he saw occurred at Saturday night crap games in which he did not participate. "Worst of all," he said, "I failed to measure up to my boyhood paper heroes."

The fate of Lloyd Whitlow, Jack's first Aviation Cadet roommate, was quite different. Whitlow piloted Boeing B-17 "Flying Fortress" bombers in 38 missions over Europe while serving in the famous Eighth Air Force during World War II. Though he departed the service in 1946 to complete college, he later flew in the United States Air Force Reserve during the Korean War. Lloyd eventually became a United Airlines commercial pilot for 31 years and achieved the rank of Captain. "It was a very rewarding and interesting job," Whitlow reported. Yet, he never forgot Jack and Webb's fascination for Cadillac automobiles.

Lloyd tracked Webb's rise to prominence through radio and television, but due to his flying schedules and family demands, Whitlow never found the time to visit Jack. "Something," Lloyd said, "I will always regret not doing." However, once during the mid-1950's when Lloyd was driving through Hollywood and following a new Cadillac, his thoughts were once more of Jack. Out of curiosity, Lloyd pulled alongside the luxurious convertible and easily recognized his Army friend. Lloyd sounded his horn, but was ignored until he lowered his car window and shouted to Jack. The two Cadet buddies immediately pulled over to the curb for a spontaneous and happy reunion.

Lloyd was transferred to Chicago and hoped to meet Webb once more on one of his commercial flights. He never did, but he spoke with *Dragnet's* Ben Alexander who Lloyd gave a business card to pass on to Webb. Perhaps Alexander overlooked delivering this card, since Lloyd never heard from Jack again. Nonetheless, as a commercial airline Captain, Lloyd met many famous and interesting people. Lloyd recalled that both he and Jack had fascinating and successful careers, "but the best and the most outstanding celebrity that I have known is my old roommate, Jack Webb!"

Though Jack never had great success in the air as a pilot, he took off into a new, emerging type of "air." This new "air" would launch Jack to heights that others could only dream of achieving. Interestingly, Jack would take this leap on a borrowed $40 in travel money and an empty half-hour on a Sunday night in San Francisco.

"For eight or nine weeks
I was everybody's hot cake."

After Jack was discharged from the Army in January 1945, he returned to Los Angeles and lived with "Maggie" and "Gram" in the apartment on Marathon Street. He invited his Army buddies to visit him. Herm Saunders, who was still in the service, often had breakfast at the apartment with Jack.

Webb took several odd jobs to make ends meet, including selling snake skin belts. However, nearly twenty-five years old, he needed to pursue a more meaningful career. He dismissed becoming a commercial artist because he felt the field was too competitive. Instead, he chose radio, in which he had excelled in high school.

Accompanied by Herm Saunders, Webb auditioned at station KHJ in Los Angeles for their San Francisco sister station KFRC. A demonstration recording was also sent to radio station KGO in San Francisco. KGO was impressed enough to invite Jack to visit the station for further talks. Jack borrowed $40 from Saunders for travel and relocated to the Bay Area city to begin his radio career.

Jack's Uncle Frank Smith and Aunt Faye lived in San Francisco and had associates with connections to radio there. Frank owned a clothing store, and if need be, Webb could work there while awaiting a coveted broadcasting opportunity.

Demand for broadcasters increased in San Francisco when a United Nations Conference on International Organization convened there from April to June 1945 to promote world peace. However, quality radio talent was in scarce supply, as many broadcasters were still in military service.

Playing disc jockey

Cosmopolitan Magazine —
Courtesy of Jack Webb Archives

World War II with Japan did not end until August-September 1945. The UN Conference would continue for months. Following debate and ratification, a United Nations (UN) charter became effective on October 24, 1945. The UN event was reported worldwide, and radio, as the medium of the day, needed additional broadcasters to cover the ongoing story.

The KGO management temporarily hired Webb, and from that moment on his life became one of ambition and dedicated work. On his third work day, an excited woman ran through a KGO station corridor where Webb was standing in awe of his new job. In her excitement she asked, "Hey boy, are you an announcer?" Jack replied that he was and remembered that the woman "grabbed my arm and hauled me like a sack of beans," proclaiming she was scheduled to broadcast at that very moment and demanding, "Put me on the air!" Webb recalled, "I walked into the studio as nervous as a pup at a dog show, and I got her on the air. This was my debut on radio in San Francisco, and the jittery lady I didn't know was Miss Hedda Hopper." Hopper, an actress and a Hollywood celebrity gossip columnist for 28 years, could make or break aspiring radio announcers or rising motion picture stars.

Since his only broadcast experience was what he acquired at Belmont High School, Jack constantly asked questions of the KGO staff and learned all he could about the business. For hours, he practiced modulating his voice and studied radio sound effects. As a disc jockey, announcer, narrator, and writer he discovered, "On local radio you do everything but design [radio] tubes." Throughout his life, Jack believed that "radio is [was] the theater of the mind."

After Roy Knight was discharged from the Army, Jack persuaded him to move to San Francisco and perhaps work for KGO. However, the station never employed Roy. Knight later prospered from owning a large automobile dealership. During this period, Webb had a bout with ulcers caused by the pressure of having to be in a precise spot at an exact moment, as demanded by "live" radio.

Webb was briefly dismissed by KGO to vacate his position for a regular announcer returning from military service, but was promptly rehired. His first reporting assignment in San Francisco was covering the August 15, 1945 "VJ Day" (Victory over Japan) celebrations when Japan surrendered, ending World War II. On Market Street, Jack spotted a sailor fresh off a battleship and seriously asked the young man what he planned to do since the war was over. The sailor replied, "Why sure! I'm gonna find me a hayloft and a hot little chick to go with it." Jack was dumbfounded and caught off guard. He recalled the experience as the only time in his radio career that he was stuck with a "sizable hunk of dead air." Thanks to that unknown sailor, Webb reported, "nothing ever seemed to rattle me again." On May 2, 1946, Webb calmly reported for KGO on the U. S. Marines and civilian police efforts to end a riot at the famous Federal Alcatraz prison in the San Francisco Bay.

Though Jack became an accomplished radio actor and announcer, he characterized his early career as "about as romantic as playing 'post office' in an old maids' club." He reported to work at 4:30 A.M. daily as a wake-up disc jockey for a program called *The Coffee Club* where he chiefly pushed buttons on a console and engaged in what he called "smart songs and snappy chatter." However, once more, good fortune smiled on Jack when he worked with a fellow disc jockey whom he only identified as a chief announcer for KGO. The veteran broadcaster arrived at the station at 6:30 in the morning and downed a paper cup full of rye whiskey in one swallow and a generous helping of snuff before going on the air. Much of his chatter with Webb concerned an ambition to own a chicken ranch, but at 7:00 A.M. sharp, the man was on the air. Jack, recalling that his mentor never made a mistake, shared, "At KGO, he taught me everything he knew about radio announcing, and he was a master." The seasoned radiocaster eventually retired and bought his chicken ranch.

At KGO Jack was well liked, and with the assistance of ABC staff writer Jim Moser and Director Gil Doud, Webb began his first weekly broadcast in early 1946. The show was called *One Out Of Seven*. The station staff reviewed the top news story each day derived from the major news services, including the International News Service (INS), Associated Press (AP), United Press (UP), and other "authoritative files." Only one story from the week's worth of news was selected to air— hence, "One Out Of Seven." Webb was the entire cast, and his associates branded him the "man with a hundred voices—all alike."

One Out Of Seven had Webb standing before three microphones, where he dramatized President Franklin D. Roosevelt, Soviet Premier Joseph Stalin, and British Prime Minister Winston Churchill regarding significant world news of the week. Jack also did a variety of dialects that ranged from black to Jewish. In his *Tune In Yesterday*, critic John Dunning described the program as a "strong opponent of racial injustice," exposing hate mongers and bigots long before the national self-investigation and reforms of later years.

No one was exempt from being targeted on *One Out Of Seven*, a fact that was evident during the broadcast on February 6, 1946. Webb and others criticized Mississippi Senator Theodore G. Bilbo, who was no friend of minorities. Webb's narrative was most effective in what Dunning called "truly a gutsy show for radio of the era."

Jack also convinced KGO's management to allow him to do comedy, and he lured live studio audiences by persuading a local florist to donate free gardenias for those attending his broadcast. When he learned the daughter of the KGO general manager suffered from cerebral palsy, Jack raised money on the air for cerebral palsy victims, a charity he enthusiastically supported for the remainder of his life.

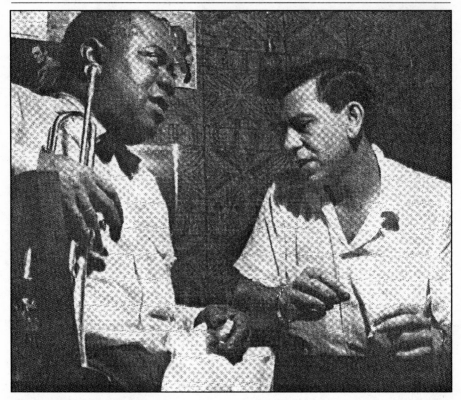

One of Jack's personal favorites — Louie Armstrong

Courtesy of Jack Webb Archives

Webb's first great break came shortly after he met Richard "Dick" Breen, "a round-faced, voluble Irishman" (*Time*, 3/15/1954). The Fordham graduate joined the KGO station staff as a writer-producer soon after he was discharged from the Navy. Webb was immediately impressed with Breen, and later said, "I met and had the privilege of working with the finest young writer I've ever known. It was his writing skill that put me on the road to becoming an actor." Breen was equally impressed with Jack. The team later became roommates, sharing Webb's $30.00 a month room.

Jack Webb's career as a rising radio celebrity took off when KGO had to fill an empty Sunday night half hour spot for a limited number of west coast ABC stations. Fascinated by San Francisco's *Embarcadero*, Breen wrote *Pat Novak For Hire*, a radio thriller that entertained audiences with sex and violence. Dunning called the program a "hard-boiled private-eye show about waterfront crime." For realism, the show used the background sounds of foghorns and lapping water in San Francisco Bay. The script was loaded with similes, and during the first episode, Breen urged Webb to depart from his normal aggressive delivery and instead underplay

"Novak's" role. The suggestion was significant as related to *Pat Novak*, and even more so later when Jack adopted the technique to downplay "Sergeant Friday's" personality on *Dragnet*.

Critic John Dunning described the character "Pat Novak" (also called "Patsy") as "a tough, fast-talking, fast moving private eye." Webb played the role for 26 to 28 weeks. Tudor Owen played "Jocko Madigan" ("Novak's" assistant) and Raymond Burr played "Inspector Hellman." The series was announced by George Fen-

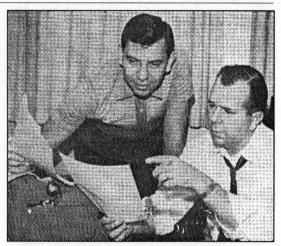

Jack going over a *Pat Novak* script with writer Dick Breen.

Cosmopolitan Magazine —
Courtesy of Jack Webb Archives

neman and directed by William Rousseau, both of whom went on with Webb to greater days. The series was an instant success, winning the praise of radio critics and fans who enjoyed what Dunning dubbed Jack's "smart mouthed delivery." *Novak's* high ratings earned Webb a small amount of fame and fan mail, and Jack admitted, "I confess, I liked the flavor." Most importantly, "Pat Novak" was the character who in 1946 first propelled Jack to warrant attention as a radio tough guy. The achievement is ironic since Jack was never considered a "tough guy" in real life, and there is no record of his ever being in as much as a schoolyard fight.

Webb's teaming with Breen at KGO was short-lived. Breen quarreled with the station management and resigned after receiving an offer to work for Academy Award winners Charles Brackett and Billy Wilder in Hollywood. Packing his large collection of jazz records and other belongings into his 1941 Buick convertible, Webb resigned one hour later, departing *Pat Novak For Hire*. The role was picked up by Ben Morris, but "his portrayal was dull compared with Webb's," according to critic Dunning. Jack's fans protested his departure, resulting in a 1947 summer series called *Johnny Madero, Pier 23* on the Mutual Broadcasting Network. The show reunited Breen and Webb and was a near copy of the *Novak* format.

Johnny Madero played on Mutual Broadcasting Network radio on Thursday nights from April 24 to September 4, 1947. Film and radio author John Dunning states the program was "notable as Jack Webb's first significant appearance with his now famous staccato style and has direct ties to Webb's other hardboiled role, *Pat Novak For Hire."* However, both characters were removed from Webb's portrayal of "Joe Friday," who emerged from *Dragnet* two years later. Although *Johnny Madero* aired for only a summer, the character led the way for the reappearance of *Pat Novak* in 1948. Webb returned to the role on a coast-to-coast ABC hookup. *Madero's* sidekick was a waterfront priest named "Father Leahy," acted by Gale Gordon. William Conrad played "Warchek," Nat Wolff directed the show, the music was by Harry Zimmerman, and Tony La Frano was the announcer. Others responsible for the program were Lou Markheim and Herb Margolis who wrote much of "Madero's" dialect.

After Jack returned to Los Angeles on the heels of Dick Breen, he lived in the Marathon Street duplex, preparing to begin a career again. With two years of radio under his belt, and *Pat Novak* and *Johnny Madero* on his resume, Webb sensed the time was nearing to make it big. In what Jack called "blind free-lancing confidence," he played numerous small radio parts on major radio shows as a police officer, gangster, burglar, and villains. Jack would later recall that "for eight or nine weeks, I was everybody's hot cake." He soon had screen and voice tests and visited casting directors for Hollywood movie studios.

The future looked auspicious enough for Jack professionally. Personally, the summer of 1947 would see him marry a young, talented, beautiful woman, who, in her own way, would rival him.

Julie, Lisa, Jack and Stacy

Courtesy of Jack Webb Archives

"The magic carpet unraveled and I couldn't get a job."

O ne 1941 evening when Jack was living with Gus and "Gram" on Marathon Street, the two young men decided to visit a malt shop on the opposite side of Vermont Avenue. On their way, they approached two girls talking in front of a large apartment house. One was fifteen-year-old Julie London and the other was Caroline Woods. Gus and Jack flirted with the teens in a chance meeting that eventually joined two of the premium entertainers of the 1950's as husband and wife.

Julie London was born Gail Peck in Santa Rosa, California on September 26, 1926. Her parents were vaudeville and radio singers, and her father had a San Bernardino radio show. The family later opened a photography

Out for dinner with wife Julie London

Courtesy of Jack Webb Archives

business that the Depression ruined. However, despite any loss of income, Julie's parents made certain their daughter lived comfortably and had a normal teen life.

When the Peck family moved to Hollywood – "just one step ahead of the truant officer," according to *TV Guide* – Julie's school grades were poor. She was more mature than the other children and, thus, became bored with her peers. London recalled, "A doctor decided I was allergic — literally allergic — to school. I stopped going. Even my sense of humor was more adult than that of the other kids. They thought I was a real idiot because I didn't talk their language, and I thought they were childish, so we didn't mix too well."

Then teenage Julie had met Jack Webb, six years her senior. Julie's parents expressed no objections to the meeting. They also approved of her withdrawing from school to work in Nancy's Department Store. The elegant women's store was located on Hollywood Boulevard where Julie worked as an elevator operator at age 16, though she listed her age as 19 to get the job. She also worked for a time at Brooks Brothers Department Store.

Jack and Julie dated for a year until he went into the Army, after which they did not see much of one another for about a year. London was, in the meantime, "discovered" at Nancy's Department Store by agent Sue Carol, who later became actor Alan Ladd's wife and an agent for Webb. Julie was initially signed as an actress for $250 weekly, but she kept her elevator job for four years earning $19 a week. She soon assumed the stage name of Julie London, as listed in the credits of her first film in 1944. Daughter Stacy recalled that Julie picked up the London name, because she was attracted to the English city as well as the sound of the word.

Julie sang periodically with local bands in her teens, although becoming a singer was not her original goal. Instead, she aspired to act in motion pictures and was fortunate to have an employer who excused her from work to play bit film parts that occasionally came along. State laws, however, required juveniles to attend school. So, Julie attended and graduated from the Hollywood Professional High School in 1944. At age 18, she had matured to become a beautiful and appealing young woman, whose acting career seemed to have found its course.

London's first two film appearances were a small part in *Jungle Woman* followed by a larger role in *Nabonga* in 1944. *Jungle Woman* was directed by Sam Newfield with a cast including Buster Crabbe and Fifi D'Orsay. Film critic Leonard Maltin calls the movie an "incredible cheapie" about a plane crash survivor (London) making friends with a local gorilla and "good for laughs, anyway." The film was later re-titled *Gorilla*. The film *A Night In Paradise* followed for Julie in 1946.

A starlet, London was photographed by *Esquire* magazine as a World War II pin-up girl in a prone pose wearing what the magazine called "a wet metallic drape." While Webb was stationed at Laughlin Field in Del Rio, he saw Julie's picture on a barrack's wall and boasted to her admirers that he knew and dated her. When Webb was mocked and doubted, he wrote Julie a letter, and she replied confirming his story. Jack's influence and status in the barracks immediately rose.

When Webb was discharged from the Army and returned to Los Angeles, the two resumed dating. Jack then frequently dressed like a college student with black and white saddle shoes, an Angora sweater, and shirt open at the neck. The style was to hide any appearance of poverty. The couple enjoyed attending the movies. Regardless of how terrible a film might be, Julie recalled that Jack always spotted some part that interested him: "We'd sometimes sit through double features twice so Jack could see a certain little bit of business. In a way, he was going to school." In theaters or at intermissions when Julie was performing, the two engaged in youthful "necking." They reportedly also saw one another in San Francisco while Jack was doing *Pat Novak* at KGO. They resumed regular dating again when Webb followed Dick Breen to Hollywood. The Southern California climate and dating Julie must have agreed with Jack, as his ulcer soon disappeared. In July 1947, Jack and Julie were wed.

For about one month, the near penniless newlyweds shared apartments with friends, such as Tommy Thompson and Dick "Moe" Turner and his wife. About the only income Jack received was from writing film scripts. He reportedly was so persistent with his screenplay offerings that he was sometimes given $10 to $20 just to vacate a lot. When he earned no money for the day, Webb quipped, "It looks like tomorrow I'll be breaking light bulbs again."

Before long, the two moved into a duplex at 3936 Marathon Street. Their bedroom was decorated with a large bamboo valance designed by Jack and Gus Stamos, which had accessible light switches to program reading lights and indirect lighting to create a romantic atmosphere. A huge stereo system was constantly in use, and a telephone was installed as Jack waited for the "big money calls." The phone calls did not come and Webb was suddenly a forgotten man. "The magic carpet unraveled and I couldn't get a job."

Within nine months the marriage faltered and the couple separated for nearly a year. Julie recalled that being married to "a struggling bit actor as intense and ambitious as Webb involved some difficult psychological problems," and separation seemed to be the best decision for both of them. She remembered that without any "preliminaries" or "big scenes," Jack left home one morning only saying good-bye. She telephoned him several days later to see if he was coming home. He never did. Several of Jack's friends recalled that Julie was not without her faults while others considered her polite and fun.

During the separation, Webb shared a sparsely furnished apartment

Preparing for a radio performance

Donated by Harry Bartell

with NBC announcer Eddy King. Money was so scarce that luxuries were unaffordable. As a cocktail, Jack drank a homemade brew his landlord introduced to him. "Slivovitz" was a concoction of cherries and pure alcohol, which Jack recalls "tasted like a red-hot rivet and unscrewed the top of my head." He took any job that he could find, while he and Julie attempted to save their marriage. Finally, Webb's professional film debut came in the 1948 with the Eagle Lion production *Hollow Triumph*. Paul Henreid and Joan Bennett were in the cast. The picture was later re-titled *The Scar*. In 1949, Jack had a brief part in *Sword In The Desert*.

On the motion picture lot, he pursued his quest for film knowledge as relentlessly as he did with radio. Webb placed himself in the role of the soundman, light man, director, stage carpenter, and most any position having to do with making films. Perhaps without realizing it, Jack was preparing to become a film director and producer and learning much that would be valuable for him in a new industry about to become an international phenomenon — television.

William Conrad (radio's *Matt Dillon*) and Webb occasionally worked together in *Escape*, an excellent radio series of "high adventure" programs to first air on CBS on July 7, 1947. The program, chiefly an anthology with no star, remained on radio until 1954. Ron Lackmann, in his book *Same Time ... Same Station,* describes the series as one which "usually presented protagonists in very difficult, almost impossible to overcome situations." Lackmann tells of one series tale that had "three men trapped in a lighthouse as millions of rats from a deserted ghost ship covered the place, trying to get in as they searched for food." Others in *Escape* who worked with Jack then and later were narrator Paul Frees, Harry Morgan, Virginia Gregg, Frank Lovejoy, and Barton Yarborough. *Escape* was produced and directed by William N. Robson and Norman Macdonnell.

In the summer of 1948, Webb returned to radio as *Jeff Regan, Investigator* for CBS. The character was the same tough detective role Jack played as *Pat Novak* and *Johnny Madero*. Wilms Herbert played "The Lion," "Regan's" boss. The show was written by E. Jack Neuman and produced by Sterling Tracy. In 1949, Jack abandoned *Jeff Regan*. Frank Graham next played the part. The story character underwent a significant change from Webb's "Regan" having a chip on his shoulder to Graham's "Regan" being a defender of the underdog.

Webb's *Pat Novak* fans demanded his return in 1948 and 1949. *Novak* was broadcast by ABC from coast-to-coast by February 1949 and billed as "the network's 'most unusual' crime-detective series," resuming "Novak's" career from where it had paused. The dialogue was fast and filled with cliches made for Webb's smart-mouth quips. In fact, Jack's *Novak* cliches and his purple dialogue, such as the following, made the series a success:

> The street was as deserted as a warm bottle of beer ... a car started up down the street and the old man couldn't have made it with a pocketful of aces ... I caught a glimpse of the license plate in a dull, surprised way, the way you grab a feather out of an angel's wing.

With the resurrection of *Pat Novak*, Webb was dubbed by *Time* magazine as the "ultimate radio hard boiler." Jack was so successful that he was parodied on a competing program *Richard Diamond* with "Pat Cosak" who copied Jack's "Novak" mannerisms. *Broadway Is My Beat* was another 1949 CBS detective story that imitated Webb's tough cop character for "Danny Glover" played by Larry Thor. Jack also contributed to *Dr. Kildare* in 1949-1950. The *Dr. Kildare* movies and radio programs were as popular in the 1930's-1940's as Richard Chamberlain's "Dr. Kildare" or the later television offering of *Marcus Welby, M.D.* The earlier "Kildare" programs offered acting opportunities for Stacy Harris, Paul Frees, Raymond Burr, and featured music by Walter Schumann. All of these people later worked with Webb at his Mark VII Productions studio when he became a star.

In 1949, Jack and Julie reconciled and moved into a modest house on Serrano Street. The success of their marriage required that they spend more time together. They even acquired a dog as a family pet. By then Julie had appeared in *The Red House* (1947), *Tap Roots* (1948), and *Task Force* (1949). Jack, although active in radio, was still searching for his "pot of gold" to support a wife who was expecting their first child. He would not have imagined or believed that he would find the end of his rainbow at night in the back seat of a police squad car.

**Somehow he managed to
find time to relax and do
the mowing.**

Look Magazine — Courtesy of Jack Webb Archives

Radio Dragnet — "Don't change a thing! Keep it just as it is."

Webb had unsuccessfully attempted to create several new radio shows, when he landed the part of forensic chemist "Lieutenant Lee Jones" in the film *He Walked By Night*. The 1948 cast included Richard Basehart and Scott Brady. The movie, based on a true case concerning the murder of a California police officer, was the embryo for Webb's *Dragnet*. The word "dragnet" was used in the picture several times, as was the *Dragnet* disclaimer, "Only The Names Are Changed To Protect The Innocent." The Los Angeles City Hall also appeared on screen — all to be associated with Webb's sensational radio, television, and film creation of *Dragnet*.

Jack recalled that he had little interest in police officers when he was a boy, and that he did not know any policemen. "There were too many other interesting characters in the neighborhood," Jack would say. However, during the filming of *He Walked By Night*, Detective Sergeant Marty Wynn took Webb aside and approached him for a project. This Los Angeles Police Department (LAPD) technical adviser informed Jack that he had access to the Department's files, most of which were in the public domain. Wynn suggested that Webb use the LAPD file resources to produce a series of *realistic* police stories in a format similar to *He Walked By Night*. Jack's immediate indifference was due partly to the number of current police programs already available, including *True Detective Mysteries, Gangbusters,* and *Mr. District Attorney*.

The rotund and cheerful Detective Sergeant concurred there were indeed such programs, however added, "It rankles every damn cop in the country when they hear those farfetched tales about crime. Why don't you do a *real* story about policemen?" Webb remained unmoved, but informed Marty that being "farfetched" was why their ratings remained high. Wynn then touched on what became the essence of *Dragnet*, "And they're all jazzed up and the detectives are all supermen, and they do it with mirrors. *Real cops don't work like that.*" Jack seemed disinterested. Marty forgot the conversation soon thereafter.

Three weeks later, Jack visited the Elysian Park Police Academy, where Detective Wynn was taking a refresher course concerning the rules of evidence and criminal law. Webb, showing more interest in law enforcement, inquired if he could ride with Wynn and his partner, Detective Vance Brasher while they were on duty. Night after night, Jack sat in the back of a police cruiser, listening to what he characterized as "radio's unemotional reports of crime and human weakness," while observing every reply and procedure of the two officers.

Jack inquired about such topics as forcible entry, frisking suspects, and asked Marty to speak like a cop. Marty replied, "We don't talk any different than you do." Webb then asked, "What would you do if you had a suspect?" Wynn answered, "Why, I'd go down to R & I and pull the package." Jack replied, *That's what I mean!"*

("R & I" is the "Records and Identification" section at the police department and "package" is a "criminal record." See the Glossary at the back of the book for more "Dragnetese" and translations.)

Nearly a year passed before a financially strapped Webb realized the genius of Detective Wynn's suggestion. Jack had become increasingly fascinated with police work, and he came to believe deeply that police officers were men and women trying to improve their lives and profession against a daily backdrop of high drama and tremendous odds. So, despite (and due to) Julie's pregnancy and their dwindling financial resources, Jack dropped everything to create *Dragnet* for radio in 1949.

He unquestionably relied on ideas learned in *Pat Novak, Johnny Madero*, and *He Walked By Night*. Webb first considered setting the story in San Francisco, but better radio production facilities and a large metropolitan police force were available in Los Angeles. Jack admitted that he knew nothing about police departments. His desire was simply to create and produce a police-type radio program that was as realistic as possible.

To achieve that goal Detective Sergeants Marty Wynn, Vance Brasher, and Detective Captain Jack Donohoe read through the LAPD files for suitable stories and offered Webb technical advice. Jack frequently visited the Department gathering color for his stories. One detective recalled, "He'd come down and they'd get a hot-shot call [robbery in progress], and he'd roll with them." Jack studied police codes and procedures and after observing a robbery in progress from the station, he wrote:

> There was always something going on, like robbery, a hot detail. A cop would come in: 'Those #@&*! just knocked off the Western Union at 7th and Flower.' The same gang had knocked over three places in the last few hours ... they (the detectives) start checking for the pattern, to see if they can figure where the gang will hit next ... but they're very calm; they don't shriek and yell. It's a business. That's what we try to do in *Dragnet*.

Webb narrated the pilot story in his short-clipped delivery, giving the program an official sound. However, *Dragnet* could not get off the ground without the endorsement of the Los Angeles Police Department. Detective Wynn requested an audience with Deputy Chief Joseph F. Reid at City Hall, where Jack's creation was previewed in Reid's office. Wynn, Brasher, and Webb were nervous as Chief Reid simultaneously leafed through a stack of papers on his desk until his reading of Webb's story was complete.

All apprehension ended when Chief Reid approved the format, though he insisted that all Los Angeles Police Department information must be accurate.

The Chief and others in law enforcement had little tolerance for Hollywood's past portrayals of law officers from the *Keystone Kops* through the brutal, bumbling, rogue "cops" typically seen in the movies. Any use of the word "cop" caused some sensitivity for which Webb was always attentive. Nevertheless, the slang expression often made for better script than more respectable words, though the LAPD could endure the realistic use of the word "cop." Police Chief Clemence B. Horrall, who later endorsed Webb's portrayal of police officers, told Jack, "You're on the right track. You don't make heroes of cops and you're reflecting the day-to-day drudgery of police work." Specifically, *Dragnet's* guidelines were: (1) To never glorify or defame police officers; (2) To represent police as average or regular human beings; and (3) All dramatizations must follow the facts of a genuine LAPD case.

Interim Chief William A.Worton cooperated with Webb from 1949-1950, as did Chief William H. Parker during his tenure beginning in 1950. However, Parker also was critical of radio and Hollywood's past image of police officers, complaining that motion pictures mostly glorified

"Machine Gun Kelly," John Dillinger, and other criminals, rather than the police. Yet, since the LAPD and Webb had made previous agreements, Parker relented and eventually became an ardent supporter of *Dragnet*. He later assisted television *Dragnet* and received credits on each show. However, there was never an "official," or legal relationship between Webb and the Department, whose support added realism to *Dragnet* and helped reduce production costs. Despite the lack of a formal agreement, the department would support Jack in all his endeavors for the rest of his life.

Quickly discarding such show titles of "The Cop" and "The Sergeant," Webb, without hesitation, preferred *Dragnet*. The word is defined as, "A system of coordinated procedures for apprehending criminal suspects or other wanted persons." However, Jack realized that even with LAPD's blessing, *Dragnet's* realistic approach to police work could be hard to sell commercially. The problem was that Webb wanted – and the Department demanded –his creation to be more fact than fiction, portraying officers as human beings who do dangerous jobs for low pay. He was also trying to get away from any "dumb-cop" stereotypes. Moreover, Jack realized that some viewed police officers as not what he called "being normal, plain guys working for a pay-check." This bias might have created a mental block to *Dragnet* for radio executives, who were accustomed to police stories in the traditional tough-guy style.

As *Dragnet* was minus the gore and violence associated with other police stories, many — including some of Jack's writers — did not understand that violence could be portrayed by suggestion and innuendo, as was done by Webb. Jack would explain that "we often went for months without anyone on the show getting so much as a blister. It seemed that where there were cops, there had to be robbers. And where there were cops and robbers, there had to be violence. Policemen don't always shoot-'em up or get into brawls with thugs and hoodlums." Few saw that much of a police officer's work is routine. However, *New York World-Telegram And Sun* reporter Harriet Van Horne in December 1951 rated *Dragnet* as "one of radio's more intelligent (and less bloody) crime programs" and praised the show for its emphasis on "the people who enforce the law rather than on those who break it."

Dragnet was one of the first radio programs to "break the unwritten taboo against dramatizing sex crimes," and it was the first show to extensively introduce the language of police officers to the public. For example, "KMA 367" requested a radio check and "390" identified a drunk. "MO" was a "method of operation," and "R and I" meant "records and identification." Per episode, Webb's demand for accuracy also required as many as five radio sound effects men who could produce over 300 sounds.

Jack vividly recalled that when he first offered *Dragnet* to CBS in Hollywood, he was "given the cold-shoulder" and lectured "it'll never work." He was informed that there was too much attention to detail and that the pace of the stories was too slow: "You don't even see the crime committed. And you can't tell true stories because you'll get sued every week." Webb argued that he was changing every person's true name to avoid lawsuits. Nevertheless, he was again told, "Sorry!"

Jack next approached NBC, which had recently lost many stars to CBS and had an excess of open-air time. Program Director Homer Canfield praised Webb's scripts and after three auditions, weeks of rewriting, fine-tuning the characters, and organizing an orchestra for background music, the show was awarded one of the lowest-rated half-hour slots in radio.

Dragnet was born in NBC's Los Angeles Studio H on station KFI and went on the air for transcontinental broadcast on June 3, 1949 at 8:00 P.M. The program was initially intended as a summer replacement show. Webb received $150 each for the early episodes. Two years later, *Dragnet* catapulted to the nation's premiere radio show.

NBC gave Webb a contract with a four-week cancellation arrangement, allowing the network to shelve *Dragnet* with one week's notice. Four times the program received a reprieve as Webb and his staff worked feverishly to improve the show. After 18 weeks on a "sustaining basis," the Liggett & Myers (L&M) Tobacco Company agreed to stand-by *Dragnet* by advertising L&M's Fatima Cigarettes. For seven years, the program was singularly sponsored by Liggett & Myers, who made Fatima, L&M, and Chesterfield cigarettes. Webb recalled, "I could not possibly foresee that we had lightning in a bottle, nor the violent impact the show would have on my personal life."

Dragnet was synonymous with Detective Sergeant "Joe Friday," who became endeared to the American public with his terse "Just the facts, ma'am" and "My name's Friday — I'm a cop" signature sayings. Webb was accused of taking the name from Robinson Crusoe's man "Friday" or the day of the week. Others guessed that Webb adopted "Friday" because the name was easy to recall and was race-neutral. Jack claimed, "I really don't know where the name came from." Nevertheless, he wanted the name to represent a composite of many officers with no connotations whatsoever. He said the detective "could be Jewish or Greek or English or anything. He could be all men to all people in their living rooms." For Jack, the identity was unique, yet commonplace.

"Sergeant Friday" became as well-known to Americans as "Sherlock Holmes" and "Dick Tracy." In his under-played character, "Joe" was, according to Jack, "a quiet, conservative, dedicated policeman who, as in real life, was just one little cog in a great enforcement machine." He was cast with a "neutral character," who had no childhood, religious or educational backgrounds, no war record, or any personal side. A psychologist might suggest that such a character was a projection of Jack's life. Webb declared that "Joe" was neither "a comic nor a slug-'em-and-love-'em policeman. He was simply a man with police training and intelligence,

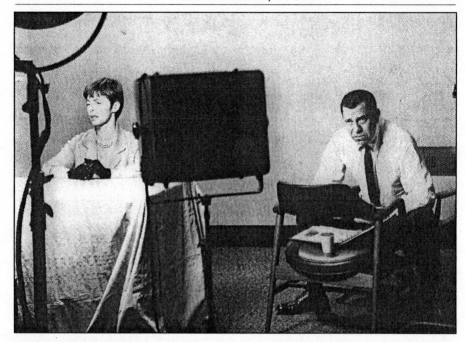

Peggy Webber with Jack on the set of *Dragnet 1967*

Donated by Peggy Webber —
Courtesy of Jack Webb Archives

whose job was crime detection and who didn't get into a tizzy about anything." Neither was "Friday" a super-sleuth-type who mostly worked alone. "Joe Friday" was "a department man, a professional detective working in league with others." Webb recalled:

> I wanted him to be the steady, plodding kind of cop the public never really understood or appreciated or ever heard about. I wanted ed him to be an honest, decent, home-loving guy — the image of 50,000 real peace officers who do their work without the help of beautiful, mysterious blondes, hefty swigs from an ever-present bottle and handy automatics thrust into their belts or hidden in their socks. I called him "Joe Friday."

"Joe's" radio *Dragnet* partner was "Sergeant Ben Romero," played by Barton Yarborough until Barton's death in 1951. On radio, Yarborough played "Cliff" in the highly acclaimed *One Man's Family* and "Doc Long" in the original *I Love A Mystery*. In *Dragnet*, "Romero" was a family man with attendant family problems. "Joe" simply lived at home with "Ma Friday."

Peggy Webber and Virginia Gregg were two of Jack's favorite actresses, who remained with him throughout their careers. Both Peggy and Jack came from similar back-grounds. They first met when they worked on *Escape*. Though the two worked together in radio on *Pat Novak* and *Pete Kelly's Blues*, Peggy was recruited for radio *Dragnet* while she was making *This Is Your FBI*. Webber did over 100 *Dragnet* radio episodes and appeared in various Mark VII produc-tions. In her professional career, she considered playing "Ma Friday" on the radio series and being the mother in the *Big Mother* television episode as her best, most enjoy-able, and favorite roles. Though Peggy admits that she and Jack had their dis-agreements, she explained that they "had a strong affection for each other." Webb fondly referred to her as "Ma" and "Little Fella." He was like a big brother to her. As a pro-ducer and celebrity, Webb confided in Peggy, whom he considered his lucky

Checking a script before an NBC Radio performance

Courtesy of Jack Webb Archives

rabbit's foot. She would recall Jack often saying, "I always win, when I work with you."

Virginia Gregg, a regular in numerous Webb productions, once joked that, "Jack Webb is my mentor and favorite friend. He's everything to me but my lover — damn it!" Virginia apparently entered the acting field via playing the string bass in a radio station house orchestra. She took acting classes at the Pasadena Playhouse and soon went into radio acting, where she excelled.

Some of Webb's other regulars from the early *Dragnet* radio days include Stacy Harris, Raymond Burr, Jack Kruschen, Whit Connors, Vic Perrin, Harry Bartell, Herb Ellis, Olan Soulé, Herb Butterfield, Parley Baer,

Wilms Herbert and Ralph Moody. Yvonne Peattie and Joyce McCluskey participated less, while others appeared for only one production shot. James B. Moser scripted the episodes.

William Rousseau first directed *Dragnet*, but Jack quickly assumed the responsibility, knowing exactly how he wanted each story to resolve. The program was not performed in the presence of live studio audiences as some other shows were. There were two broadcasts: The "East Coast Rehearsal" at 4:00 P.M., sent by long distance telephone lines from Los Angeles to Chicago and New York; and the west coast re-performance at 7:00 P.M. The announcers were Hal Gibney and George Fenneman. Walter Schumann wrote the story music. The "Dumm—de-dum-dum" theme was arguably the most famous four musical notes in the United States during *Dragnet's* zenith. The musical phrase was also recognized in other parts of the world. In 1952, Peggy Webber heard the *Dragnet* theme while living in Japan and remarked, "Once you heard it, you didn't forget it."

For effect and protection against libel suits, Jack created *Dragnet's* introduction and epilogue. Preceding each story was the program music and the proclamation:

> Ladies and gentlemen: The story you are about to hear is true. The names have been changed to protect the innocent. For the next thirty minutes, in cooperation with the Los Angeles Police Department, you will travel step by step on the side of the law, through an actual case, transcribed from official police cases. From beginning to end, from crime to punishment, *Dragnet* is the story of your police force in action.

Each program ended with a brief synopsis of the sentencing of the criminals and the fate of the victims.

When the first few radio episodes did not go well, Webb dropped his lead writer and relied on his friend Jim Moser. This change proved fateful, as Moser's writing talents turned around *Dragnet*. A growing group of loyal listeners soon followed.

Radio audiences were attracted by Webb underplaying "Friday's" role and his novel emphasis of real persons caught up in crime. A $20 robbery was as significant on *Dragnet* as one concerning a $20,000 crime.

LAPD officers learned about radio scripting and visited the studio to read over *Dragnet* stories and identify inaccuracies during their time off. Sometimes, while consuming cups of coffee, the detectives examined scripts through the night. For their labor, officers received $25 a week. Department assistance was also rewarded by Jack's donations to the LAPD Policemen's Benevolent Fund. Among the police and radio staffs, Detective Brasher recalled, "We didn't know what they wanted, they didn't know what we wanted." Always concerned with libel, names and infor-

Chief Parker and an NBC executive at a *Dragnet* radio performance

Picture donated by the L.A.P.D. —
Courtesy of Jack Webb Archives

mation were slightly altered to avoid potential lawsuits. Nonetheless, several did occur.

An unexpected boon assisted the struggling program when columnist John Crosby endorsed *Dragnet* in the *New York Herald Tribune*. Crosby was impressed with the laconic way the police talked and how they approached their cases as a day-in-day-out job. He praised the program's honesty. More significantly for the show's future, Crosby's report apparently influenced NBC's New York executives, who telephoned their Hollywood offices and declared: "Don't change a thing! Keep it just as it is!"

Webb faced ownership difficulties as *Dragnet* was born. Jack's theatrical agent was George Rosenberg, a notorious Hollywood agent in 1948. Rosenberg and his assistant Mike Meshekoff suggested that Jack needed a "Sam Spade" detective-type character in *Dragnet* and warned Webb that his reliance on actual LAPD cases could result in his being sued. Jack ignored the warning and pushed forward.

Rosenberg loaned Webb $300 to pay-off a note on an old car. Rosenberg also agreed to pay Webb a $300 weekly salary. With pressure from Liggett & Myers, Rosenberg persuaded NBC to put up $38,000 to have a television *Dragnet* pilot aired. Following L&M's investment, Webb and Meshekoff agreed not to receive a salary for the initial 13 weeks of production. *Dragnet's* title was placed in Rosenberg's name, leading him to believe that at least a part of the show belonged to him. Jack disagreed, called Rosenberg a "veritable kidnapper," and a nasty fight ensued. Eventually, through Meshekoff, an out of court compromise was reached and Webb retained *Dragnet's* ownership. However, Rosenberg walked away with an undisclosed, but significant, percentage of the show's profits for its production life.

By this time, Meshekoff had departed the Rosenberg agency to become a *Dragnet* producer, receiving a 25% interest in the show. Soon, Webb had his revenge. Rosenberg recalled, "I got a letter from Webb and what the hell do you think it said? Webb was discharging me!" In January 1954, Jack's new business manager, Stanley Meyer, also fired Meshekoff. Rosenberg sued Webb for $300,000 and was awarded $625 weekly from *Dragnet*. Meshekoff eventually emerged with more than a million dollars. Both suits were settled out of court. Jack warned that Hollywood was "full of guys who are expert at riding on your back and putting their hands in your pocket."

Dragnet continued attracting larger radio audiences and received fan mail chiefly from women who confessed they had never submitted fan mail before. The women approved of the program's "grown-up approach," considered Jack to be handsome, and were fascinated by Webb's down playing "Joe Friday's" role. In 1950, Jack nearly won two Peabody Awards, as *Dragnet* joined the top ten radio listings and rose to the number one spot that year.

Webb recalled, "Remembering that talk with [Detective] Marty Wynn now, I get a little queasy thinking how I almost missed the boat." Though Jack clearly caught the boat to professional stardom, his boat to family happiness would soon be hitting some very choppy waters ahead.

"I can't stop working."

In 1950, Jack and Julie were living in an unimpressive white, frame stucco house on Serrano Street in Los Angeles. For the first time in his life, Jack lived in a house belonging to him. He was making enough money to provide medical attention for his mom "Maggie" and grandmother "Gram." Apparently, "Maggie" was separated or divorced by the early 1950's, and for some time, she lived with Julie and Jack.

Alcohol remained a problem for "Maggie. She too often retreated into the privacy of her room with a large amount of liquor and remained there for days. On one occasion, the police summoned Jack when she was drunk and had walked into the ocean. "Maggie's" conduct was not beneficial to Jack and Julie's marriage. Yet, the two did spend more time together play-

Jack and Julie with daughters Stacy, 3, and Lisa, 6 months

McCall's Magazine —
Courtesy of Jack Webb Archives

In the pool with Patsy

TV Starland — Courtesy of Jack Webb Archives

ing records and enjoying country rides. They even added a dachshund pup to the family. They enjoyed jazz music and often visited Hollywood's Bantam Cock Club & Restaurant to listen to The Herm Saunders Trio perform.

Their first daughter, Stacy was born on January 11, 1950. The child was named after actor Stacy Harris, who starred in many *Dragnet* episodes and in *Appointment With Danger* in 1951. The Webb's normally well-behaved dachshund welcomed Stacy to the family the day she arrived from the hospital by urinating on Stacy's crib – a story that Stacy joked about for the remainder of her life. The family found it less humorous that Jack spent much of his time in the early 1950's on the Disney studio lot producing and improving *Dragnet*, rather than being at home with Julie and their new baby.

Jack's rising celebrity fame was apparent when a Los Angeles motorcycle traffic officer, who immediately recognized "Joe Friday's" distinctive voice, stopped Webb for a traffic violation. Jack was lectured that "Sergeant Friday" should know better than to run a traffic light, and the officer promptly ticketed Webb. Similar situations occurred throughout Webb's life, even among his friends. In the late 1960's, Jack was stopped for speeding on the Ventura Freeway. As the officer approached Jack's Cadillac and recognized who was driving, he said, "Oh, excuse me sir, I'm sorry, I didn't mean to pull you over." Webb replied, "Son, if I deserve the ticket, I want you to give it to me."

At first the officer refused, but after a stern law and order lecture from Webb, Jack was issued the citation. Later that week a rumor surfaced concerning an officer who was demoted for writing "Sergeant Friday" a speeding ticket, but the story was never substantiated. Several years later the same officer unknowingly cited one of the *Adam-12* cars for being illegally parked on Colfax Avenue.

James Bacon wrote for the *Los Angeles Herald Examiner* and had sev-

Halls of Montezuma, with Richard Widmark (left) and Richard Boone (right).

Courtesy of Jack Webb Archives

eral small roles in _Dragnet._ After filming one episode, a traffic officer stopped Bacon for speeding. Desperate and hoping mention of Webb's name may help, James informed the policeman, "I just finished playing a cop with Jack Webb." The traffic officer replied, "That's what they all say," and issued Bacon a ticket.

In 1950-1951, Webb remained active in radio, and he appeared in a number of movies with rising stars. Jack recalled, "If you went out for popcorn, you missed me in any number of films." One of his most outstanding performances was in _The Men,_ directed by Fred Zinnemann. The story was set in a veteran's hospital for paraplegics and dealt with rebuilding the physical and psychological lives of crippled World War II men. The 1950 picture was Marlon Brando's debut, and starred Brando and Teresa Wright. Jack's role was the paraplegic, "Norm." The film received an Academy Award nomination for the best story and screenplay. Webb also appeared as "Correspondent Sergeant Dickerman" in _Halls Of Montezuma_ with Richard Widmark, Jack Palance, Robert Wagner, Karl Malden, Richard Boone, and Martin Milner. The excellent cast made-up for some of the character stereotypes in this World War II story about Marines fighting in the Pacific theatre.

Dark City was Charlton Heston's film debut

Courtesy of Jack Webb Archives

Webb appeared as "Augie" with his future *Dragnet* companion Henry (Harry) Morgan in the 1950 film *Dark City*. The crime story cast Lizabeth Scott, Dean Jagger, Don DeFore, Ed Begley, and Charlton Heston in his film debut. *Sunset Boulevard*, released in 1950, was a story about a Hollywood silent film star who lived her life in a glorious past. Billy Wilder directed, and Gloria Swanson, who played the lead, was nominated for an Academy Award. The picture won three Oscar's for writing. The cast included William Holden, Eric von Stroheim, Nancy Olson, Buster Keaton, and the legendary Cecil B. DeMille. The picture reunited Jack with Hedda Hopper, whom he first met as a neophyte KGO radio announcer in San Francisco.

In 1951, Jack had a role in *You're In The Navy Now*. The World War II comedy included Gary Cooper, Jane Greer, and Eddie Albert (who in real life had served as a World War II U.S. Navy combat officer at Tarawa with the Marines). Lee Marvin and Charles Buchinski (Bronson) made their film debuts.

In the same year, Jack appeared in Paramount's *Appointment With Danger.* The film concerned postal theft. The story was taken from actual cases in the files of The Postal Inspection Service. The screenplay was written by Richard Breen and Warren Duff and starred Alan Ladd with Phyllis Calvert, Paul Stewart, Stacy Harris, and Jan Sterling. Harry Morgan and Jack Webb ("Joe Regas"), cast as villains, were totally out of character with their future police officer roles. Leonard Maltin notes the "best bit" of the movie is Ladd "dropping Webb on a handball court." "Regas" was involved in various brawls throughout the picture, which climaxes when he and Postal Inspector "Al Goddard" (Alan Ladd) engage in a gunfight. Fortunately, Webb played his last part as a villain in *Appointment With Danger,* as criminal roles did not suit him.

A promotional shot for *Pete Kelly's Blues* radio program

Courtesy of Jack Webb Archives

Many of Jack's associates believed that his forte was in radio. *Pete Kelly's Blues* aired on radio from July 4 to September 19, 1951. The 1920's and jazz idol Bix Biederbecke were Jack's inspirations for a radio story set in Kansas City during the Prohibition years. The decade always held an interest for Webb who wrote:

> Then I got interested in the era. If they didn't like the way a guy parted his hair, they knocked him off. And it was the only time when the cream of society was on cozy terms with the hoodlum element. They had to be, what with bootleggers on their back

stoop. And wacky? Man! There was marathon dancers and flagpole sitters and flappers and hip flasks and raccoon coats and Lucky Lindy and Dempsey-Firpo. Wonderful!

"Kelly" was a musician who played the cornet in a speak-easy with his "Pete Kelly's Big Seven Band." The first 13 scripts were written by Dick Breen, who later wrote *Kelly's* film script. Jack's school classmates "Chuck" Anderson and Gus Stamos attended the program Press Review for which Jack and Julie rented a large Hollywood nightclub. "Chuck" Anderson characterized *Pete Kelly's Blues* on radio as "one of Webb's best showings," which served as the platform for his 1955 film and a 1959 made-for-television series.

In 1950, Julie appeared in *The Return Of The Frontiersman*. In 1951, she appeared with Rock Hudson in *The Fat Man*. However, she again happily interrupted her film career for family.

Jack and Julie's second daughter Lisa was born on November 29, 1952. However, professional satisfaction was no substitute for marital contentment, and the on-and-off-again marriage ended when Julie filed for a divorce in August 1953. She believed that Webb's frantic schedule and his "compulsion to work" ultimately caused their divorce. She said that "she could not hurry or worry with him — nor understand why he hurried and worried so much himself." Jack agreed that his "work demands got too heavy." The projection room became his home. He would recall:

> We were lost ... I never could adapt myself. I never got home on time for dinner. When I did get there I was usually too tied up in my own problems to be a companion for my wife. I never saw the kids except for two minutes in the morning, when I left for the studio, and on Sunday. And then maybe I'd get a call from the studio at nine o'clock Sunday morning and have to be there at nine-twenty. I can't stop working, or worrying about the show. I'd go crazy if I tried. So our marriage got to the point where love wasn't enough.

Others shared that Webb was so determined to succeed that he would not even take the time to use his own swimming pool. Many believed that he was driven by his fear of living in poverty again.

On another occasion, Jack offered that "if marriage makes your life a living hell — not that I am saying mine was! — you simply have to take the only way out." The break-up and divorce was traumatic for both of them. Julie became depressed. Jack was resentful for awhile, though Webb's *Dragnet* partner Ben Alexander helped him get through the bad feelings of divorce. Jack's high school girlfriend, Margaret MacGregor asserted that leaving Julie was the dumbest thing that Jack ever did.

After the marriage failed, Julie and the two children first moved to Paris, France for about one year and then to Palm Springs, California. The divorce was final in 1954. Both Jack and Julie claimed their settlement stories were exaggerated. Julie reported that she received a $100,000 lump sum, $18,000 a year alimony, her car, and money from the house that she and Jack owned. Trust funds were established for the two children. In August 1954, Jack reported that Julie received a cash settlement of $250,000, insurance for her and the children, $1,800 monthly alimony, and $350 a month for child care.

Appointment With Danger, with Alan Ladd marking Jack's last role as a criminal

Courtesy of Jack Webb Archives

Some reported that Jack was not paying Julie sufficient support, but others said that she received a million dollars. Webb could never understand why people wanted to deal in another person's misery. The truth, according to Jack, is that he and Julie divided their property, and he paid her $1,500 a month alimony and $350 monthly child support. No documents were seen to verify any settlement. But Webb stated that he "was very happy to pay" Julie, since she "was entitled to it, for having been my wife and the mother of my children."

Following their separation and divorce, Webb appeared around Holly-

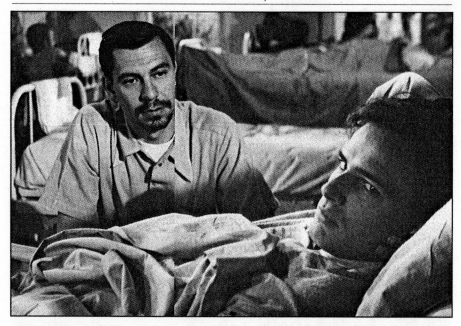

The Men, **1950, Marlon Brando's film debut. Jack played "Norm," a paraplegic. The film was nominated for an Academy Award for best story and screenplay.**

Courtesy of Jack Webb Archives

wood with beauties Dorothy Towne, Myrna Hansen (Miss USA 1953), and Mamie Van Doren riding in Jack's white convertible Cadillac. He and Julie remained on good terms for the sake of the children and were friends for the rest of Webb's life. Some maintained that Jack and Julie still loved one another long after their divorce.

Julie enjoyed a remarkable film, television, and music career, in many ways the equal of Jack's. Among her career highs were having her "star" added to the Hollywood Walk Of Fame, and performing in the White House for President and Mrs. John F. Kennedy. However, Julie related on several occasions that she was "terrified by live audiences," and gladly left the club circuit "for the most part, without a backward glance."

Ironically, her greatest hit record, from her first album *Julie Is Her Name*, was originally intended for Ella Fitzgerald to sing in Jack's film *Pete Kelly's Blues*. When the ballad was omitted from the film, Julie performed the song for the Liberty label and made recording industry history. The record immediately sold over 800,000 copies and continued climbing on the charts to pass the one million mark. Still a standard for singers today, the song was entitled *Cry Me A River*.

"My name's Friday. I'm a cop!"

The United States returned to an Asian war in Korea from 1950-1953, as "suburbia," jet aircraft, and television were becoming more commonplace. On September 4, 1951, the first transcontinental television program aired when Americans witnessed President Harry S. Truman address the Japanese World War II Peace Treaty Conference in San Francisco. The event was carried from New York to San Francisco via 107 concrete and steel towers placed 28 miles apart, transporting signals by microwave relays for an estimated 14,670,000 people to view. The technological achievement tremendously opened an infant television industry, which by 1952 was beginning to overtake motion pictures and radio as the nation's primary entertainment source.

As more and better receivers were built, viewers were drawn to TV to see Arthur Godfrey, Milton Berle, Sid Caesar, Red Skelton, and others who became a part of television's "Golden Age." The queen of the black and white era was Lucille Ball. *Babaloo*, her first episode of *I Love Lucy*, premiered on CBS on October 15, 1951. Other new programs that year were television portrayals of *Amos 'N Andy* and the soap operas of *Search For Tomorrow* and *Love Of Life*. Edward R. Murrow first appeared on *Hear It Now*. The November 18, 1951 telecast carried live images of the Statue of Liberty and San Francisco Bay, as Murrow observed, "We are impressed by a medium through which a man sitting in his living room has been able, for the first time, to look at two oceans at once."

During the late 1940's and very early 1950's, a small number of television stories featured romantic detective rogues in programs such as *Lights Out, Inner Sanctum, Barney Blake, Police Reporter, The Big Story, Man Against Crime, Ellery Queen, Mark Saber, Rocky King, Inside Detective*, and *Martin Kane - Private Eye*. Meanwhile, the radio version of *Dragnet* retained its popularity and ratings. In 1951, the Liggett & Myers Tobacco Company cautiously considered risking "Sergeant Friday's" transition to television. Webb recalled, "Chesterfield cigarettes took the gamble with me."

Jack with Mike Meshekoff put together a sample television pilot from one of *Dragnet's* many radio scripts, and the episode "clicked." Working with little production capital and rented cameras, Webb quickly organized a staff to select stories and assembled a cast to meet production demands. Sixteen and eighteen hour work days were common in *Dragnet's* early years, when as much as five days were necessary to produce one 30-minute TV show.

Filming television *Dragnet* began early on the morning of Columbus Day, 1951. The work was arduous, but Julie London offered the cast some

STUNNING JULIE NEWMAR:

HOW A BEAUTY STAYS THAT WAY

see page 18

TV GUIDE

LOCAL PROGRAMS
FEBRUARY 2-8
15¢

JACK WEBB

On the cover of TV Guide, February 2, 1963

relief when she visited the set delivering baskets of food, at times outfitted in boots and fur coat. Webb received an order on December 5 for 13 programs to begin airing the following month. The Los Angeles Police Department came to Webb's rescue by permitting him to film scenes in its offices, which gave the episodes a documentary appearance. The premiere episode was completed in two days, but Jack was not pleased with the results.

Jack saw a need to bring the camera in closer for tight shots, as most viewers had small television screens (14-inches), making distant scenes difficult to see. Though consuming an additional two days of filming, Jack improved the look even more by shooting the actors from their chests up to emphasize faces, intensify the drama, and to bring the viewer closer to the subject.

Jack relied mostly on radio actors who had mastered acting with their voices while reading from a script. Whether out of necessity or creativity (or a bit of both), Jack pioneered the use of teleprompters in filmmaking. This innovation, placed to the side of the camera, displayed an actor's lines in large print allowing the actor to read the script. The teleprompter saved hours of memorization and eliminated retakes caused by an actor forgetting lines. However, reading script from a teleprompter, in the opinion of some, took away from truly acting the role.

The very first television *Dragnet* was a preview broadcast presented in a special edition of a *Chesterfield Sound Off Time* televised on December 16, 1951. This episode, entitled *The Human Bomb*, starred Webb with Stacy Harris and Raymond Burr (later known for his own roles as "Perry

Mason," "Conrad," and "Ironside"). The 26-minute broadcast was billed as "a real-life thriller" about a deranged man (Harris) who threatened to blow up the Los Angeles City Hall and jail if his incarcerated brother "Sam Edwards" was not released. The story was a total success with Webb's sponsor, the public, and even television's critics. However, NBC preferred that *Dragnet* be produced in New York. Webb was adamant about remaining in Los Angeles, and with the support of the Liggett & Myers Tobacco Company, Jack prevailed. He then received $38,000 to produce an NBC premier and presented *The Big Mother* episode to the country on January 3, 1952.

Dragnet* was initially scheduled to appear each Thursday night from 9:00 to 9:30 P.M., sponsored by Chesterfield cigarettes. However, the show's success was so sudden that Jack did not have ample episodes in reserve for a weekly appearance. This

Barton Yarborough as "Sergeant Ben Romero" in the pilot television episode of *Dragnet* — "The Human Bomb," aired on December 16, 1951.

Cosmopolitan Magazine —
Courtesy of Jack Webb Archives

shortage of shows, from January to March 1952, required that *Dragnet* be alternated with a dramatic anthology called *Chesterfield Presents*, also known as *Dramatic Mystery*. From March 20 to December 25, 1952, *Dragnet* alternated Thursdays with the popular *Gangbusters*, which had also made the transition from radio to television. *Gangbusters*, however, was intended to be only a temporary substitute until Webb could consistently produce a weekly *Dragnet* show. Jack appeared at the end of each *Gangbusters* episode to inform the viewers that "Joe Friday" and his officers could be seen the following week. In 1953, *Dragnet* became a weekly television show, filmed in Burbank at the Walt Disney Studio.

Webb returned to the best of radio *Dragnet* for television. He considered Lloyd Nolan for the role of "Joe Friday," so that Jack could devote his time to directing. Nolan was then acting in *Martin Kane - Private Eye*, which ran on radio from 1949 to 1954. Webb eventually abandoned the idea of Nolan as the lead actor and decided to portray "Friday" and to narrate television *Dragnet* himself in his no-nonsense, impassive voice.

While a radio program required only one room to produce, television production demanded sets, which Webb neither had nor could afford at first. In the beginning years, Jack also lacked sufficient camera crews and had to direct, cast, and edit the television filming himself. His fanaticism for detail was evident in his very first TV films. He soon became known as a stickler for facts. Story locales and time periods were required to be exact. Calendars and telephone extension numbers were authentic, and even doorknobs were replicated to match those in the Los Angeles City Hall. Period ashtrays were filled with actual discarded cigarette butts and other aspects were duplicated to the tiniest detail. Male actors were not permitted to wear stage make-up and actresses were instructed to use only street cosmetics. Jack's goal was to have his characters appear as ordinary people and his stories to be as routine as those experienced daily by police officers nationwide. Webb recalled, "My thesis for the show — and perhaps this was what kept us on top so long — was realism pitched in a low key."

Before long, "Joe Friday" and his partners became television household names. Barton Yarborough, who played "Friday's" partner "Sergeant Romero" on radio, appeared in the first few television episodes, but Yarborough unexpectedly died from a heart attack. His character, "Sergeant Romero," was written out of the show also as a heart attack victim. His role was resurrected briefly in 1952 by Barney Phillips as "Ed Jacobs." In 1952, Herb Ellis played "Officer Frank Smith" until Ben Alexander was selected for that role from 1953-1959.

His *Dragnet* character of "Frank Smith" overshadowed Alexander's impressive film career. Ben was born in Nevada and came to Hollywood as a child actor at the age of three. At four he appeared in silent films, and worked with directors D. W. Griffith and Cecil B. DeMille. As one of the most active juvenile actors in Hollywood, Alexander created the original *Penrod* series of films. In 1928, he had a lead role in *Scottie Of The Scouts*, and while attending Stanford University, Ben had a second lead in Erich Maria Remarque's film story *All Quiet On The Western Front*. This classic and powerful anti-war 1930 silent film starred Lew Ayres and made film history as the third motion picture to win the Academy Award. Director Lewis Milestone received an Academy Award.

During the 1930's Alexander became a well-known radio announcer and during World War II served as a lieutenant aboard a U.S. Navy aircraft carrier. Following the war, he acquired a motel and several gas stations, which became profitable businesses, often managed by some of his former Navy buddies. He also created several moneymaking television programs and ultimately lived the good life in San Francisco with his wife Lesley.

In 1952, Ben had no intention of returning to an acting career, although he did appear on a number of quiz and variety programs. According to *TV Guide*, Ben visited Los Angeles weekly to "ride herd on a quickie-type quiz show" called *Watch And Win*, whose format he profitably leased to other stations around the country.

Ben Alexander (l) joined *Dragnet* as Officer "Frank Smith" in 1953

Courtesy of Jack Webb Archives

Webb became interested in Alexander after he saw Ben and Lesley perform as hosts of a Saturday night audience-participation television program called *Party Time At Club Roma,* which Ben also produced and aired in 1950-1951. Strangely, when Jack contacted Alexander, Ben was coincidentally interested in *Dragnet*. Since Alexander was well off financially, the veteran actor only wanted to appear in *Dragnet* for professional satisfaction and fun. Ben asked Jack, "Do you suppose you fellows would ever have a bit where you could use me? I'd get a kick out of it." Jack informed Ben that he had little money to budget for talent, but Ben, replying that money was not a problem, explained, "I don't want to be tied down to any role where I have to be at a studio every day. Lesley and I are happy the way we are. I just want to play a character bit." That night Jack expanded the role of "Frank Smith" using the same name for the character as Webb's

San Francisco Uncle Frank Smith. The part of the new "Frank Smith" suited Ben's personality.

The following day, Ben informed Jack that he would do no more than four episodes, though he eventually made scores of shows from 1953-1959. Alexander enjoyed working on *Dragnet* so much that he and Lesley moved to Los Angeles and built a house in Hollywood Hills. Having departed his beloved San Francisco, Alexander said with mock bitterness, "This was the terrible act that Jack did to us." He shared that Jack's genius was the only thing that could have convinced him to move to Hollywood. The two men remained close friends for the rest of their lives.

Alexander also assisted Webb with research and with the younger actors, who appreciated Ben's easy-going style. As "Joe Friday's" partner, Ben brought a touch of humor to *Dragnet*, worrying over such mundane problems as what his stage wife "Faye" had packed in his lunch.

In the earliest episodes, "Friday" had a fiancée "Ann Baker," played by Dorothy Abbott. However, in the January 5, 1956 *Dragnet* episode, former model Marjie Millar became "Friday's" new girlfriend, as actress Dorothy Abbott had other commitments. Millar, who fit the image of the "all-American girl," was cast as "Sharon Maxwell," a Civil Service secretary employed in the Record Bureau of the LAPD. "Joe" was later impressed with a policewoman "Dorothy Miller" played by Merry Anders in the *Dragnet* episodes of the late 1960's.

A personal friend, and one of several regular actresses for Jack, was Peggy Webber who played "Ma Friday" on both radio and television *Dragnet*. She was approached by Webb and writer Jim Moser to portray the role of a woman who steals a baby after her child died at birth in *The Big Mother* episode on television. This was Webb's first show done in close-ups. Peggy recalled that this episode revealed to her "what an innovator Jack really was."

Television *Dragnet* was one of the first reality-based drama series and established video drama guidelines for years. The format mostly followed the radio style of treating each episode as an active criminal case. "Joe Friday" and his partner investigated true LAPD case stories altered for television to avoid possible lawsuits. Other episodes had such diverse titles as, *Hit And Run, The Big Girl, The Bad Girl, Doting Mother, Kid Bandits, Counterfeit Cop, Big Betty* and many more.

Webb believed that "the greatest drama of all is found in the true experiences of life." One radio *Dragnet* episode which attracted protest when performed on television in the 1950's concerned a serviceman's wife who gave birth to a child fathered by a lover while her husband was stationed overseas. When the husband returned home, the unfaithful wife explained that she found and took the baby as her own. The story generated intense debate because many viewed the story as too sensitive for airing on TV. On another occasion, Webb was rebuked by the National Rifle Association regarding his ".22 Rifle For Christmas" *Dragnet* story of a boy who was accidentally shot with a rifle. On the other hand, Jack was praised for his episode regarding traffic safety, which trucking companies, the military, police organizations, and insurance companies requested for use in their training classes. Frequently, as a civic service, Webb only charged shipping expenses for institutional or educational use of a film.

Dragnet's radio and television announcers were George Fenneman and Hal Gibney. However, each 30-minute program opened with Webb as "Sergeant Friday" speaking in his succinct and clipped style, "This is the city — Los Angeles, California. I work here. I carry a badge. My name's Friday. I'm a cop." The badge was LAPD Badge Number 714.

A Los Angeles Police Department *Dragnet* adviser explained that "Jack had a thing for sevens. That's where he got 714; seven plus seven is 14." Legend has it that Meshekoff and Webb

Dragnet sheet music, 1953 Dumm-de-dum-dum ... In November 1953, an arrangement of Dragnet's music by Ray Anthony's Orchestra skyrocketed to #3 on the popular music charts.

Courtesy of Jack Webb Archives

created the seven-character "Mark VII" designation for Webb's production company during a coffee break. Even the word *Dragnet* contained seven letters.

Walter Schumann scored *Dragnet's* music, assisted on television by Frank Comstock, Nathan S. Scott, and Lynn Murray. Aside from the trademark "Dumm—de-dum-dum" theme, the show's music included *Dragnet March* and *Danger Ahead*, each woven throughout every episode. When danger and apprehension appeared, the music could erupt "in a loud, sud-

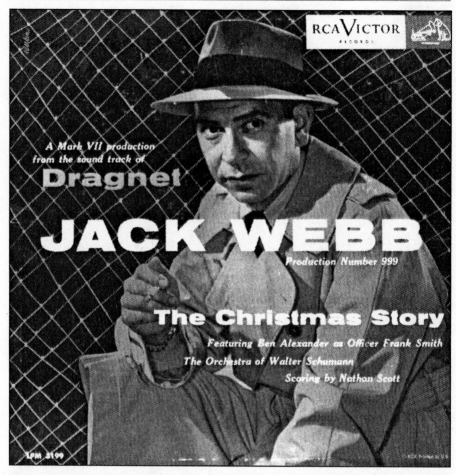

RCA VICTOR
RECORDS

A Mark VII production from the sound track of

Dragnet

JACK WEBB

Production Number 999

The Christmas Story

Featuring Ben Alexander as Officer Frank Smith

The Orchestra of Walter Schumann

Scoring by Nathan Scott

LPM 3199

The Christmas Story record album from one of the most famous *Dragnet* episodes of the same name.

Courtesy of Jack Webb Archives

den 'stinger' after an especially significant revelation or denouement," only to later reappear.

In November 1953, an arrangement of *Dragnet's* music by Ray Anthony's orchestra skyrocketed to number three on the popular music charts. Following this success, Robbins Music sued Schumann, arguing that Schumann copied his score from a motif written by veteran film composer Miklos Rozsa for *The Killers*, produced in 1946. Though no complaints were registered when the music was used on *Dragnet* radio, Robbins Music won the case against Schumann. The court ordered that Rozsa should be credited, but Rozsa's name never appeared in the credits at the end of each show, though Shumann's name did. Schumann did not appeal the decision, perhaps because he was in poor health and died shortly after the court case ended.

Following *Dragnet's* signature four musical notes, an announcer proclaimed: "Ladies and gentlemen, the story you are about to see is true. The names have been changed to protect the innocent." Each story ending concerned the trial results or hearings of those involved in the case or incident, preceded by a teaser (such as the one below) to capture the audience several minutes more for a commercial announcement:

> The story you have just seen is true. The names were changed to protect the innocent. Harold Ruston was certified by a juvenile court to be tried as an adult. On February 20th, trial was held in Department 184, Superior Court, of the State of California, for the County of Los Angeles. In a moment the results of that trial.

Following the teaser, more *Dragnet* music played, and the commercial appeared next. The final scene was the impressive anvil and large hammer-in-hand imprinting the Mark VII Limited trademark in the style of J. Arthur Rank's hammer and gong. Lewis Grossberger vividly recalled the Mark VII imprint in this *Rolling Stone* magazine account:

> Finally would come the grand, mysterious climax. This huge, hairy paw would slam down a hammer on top of a stone slab. *Clang!* Away came the hand and there, left printed across your screen, was the totally anticlimactic message: A MARK VII LTD. PRODUCTION. It was Webb's production company signing off, but the effect was at once mystical and official, as though God Almighty had just reviewed the case and upheld the verdict.

Daughter Stacy recalled that her father used a burly set construction supervisor's hands for the Mark VII television insignia used in the 1950's. The original tape was used until it began showing wear. When *Dragnet* was revived in 1966, a new and updated tape loop was needed for the insignia, and for this tape, Jack's arms and hands were pictured. Stacy and an audio unit visited numerous Chatsworth area blacksmith shops in the San Fernando Valley (in Southern California) to record an anvil striking a die. After reviewing each recording several times, Jack eventually decided on the precise sound he believed would be best for the *Dragnet 1966* television movie and the *Dragnet 1967* series. Later, the hand and die scene was used on *Adam-12*, but was retired for that and most other Mark VII productions. Apparently, the use of "Limited" in the Mark VII title was copied from the business of Robert Kirk, Limited, where Webb's Uncle Frank Smith in San Francisco was once employed. The usage sounded sophisticated, British, and appealed to Webb. Besides, the word "Limited" has seven letters, Jack's favorite number. He preferred the use of "Limited" to "Productions," though he frequently used the name "Mark VII" by itself.

Often overlooked are the people responsible for the nuts-and-bolts operations of successful companies, such as Mark VII. James R. "Riff" Rodgers was described as Webb's "right hand man," who was associated with the life and growth of the Mark VII company from 1952 to 1962. Rodgers grew up in the theater business with 20th Century Fox, primarily managing groups of theaters on the West Coast. He later worked as a Theater District Manager for Warner Theaters until the United States Supreme Court broke up the monopoly that allowed film companies to own all properties and theater chains. "Riff" saw a bleak future remaining with managing theaters and joined Webb's fledgling production company as a Vice-President and Treasurer in 1952. Webb and Rodgers enjoyed both a harmonious business relationship and a good friendship.

"Riff" and Ann Rodgers and their children, Ron and Nancy, enjoyed social gatherings with Jack and his wife until Jack began working for Warner Bros. in 1962. Rodgers once worked for Jack Warner and knew that he and Warner would strongly disagree and wisely sought new employment elsewhere. He joined Bing Crosby Productions and eventually became the head of the company under Cox Enterprises until his death in 1986.

In 1952, Jack purchased his first Cadillac, but hastened to add that it was not a new one. More significant was his receiving a 1952 Emmy nomination from the National Academy Of Television Arts And Sciences for being the "Best Actor." In 1952 and 1953, *Dragnet* received an Emmy for the "Best Mystery, Action Or Adventure Program." Further, in 1953 Webb was nominated for an Emmy as the "Best Male Star Of A Regular Series" and the "Most Outstanding Personality." In 1954, his *Dragnet* nominations were for "Best Actor Starring In A Regular Series" and "Best Director (Film Series)" for *The Christmas Story*, a *Dragnet* episode.

The very popular holiday story concerned the secret removal and return of the Christ Child statue from its altar cradle in a church by a young boy. Webb selected unknown child actors Paco Mendoza to play the lead and six-and-a-half-year-old Jose Cariocoa, who had never acted professionally. Jack commented that Paco "was able to express the full innocence of the theft with great feeling and sensitivity." Since the Christmas episode marked the first time that color was used for a major network television program, many new technical problems arose. Father Louis LeBihan, from whose San Francisco church the Christ Child was "stolen," served as Webb's technical adviser. Much of the production was filmed at Our Lady Queen of Angels Church in Los Angeles. The choral music was composed and conducted by Walter Schumann and *The Christmas Story* soundtrack was issued by RCA Victor (LPM and 45 Extended Play recording 3199. The episode was Production No. 999).

In 1954, Ben Alexander was chosen for an Emmy for his work in *Dragnet* as the "Best Supporting Actor In A Regular Series." Edward Coleman

Talking business with Riff Rodgers, Jack's "right hand man" at Mark VII Limited, Webb's production company.

Courtesy of Ron Rodgers

was selected for the "Best Director Of Photography" for his work on *The Big Bible* episode, and Jack received an Emmy as the "Best Director" for *Dragnet* in 1953.

The *Dragnet* Christmas episode of the 1960's was almost identical to its 1950's predecessor. Webb used virtually the same Richard Breen script that concerned a missing statue of the child Jesus from a church nativity scene. Others in the remake included Bobby Troup, Harry Bartell, and Barry Williams.

As late as 1959, Webb was critical of the Emmy Awards and either from scheduling conflicts or disdain, once had a *Dragnet* Emmy accepted on his behalf by James R. "Riff" Rodgers, Mark VII's Treasurer and Vice-President. Jack also once withdrew his name and *Dragnet* from the nominations. He explained, "Even though I won three of these statuettes, I have felt that these prizes don't mean anything because there are too many of them, and the selections are not equitable. The annual awards show is a sorry performance that makes me ashamed." He was encouraged, however, by a forthcoming revision of the awards' qualification criteria then under study.

More laurels were bestowed upon Webb who received the *Look* magazine TV award in 1953 and 1954 for the best direction given to "individuals who most effectively utilized the skills of actors and technicians in television presentations." Webb also received *Billboard's* 1954 choice award as the best actor, and *Dragnet* was selected as the best television show (both determinations made by television, motion picture, and advertising executives).

In entertainment and law enforcement circles, *Dragnet* was praised for its public service achievements. One notable *Dragnet* television episode exposed a TV repair scam, which was instrumental in bringing about legislation in California and Pennsylvania for the examination and licensing of television repairmen. RCA used Webb's program and script for the indoctrination and instruction of its employees.

Jack's association with law enforcement would continue for the rest of his life and beyond. Since 1993, the LAPD Historical Society has held the annual Jack Webb Awards to celebrate individuals in the community and business who have – like Jack – made outstanding contributions to law enforcement or children's issues. This black-tie affair, held in Beverly Hills, is attended by many celebrities and serves as a fund raiser for the Police Historical Society. Jack "My-name's-Friday-I'm-a-cop" Webb would be proud to lend his name to such an event.

A collection of *Dragnet* memorabilia from the 1950s.

Courtesy of Jack Webb Archives

"It is the most realistic police program on television."

Dragnet's success made Webb and Mike Meshekoff wealthy. By 1954, the series earned more awards and citations than any other television program of its kind and commanded an impressive 38 million viewers each Thursday from 9:00 to 9:30 P.M. The show's greatest competitors were the *Arthur Godfrey Show* and *I Love Lucy*, which on April 7, 1952, became the first televised program viewed in over 10 million homes. Jack topped *I Love Lucy* only once — on November 20, 1953, when the comedy fell to number two behind *Dragnet*. Webb was, nevertheless, among the most popular male television actors through *Dragnet's* initial 1952-1959 television life.

Though Jack enjoyed his new found fame and wealth, he wanted to remain in touch with his long-time friends. When "Moe" Turner visited Jack in Los Angeles, Webb usually dropped everything – even when at work – to chat with Turner. On one occasion, Jack offered "Moe" a Mark VII position, but Turner decided to remain in aviation.

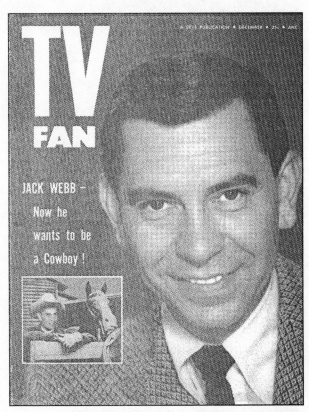

JACK WEBB – Now he wants to be a Cowboy!

Jack appeared on many magazine covers. This one suggests he wants to be a cowboy.

TV Fan — Courtesy of Jack Webb Archives

Jack signing autographs in New York City. "Once I start signing autographs, I stay until I'm finished."

McCalls Magazine —
Courtesy of Jack Webb Archives

When Roy Knight was flying for the U. S. Air Force Reserve, he landed at the Burbank Airport on weekends and was met by a Mark VII studio car. Jack offered Roy an Assistant Director's position, but Knight did not accept the appointment, as he did not want to leave his lucrative pilot's job. Webb's partners were happy that Roy declined the offer, because Knight was not a union member, many of whom were then unemployed. Roy recalled that the last time he saw Jack was when the two visited a number of clubs to interview small jazz combos for Jack's film *Pete Kelly's Blues*. However, during his rise to fame, Jack did lose contact with Gus Stamos and some other friends.

Fame made Jack the object of autograph seekers, a target for gossip columnists, and the subject of nightclub impressionists. With his celebrity status came the occasional personal insult. Richard Tregaskis, a celebrated World War II correspondent known for his eye-witness account *Guadalcanal Diary* (1943), proclaimed that even Webb's most enamored fans would agree that Jack's ears were "of a size more suitable for flying than for listening."

However, Webb was flattered when he learned that Sid Caesar and other celebrities watched *Dragnet* on TV and discussed the dramas in greater detail than the show could cover in 30 minutes on television.

Moreover, Jack was recognized most everywhere he visited. As one columnist reported, Webb had "the face that solves half a hundred crimes and never changes expression."

Police language and codes used on *Dragnet* were so popular that *TV Guide* offered, "as a public service," a *Dragnet*-to-English Dictionary in one of its issues to assist Jack's radio and television fans in understanding "Dragnetese." For example:

> We thought he was an ordinary 4127A LAMC without a package, but the make showed the caper was a 211, a carry away. When R and I checked, The FBI kickback had him a muscle-happy big time. [See the Glossary for a translation of "Dragnetese."]

People were instructed that the secret to becoming a true "Dragnetter" was in the facial expressions, which should be practiced in front of a mirror while pronouncing *Dragnet's* vocabulary in perfect monotone.

Soon after *Dragnet* was established on television, a uniformed police officer approached Webb to shake hands. The officer said, "Been wanting to meet you, Jack. My name's Friday." Webb, assuming that the officer was joking, went along with the gag, replying, "Sure, I guess a lot of you fellows get called 'Friday' since the show went on the air." The officer smiled, but explained politely, "Friday is my *real* name." And it was! Of course, it was too late to change "Joe Friday's" name on *Dragnet*, since millions of people in radio and television audiences already knew and loved the fictional detective. Surprisingly, no one thought to search the police personnel files to see if there was a true-to-life "Friday" in the LAPD. Fortunately, Patrolman Friday did not file a lawsuit, though the incident caused some minor embarrassment among the Department brass.

Many in law enforcement believed that Webb was once a legitimate police officer. Even penitentiary inmates loved *Dragnet*. One curious woman inquired if Jack learned how to fight crime while he served time in prison.

When Jack and Julie were seen in public, it was not uncommon to hear some wag hum the *Dragnet* notes "Dumm—de-dum-dum." In 1953, Stan Freberg performed the hilarious *St. George And The Dragonet*. The recording may be the only parody of a television series to sell a million copies and attain a top notch in the music charts.

Jack, Julie, Stacy, and Lisa moved into their early-American ranch-style home in 1953. The Encino mansion, located about 10 miles from Hollywood, was originally built for actor George Montgomery and his wife, singer Dinah Shore. The large home was previously occupied by Harry Karl and his wife, actress Debbie Reynolds. The house had a wing for the nursery, a large pool, and a soundproof, private projection room where Jack could view films. The den had a wall of high fidelity phonograph equipment that, according to Johnny Carson, was "worthy of a small radio station." Here, Webb could play his collection of about 6,000 jazz and classical music recordings. One bar was appointed with red carpet and blue couches. Another pleasure, parked in front of the house, was Jack's lifelong dream acquisition: a bright new yellow Cadillac convertible.

Jack gave his time to others, too. He served on the executive board of the United Cerebral Palsy Fund and participated in a Los Angeles and San Francisco telethon each year. The money raised gave him enormous personal satisfaction.

At last, Webb seemed to have the world on a string. However, with his increasing professional success came increasing professional demands. The family spent less and less time together. Jack frequently arrived home late only to take a bite or two from a warmed-over dinner that Julie had prepared for him earlier. He could never successfully balance his work with his marriage and family. The truth was that Jack was married to his work. Mark VII would not have succeeded without him — nor would his marriage. By 1953, their marriage fizzled, and Mark VII exploded.

By 1953, Webb and Executive Producer Stanley Meyer with Producer Mike Meshekoff had made 60 *Dragnet* programs, each one using about 12,000 feet of film. This output was the equivalent of 20 feature-length motion pictures — all made in less than nine months. Jack's team could produce an episode in three days at the Walt Disney Burbank Studio, where Webb had meticulously constructed a first floor Los Angeles City Hall interior set. Each *Dragnet* episode cost only $28,000 to $30,000, as casts, sets, and wasted scenes were kept to a minimum. Later, four episodes were finished in two weeks, followed by two weeks off for planning and editing. However, as in Jack's radio experience, business disagreements soon surfaced.

Jack believed that NBC's payment of $28,000 for each *Dragnet* episode was unfair, since the show brought the network $3,000,000 annually from sponsors, namely Chesterfield cigarettes. Webb's rescue from his financial dilemma was engineered in 1953, when he sold the rights to 100 completed and 95 future *Dragnet* episodes to the Music Corporation Of America (MCA). The selling price was approximately $5,000,000, of which Jack received half.

Webb never relaxed regarding *Dragnet's* quality on television or radio, though some critics claimed that a rigid production process negatively impacted the fresh creativity of the show. One problem for Jack was that his cast had a tendency to imitate his distinct voice and style. Jack continued using LAPD personnel to read scripts for technical accuracy and Detectives Marty Wynn, Vance Brasher, and Jack Donohoe now received $100 a week as technical advisors, rather than the original $25. The City Attorney's office examined each episode to discover any possible liability suit, and at least one police officer familiar with the story subject and content was on the set while filming was in progress.

Webb avoided typecasting. A thief or a murderer could appear on *Dragnet* as an ordinary citizen. *Time* magazine observed that much of Webb's success was his use of c h a r a c t e r "bums, priests, con men, whining housewives, burglars, waitresses, children, and bewildered ordinary citizens" who seem "as sorrowfully genuine as old pistols in a hockshop window."

Moreover, no detail or sentence escaped his examina-

Chesterfield ad featuring Jack with Ben Alexander

Courtesy of Jack Webb Archives

tion. Webb would stop a scene to determine if a witness should say "I can't" or "I don't remember." Jack spent so much time around the camera that one studio visitor mistook Webb for the famous actor and Producer/Director Orson Wells.

Despite the potential for use of force in police work, fighting and violence was seldom seen on *Dragnet*. Webb, who had strong moral values, would not create any episode that he would not want his children to see.

Jack seldom ignored or avoided a fan. "After all," he would say, "fans are the people we're working for." His compassion surfaced in the following remark:

Once I start signing autographs, I stay until I'm finished. I know that if I rushed off, I'd leave somebody disappointed and hurt — probably some poor little kid who was there early, but too shy to push.

He was truly flattered when the eight-year-old daughter of club owner Sherman Billingsley ran across the Stork Club restaurant to request his autograph. The famous New York Club was the meeting place of popular and publicly important people. The owner's young daughter, Shermane could have any autograph she desired. After she received "Joe Friday's" autograph, she crowed, "Boy, will the rest of the kids in my class be jealous!" On another occasion, conductor Billy May, Frank Sinatra, Jr., and Jack were dining at a restaurant when an autograph seeker completely ignored Jack and Frank but was ecstatic to have Billy May's signature. Such incidents always drew laughs from everyone involved.

Jack was attentive to his fan mail. By 1954, he received about 400 letters weekly. Every letter was answered or kept on file to create a database concerning viewers' opinions. Realizing that each letter represented approximately 10,000 viewers, if over 10 letters suggested a program change, Webb gave serious consideration to the recommendation. However, after "Sergeant Friday's" fiancée was eliminated, he refused any suggestions to inject romance into *Dragnet* for some time, explaining that he was not telling the story of "Friday's" life but that of the work of police officers and the problems they encountered every day.

For a man who placed his work above his women, he nevertheless fascinated the ladies. About 85% of Jack's early fan mail was written by women, who inquired about his clothes, taste in foods, and personal habits — including how often he shaved. Women sent him hand-knitted socks and ties. When Webb sported an identification bracelet on his wrist, the accessory created a fad among teenage girls. Since "Sergeant Friday" was unmarried, the ladies reasoned that Jack must be single, too. He received many marriage proposals. Enamored fans may have been interested to learn that Jack offered and appreciated a firm handshake, seeing the spirit of the gesture as representative of the man.

Among Webb's favorites during his adult life was his cologne of choice, "Aramis." Throughout the 1950's and 1960's he was a coffee drinker on the set, though he later preferred Sparkletts bottled water or lime Gatorade to go with his occasional doughnuts. Crown Royal and Segram's were his favorite liquors, and Heiniken and Michelob were Webb's choice of beer. Not surprisingly, he smoked Chesterfield and L&M cigarettes.

Jack was an excellent cook and once owned over forty cookbooks. Some of his preferred foods were peaches and cream for breakfast and chili dogs and most any Mexican or hot and spicy foods for lunch. Steak and barbecued ribs were his dinner favorites, which he frequently grilled at his Encino home.

Despite his love for food, he never gained weight and remained around 165 pounds until he was in his late middle age. Perhaps being trim resulted from his enormous energy or high metabolism. When he once wore a pedometer at work, the device revealed that Jack walked between 15 and 25 miles a day.

From his large personal collection of films, two of his favorites were *Casablanca* and *Gone With The Wind*. In later years, Jack's nightly work schedules surrendered to Monday night football, so he could follow his favorite team, the Los Angeles Rams. Baseball was another one of his pastimes. He always enjoyed watching Los Angeles Dodgers' games. When he took Stacy to see a Rose Bowl football game, the two flew in the Goodyear Blimp. In addition, Jack was often a guest of honor in Los Angeles parades.

Usually Webb purchased two Cadillac's a year: a convertible for the summer and a Coupe DeVille for the cooler months. He added a magnetic St. Christopher's medal, which had been blessed by the Pope, to his 1968 Cadillac convertible. He seldom, if ever, traded-in his automobiles. Instead, he sold or gave his low-mileage Cadillac's to his employees and friends. During his divorced years, he gave cars and furs to several of his girlfriends. In addition to his many Cadillac's, Jack drove a 1955 Ford Thunderbird, a 1956 Lincoln Continental, and a red 1965 Mustang convertible. In 1967, he also drove a green Corvette. He sported a favorite cream colored Chevrolet convertible and a 1971 Ford Pantera (similar to the Lamborghini). On the *Adam-12* set, Webb drove an electric powered golf cart tagged "SGT-714."

His favorite color was red, and he wore Penny loafers that exposed his red socks. While in front of the camera, Jack always dressed appropriately and wore his shirt tucked inside his trousers. As soon as he was behind the camera directing, the shirt was immediately untucked. Jack frequently changed shirts during production hours, but in his leisure hours and off the set, he preferred wearing his shirt outside his trousers. While on the set of *Dragnet 1969*, Stacy asked Assistant Director Mel Bishop what she could get her father for Christmas and Mel replied, "Buy him a shirt that 'tucks in.'" Webb's defense was that a free and loose-fitting shirt "hides my belly at my age." One of his favorite clothing stores was named "JAX," which carried a diverse line of informal shirts.

Of the 10 million homes that *Dragnet* entered weekly in 1953, only 37% of the audience were men, while the ladies comprised about 45%. As an example, during the week of April 12, 1954, Webb received 1,221 fan letters of which 1,041 were written by women and only 180 by men. The following week the ladies wrote 1,031 letters while the men penned 214. Webb commented, "Hmm, unusually heavy 'male' that week." *Time* magazine reported there was "hardly a child above the age of four" who did not recognize "Dumm—de-dum-dum," "Joe Friday's" name, or "Just the facts, ma'am." The other 18% of *Dragnet's* fans were children under age 16. *McCall's* magazine observed, "Although the show has always been considered adult fare, even the sub-teens aren't immune to Webb's sex appeal."

The magazine was also uncomplimentary to Jack. He was described as being "far from handsome," with "jug-handle ears and a tendency to stoop, which makes him look shorter than his almost six feet." Their only compliment concerned Jack's "dark, brooding eyes." Nevertheless, according to *McCall's*, even on radio before the ladies could see Webb's Irish face and dark eyes on television, women were impressed with his "intimate deep voice." Jack quietly replied that he was never an "oil painting" or a movie "glamour boy." Yet, he never had a problem arranging dates with women. He attributed his popularity with women to his screen role by saying, "It must be 'Friday.'"

When he traveled around the country, Webb went on actual emergency calls with police officers. Perhaps Webb's most loyal and devoted fans were police officers and their families, who often forwarded letters to him. Most praised *Dragnet's* authenticity and "Joe Friday" for being "a cop's cop." One Rhode Island officer, summing up his appreciation for *Dragnet's* recognition of policemen, wrote:

> It is the most realistic police program on television.... Most programs of this type feature tough, hard-punching, quick-on-the-trigger, either too-smart-or-too-dumb cops or private eyes. They don't picture police work as it really is. But your program does a fine job of showing the public just how most cases are solved, by plenty of hard, routine leg work and questioning, gathering the facts and putting them together to make the story.

Jack started in radio and had successfully transitioned to television. The natural progression for Jack at this stage in his career was to move on to movie making. Jack was about to enter the world of the big screen.

Pete Kelly's Blues — "The best damned picture I ever made."

By 1954, Jack had hit the big time. Webb owned five Cadillac automobiles and appeared on the cover of *Time* and other magazines. There was even some talk of Jack portraying a cowboy in a western film. On February 12, 1955, Webb presided as the master of ceremonies for the first telecast of the Motion Picture Academy of Arts and Sciences show announcing "Oscar" nominations for films and individuals (awarded on March 30).

In February 1954, Webb moved his antique gun collection, portable typewriter, and Bassett hound "Dudley" into a $100,000 ultramodern two-bar house on celebrity-studded Coldwater Canyon in Beverly Hills. A month later he sold the house, never having used the swimming pool. Instead, he moved into his plush office and apartment on 4024 Radford Avenue until the mid-1960's. Still, he kept his Encino home until about 1979. Mark VII business manager Stanley Meyer commented that Jack "would live in one room with a cot and a movie projector if you'd let him."

Webb's Mark VII offices, located at 4024 Radford Avenue (then Republic Studios and now CBS Studio Center), were in a $450,000 two story complex. The interior was decorated in an Early American style with much of the furniture designed by George Montgomery (then married to singer Dinah Shore). Mark VII's suite included Webb's impressive office, at least one other cork paneled office, and a private apartment outfitted with a kitchen, dining alcove, and dining room. When asked why he spent so much money for the building and apartment, Jack replied, "Most of our people spend more time here than they do at home."

Webb was devoting six days to television *Dragnet* and Sunday to the radio *Dragnet* in 1954. By then changes were occurring among the Mark VII staff, and those who did not keep Webb's frenetic pace or satisfy his demands for detail and creative contribution were fired. Jack's radio director William Rousseau was one of the first dismissed. In 1954, Stanley Meyer replaced Mike Meshekoff. Longtime *Dragnet* writer and Jack's "old pal," Jim Moser also left Mark VII. Moser and Jack disagreed on a project entitled *The Doctor*, which Moser later wrote and titled *Medic*. Jack's friend Herm Saunders began working with Mark VII Limited in Public Relations and eventually became an Associate Producer. Another of Webb's new staff was Robert "Bob" Leeds, who had been a film editor at Republic Pictures. Jack and Bob became good friends and collaborated on many productions.

Webb's unique clipped monotone delivery began to fade after several *Dragnet* television seasons, perhaps because the style was growing stale.

Jack Webb
Ann Robinson

In *Dragnet's* first feature length film, Ann Robinson played police-woman "Grace Downey" along side Jack as "Joe Friday" and Ben Alexander as his partner "Frank Smith."

Courtesy of Jack Webb Archives

Reprinted with permission from TV Guide Magazine Group, Inc., publisher of TV Guide magazine, Copyright, July 24-30, 1954 TV Guide, Inc., TV Guide is a trademark of TV Guide Magazine Group, Inc.

One study of prime-time television discusses the need for broadcast change, reporting that what was originally "a fresh and inventive style of storytelling" becomes, "through endless repetition, virtual self-parody" and even "camp." Such may have been the case with Webb's "Joe Friday's" character and Peter Falk's "Columbo" in later years. However, "Sergeant Friday" had far from lost his appeal in 1954.

Having a ready-made audience of 16.5 million television viewers and six million radio fans, logic dictated that Webb take "Joe Friday" to the silver screen. By 1954, Jack had studied movies to learn filming and motion picture production techniques. Making movies would be another of Jack's boyhood dreams come true. His favorite writer Dick Breen returned to assist Webb as a screenwriter with the Stanley Meyer production of a *Dragnet* movie. The feature length motion picture was filmed at the Warner Bros. Studios for distribution in 1954.

Webb wore the hats of actor, director, part-time writer, and film editor in the production. He was delighted that his dressing room was adjacent to Judy Garland's. The major differences between the movie and television versions of *Dragnet* were that the motion picture was filmed in color and

Lee Marvin and Martin Milner with Jack in *Pete Kelly's Blues*. The film also featured Andy Devine, Janet Leigh, and Peggy Lee.

Courtesy of Jack Webb Archives

ran for 97 minutes, while the TV episodes were shot in black and white and ran 26 minutes apiece. Webb finished the film in a remarkable 22 days at a time when the average Warner Bros. picture required about 55 days to complete.

Jack played "Sergeant Friday" as he did his low-keyed television character, wearing a moderate crew haircut, button-down collar shirts, sports jacket, and trousers that seemed a little short. Others in the cast included Ben Alexander, Richard Boone, Ann Robinson, Virginia Gregg, Cliff Arquette, Dennis Weaver, Harry Bartell, and Stacy Harris. Herm Saunders appears at the piano in one scene playing his composition of *Foggy Night In San Francisco* with lyrics by Sydney Miller.

Jack employed all of his radio and television production tricks for the film. As in television, Webb again made the most of his teleprompter, saving valuable hours of memorization and forgotten lines. Close-up camera positions were emphasized, and to achieve a natural look, very little make-up was applied.

The film opened with the brutal murder of a two-timing gangster on the outskirts of Los Angeles. "Sergeant Friday," his partner "Frank Smith," and policewoman "Grace Downey" (Ann Robinson) were charged with piecing together the case. Through a series of thorough investigations, a fistfight, and a stake out, the police learned that the murder was a joint effort, and the criminals involved were brought to justice. *Dragnet* (1954) brought in $4,800,000 at box offices but cost only $400,000 to produce. The film would also earn another estimated $9,000,000 from overseas distribution.

In 1955, before one could say "Bix Beiderbecke," *Pete Kelly's Blues* was filmed at Warner Bros. Studios. The movie served as a million-dollar, full-feature "pilot" story for a projected television series by the same name. Jack heavily invested in the picture, which was much the same as the "Pete Kelly" radio version that ran from July 4 to September 19, 1951. The film was born from Jack's love for music and he saw no reason why his history of being "Joe Friday" should prevent him from portraying a Kansas City Prohibition era musician. Jack considered himself a professional actor with the ability to play any role. However, he was well aware of the possibility of having been typecast as "Joe Friday" for life.

The picture's first few minutes have "one of the most quietly dramatic scenes ever filmed" (*Screen Stories* magazine, Sep. 1955). The opening scene centered on a cornet — no doubt recalled from Webb's youth. The memorable introduction pictures a New Orleans jazz musician's funeral, whose mourners depart the cemetery to the sound of ragtime music, played by a brass band. A cornet falls, unnoticed, from a horse drawn hearse and somehow, years later, is in the possession of "Pete Kelly" — the lead role played by Jack Webb. Herm Saunders, Jack's WWII friend and business associate, conducted the funeral music for the opening scene and the movie's background music. Webb filmed the opening scene on location in New Orleans.

Much of the story transpires in a 1927 Kansas City speak-easy, where "Pete Kelly's Big Seven Band" performs in the presence of criminals, bootleggers, a swindling club owner, and party-crazed "flappers" making the most of "The Jazz Age." Webb said, "All I wanted to do was to show a group of people of that period out for an evening of fun." Racketeer "Fran McCarg" (Edmond O'Brien) informs "Kelly" that he wants a percentage for managing the band, but "Pete" refuses him. The situation is discussed with the musicians who stand with "Kelly," but the conflict intensifies and leads to "McCarg" ordering the murder of the band drummer "Joey Firestone" (Marty Milner). The film climaxes when "Pete Kelly" and his love interest "Ivy Conrad" are caught in a crossfire in a ballroom gunfight with "McCarg" and his hoodlums. Eventually, "McCarg" is killed and his partners in crime are defeated. "Pete" and "Ivy" return to the speak-easy and resume their life.

Pete Kelly's Blues was directed by Webb, produced by Mark VII Productions, and released through Warner Bros. Richard L. Breen penned the screenplay, and Ray Heindorf wrote the title song with lyrics by the great

Janet Leigh as "Ivy Conrad," with Jack on the set of *Pete Kelly's Blues.*

Courtesy of Jack Webb Archives

Sammy Cahn. Heindorf conducted the Warner Bros. Orchestra and was the studio musical director for years. The film featured Lee Marvin as "Al Gannaway," Andy Devine as "Detective George Tunnel," Janet Leigh as "Ivy Conrad," and Peggy Lee as "Rose Hopkins."

Though Webb primarily used actors for the picture's band members, several of the musicians were professionals. The violinist was musician Joe Venuti, and the drummer was Bill Lazerus. The picture had 37 musical selections, though not all were played completely. Most memorable are the title song *Pete Kelly's Blues* and the haunting *I Never Knew*. The story music, consistent with the period, included two Negro spirituals. The film's musicians were some of the finest jazz artists in the United States. Dick Cathcart played cornet, and jazz great Matty Matlock played clarinet and arranged some of the music. Eddie Miller was featured on tenor sax and Elmer "Moe" Schneider on trombone. The other musicians included Nick Fatool on drums, George Van Eps on guitar, Ray Sherman on piano, and Jud DeNaut on the string bass. The sensational Ella Fitzgerald as "Maggie Jackson" performed several songs including the title selection of *Pete Kelly's Blues*.

Jack was completely free with his casting, selecting actors and actresses from the famous to the relatively unknown. The beautiful Janet Leigh was his choice to play "Ivy Conrad." The actress was among Hollywood's top stars in the 1950's. Her most memorable role was as the young woman in the horrid shower murder scene in Alfred Hitchcock's 1960 thriller, *Psycho*. Jack treated Janet like the star she was, sending at least two fresh bouquets of flowers to her dressing room daily. Janet, who praised Webb's personality and his meticulous directing said, "Then he works you out like a drill sergeant with a new recruit. You nearly collapse when the day is over, but you realize that your efforts are appreciated, and that he has done more for you than you have for him."

Jack hired amateur or new actors so no one would appear as a polished professional in the dance scenes. For example, the voluptuous Jayne Mansfield played the part of the cigarette girl. Others in the cast were Webb associates and stand-by's such as Martin Milner as "Joey Firestone," Herb Ellis as "Bedido," and Than Wyenn was "Rudy."

Jack's use of non-actors concerned "Moe" Turner who was on vacation in Los Angeles from his duties as a test pilot in Dallas, Texas. When he called on Jack at the studio, Webb dispatched Stanley Meyer to pick him up and come to the set. For the following two days, Turner met the *Pete Kelly* cast, and he and his wife played a cameo part in "The Everglades Ballroom" scene. Several days later Dick received a $75.00 check for his minor part. Such honesty and fair play was recalled by many of Jack's friends.

Jack astonished everyone by having Andy Devine play a detective role, a part normally not associated with him. Andy Devine was a veteran western film actor, who played Guy Madison's fat and foolish partner on television's *Wild Bill Hickok*. He was also a comic sidekick for cowboy Roy Rogers and had a major role in John Ford's 1939 classic western, *Stagecoach*. Devine accepted Webb's challenge and considered changing his normally raspy sounding voice to portray "Detective George Tunnel" in *Pete Kelly's Blues*. Devine took voice lessons, but was displeased with his new sound. With Webb's approval, Andy kept his normal scratchy-sounding voice and delighted everyone with his familiar tone.

Peggy Lee, as "Rose Hopkins," played a talented but alcoholic would-be singer, who was emotionally disturbed and abused by "McCarg." Lee, one of the premiere female vocalists of the 1950's, could pick the professional work of her choosing. Shortly before working with Jack, she received raves for her vocal performances as "Peg," "Darling," "Si," and "Am," the Siamese cats in Walt Disney's 1955 animated *Lady And The Tramp* (the first feature cartoon in CinemaScope).

Webb telephoned Peggy with an offer to play a "wonderful, yet unglamorous part." Jack warned her that much of her character's scenes would be shot in inferior lighting to enhance the depth of the role. He forwarded a script for her to read, asking that she call Jack if she decided to accept the part of "Rose." After reading the story, she immediately notified

Webb that she "couldn't wait" to be in the cast.

Peggy Lee proved to be an outstanding actress in the film. Her character "Rose" was, at heart, a good woman. She wanted to be a singer but her abuse of alcohol clouded her judgment. She became the girlfriend of a gangster who only contributed to her alcoholism. The abusive "McCarg" strong-armed "Kelly" to have her sing with his band, and in one scene Peggy portrayed a drunk and off key "Rose" singing George Gershwin's *Somebody Loves Me*. Perhaps her insane asylum scene was her most impressive. "Kelly" visits her there only to find her mindlessly serenading a rag doll, remembering little else. Peggy patterned the scene after a child she once knew who was mentally ill. The doll song was *Sing A Rainbow* written by Arthur Hamilton, who had also furnished music to Julie London.

For her role as "Rose," Peggy received the New York Film Critics Award, the Laurel Award, the Audience Award, and was nominated for an Academy Award. She was deprived of that final honor by Jo Van Fleet,

Peggy Lee played "Rose Hopkins" in *Pete Kelly's Blues* and received a New York Film Critics Award and was nominated for an Academy Award.

Courtesy of Jack Webb Archives

103

who in 1955 won the Best Supporting Actress "Oscar" for her part in *East Of Eden*. This was an ironic outcome, as Peggy was frequently visited in her trailer while shooting *Pete Kelly's Blues* by the brilliant James Dean, then filming *East Of Eden*. Peggy also competed for the award against contenders Betsy Blair (*Marty*), Marisa Pavan (*The Rose Tattoo*), and Natalie Wood (*Rebel Without A Cause*).

Jack was so impressed with her that he wanted to sign Lee exclusively to make pictures for his Mark VII Productions. Dick Breen and Webb even began preparing a TV format for Lee, but the program never matured.

Perhaps only Cecil B. DeMille spent more time researching a film than Webb, who did not overlook any detail. As on radio and television, Jack demanded the actors know their roles. In his estimation, "solid rehearsals are the best and only good insurance for good performances." Since Webb could not act as "Kelly" and direct at the same time, he devised an ingenious arrangement of mirrors on the set. The mirrors were positioned so that while Webb was acting, he could see what was happening around and behind him. Examples of his perfectionism included Jack making Photostats of 1927 Kansas and Missouri newspapers and requiring that labels for canned goods on the set carry 1927 dates. His only deviation from perfection regarded a yellow female canary named "Brigitte," who in the film was referred to as "Fred."

The score from *Pete Kelly's Blues* appeared in a number of music albums. RCA Victor issued *Pete Kelly's Blues* (LPM-1126) with a narrative by Jack and jacket liner notes written by Dick Breen. Decca Records titled an album *Pete Kelly's Blues* (DL 8166) with Peggy Lee and Ella Fitzgerald. Columbia Records released *Pete Kelly's Blues* (CL 690) with Ray Heindorf conducting the Warner Bros. Orchestra featuring Matty Matlock and his jazz band. Warner Bros. released *Pete Kelly Lets His Hair Down* (B&BS 1217) in 1958. The excellent music made Jack sufficiently happy, and he would have ignored Leonard Maltin's later appraisal of the film as being "realistic to the point of tedium." Webb was satisfied that *Pete Kelly's Blues* was "the best damned picture I ever made."

After filming the opening scenes of *Pete Kelly's Blues* on location in New Orleans, Jack and his new wife Dorothy Towne visited the nearest Cadillac agency with Herm Saunders to purchase a convertible for the return trip to Los Angeles. Dorothy was described by Helen Gould in *TV Star Parade* (August 1954) as "a cool, tall, Texas palomino blonde," who once "did some extra [acting] work and dancing." To some, she resembled Peggy Lee and was remembered as a stand-in for actress Grace Kelly.

Jack and Dorothy met after Jack and Julie were divorced. Jack, who reported that he saw only one woman at a time, was impressed with Dorothy's looks, and he observed that she was "the most frugal person" he had ever met. She apparently knew how to invest the money she inherited from her father. Dorothy had a son from a previous marriage and had recently had her second marriage annulled. Jack and Dorothy were married in Chicago on January 11, 1955.

Jack maintained his Encino house as their family home and the apartment at 4024 Radford Avenue as his work residence. However, Dorothy seldom visited him at work and mostly managed their home where she prepared the thick steaks that Jack enjoyed. She was frequently photographed with Jack for magazine stories, yet rumors were afloat as early as July 1955 of a possible separation between the two. Further, Dorothy was apparently not overly popular with many of Webb's friends and associates who had advised him not to marry her. Some found her less than exciting and thought that Webb may have just been looking for someone to keep him company when he met and married her. Others believed that Jack was a mismatch for her. Dorothy soon learned, as Julie had learned before her, that Jack's wife and family came

Out for an evening with second wife Dorothy Towne

Courtesy of Jack Webb Archives

second to his real love — his work.

The Smith & Wesson Firearms Company were among those who also loved Jack's work. In 1955, they celebrated Jack by presenting him with the first copy of a newly manufactured handgun, a 9mm automatic pistol. The gun's serial number was #714, the same as the badge number of "Sergeant Friday's" shield.

The Los Angeles Police Department moved many of its offices from the City Hall building in 1955 to a modern glass-and-steel headquarters, appropriately designated The Police Administration Building. The structure was nicknamed "The Glass House, " and, with City Hall, was made famous on *Dragnet*. The new building was later renamed "Parker Center."

In 1955, Webb created a Police Academy Trust Fund and pledged six percent of the profits that were made on the first showing of each new *Dragnet* and, later, *Adam-12* episode. The Trust Fund eventually provided appropriations for the addition of the Jack Webb Recruit Building in 1970 and the Mark VII Building in 1977. These buildings included a weight training room, classrooms, and television monitors to play *Dragnet* and *Adam-12* episodes for police training. The buildings remain in use today.

One of Jack's many contributions to the L.A.P.D.

Courtesy of Jack Webb Archives

"This motion picture will be of immense value to the Marine Corps."

O n June 27, 1956, the Los Angeles Police Department presented "Joe Friday's" Badge 714 to Jack in recognition of his law enforcement publicity, contributions to the Department, and praise of police officers everywhere. He also received a Citation Of Appreciation honoring his "engendering an increased respect for law enforcement" and "greatly enhanced public esteem for the police profession."

However, Jack apparently received no such accolades of affection in his second marriage. The rumors of marital problems between Jack and Dorothy were true, and after several separations and having no children, the couple divorced in 1957. Unconfirmed reports claimed that Dorothy received a settlement of $135,000 in cash and continued living in both Texas and California.

Though he lost his wife, Jack still had his fans. By 1956-1957, *Dragnet* was televised on Thursday from 8:30-9:00 P.M. and boasted about 35 million viewers. The fan mail convinced Webb to be more exuberant, to lessen the downplay of "Sergeant Friday's" role, and to lower the music volume. More humor was added to the script, which remained free of romance. Webb took more than 300 scripts from the Los Angeles Police Department files by 1957. For new material, he branched out into division suburb offices of the LAPD. Retired as well as active duty officers assisted Jack's research efforts. Webb believed that *Dragnet* could "go on indefinitely, if that's what the public wants."

Since his childhood, Jack loved animals and several of his productions concerned dogs. He enjoyed all canines and, at various times, had Doberman Pinschers, German Shepherds, Dachshunds, toy and full size poodles, and two huge Harlequin Great Danes. His puppy in Junior High School was named "Skippy," but was called "Ippyska" in the children's "Pig Latin" speech. The puppy's disappearance broke his heart. At age 13, Jack expressed his grief in poetry about his lost dog:

"Ippyska"

Skippy, little yellow pup,
How near my heart you were!
Now I have to give you up.
You're gone — I know not where.

You never left me, Ippyska,
Because you wanted to;
Some one took you far away,
For many wanted you.

But no one else can understand
Your every little puppy way,
And none to you will seem so grand
As you thought I was, Ippyska.

Perhaps some day when I am old,
Another dog may be my own,
But never can another hold
The place I keep for you alone.

Jack Webb (1933)

Jack loved animals so much that he could not endure completely viewing Walt Disney's sad story of *Old Yeller*. The 1957 film concerned a Texas boy and his yellow hunting dog that died of rabies.

Clearly, Jack's love of animals inspired *Noah's Ark,* his first television series since *Dragnet*. Webb produced and directed the shows, which first aired on September 18, 1956. The half-hour story was filmed in color and made in cooperation with the Southern California Veterinary Medical Association and the American Humane Association. The programs concerned two veterinarians and the pet hospital where they worked. Paul Burke, Vic Rodman, and May Wynn had leading roles, and the program's human relationships were as fascinating as the animals that were treated. The series was taken off the air in February 1957 but was revived in reruns from June to October 5, 1958. Jack believed that, with improvements, the program would have succeeded, but the network dropped *Noah's Ark* before any changes were made. Herm Saunders summed-up the show's fate succinctly when he said, "That was that!"

Turning his attention to film, Jack created *The D. I.* Perhaps no film better reveals Webb's dedication to accuracy. Although Jack's World War II Army Air Corps experience was less than spectacular, he did consider enlisting in the Marines. His Uncle Frank Smith served as a World War II Marine and Jack played the role of a Leatherneck in *Halls Of Montezuma*. So, when Webb saw an excellent script concerning the Marine Corps Recruit Depot, Parris Island, South Carolina, he jumped at the opportunity to produce the training story into a full-length film.

Webb knew that the United States Marine Corps Recruit Depot, Parris Island, South Carolina, was among the most famous military bases in the world. The historic island was inhabited by the French, the Spanish, the

English, and the Confederacy (during the American Civil War). During the 1890's, a United States Naval Station and a large timber dry dock existed on Parris Island. In 1915, the base was transferred to the Marines for the exclusive purpose of training recruits.

The evolving Marine Corps recruit program was popularly known as "boot camp." The main cog in the wheel of making a Marine was, and is, the Drill Instructor — "The D.I." Over the decades, these "enlisted colonels" demanded perfection from recruits and sometimes used training and disciplinary methods no longer permitted today. The entire boot camp psychology of organized pandemonium and chaos is difficult for the uninitiated to understand. Yet, the program produced Marines for two world wars and the Korean War without serious incident until 1956.

Webb may have considered centering the story first around a Parris

Jack Webb as "Technical Sergeant Jim Moore," the Senior Drill Instructor in the film *The D.I.* Over 50 Marines appeared in the cast out of the 350 who auditioned for parts.

Courtesy of Jack Webb Archives

Island tragedy that occurred on April 8, 1956. The event concerned an egregious training error committed by Drill Instructor Staff Sergeant Matthew McKeon, resulting in six Platoon 71 recruits drowning in a treacherous tidal stream named Ribbon Creek. The tragic misfortune, reported worldwide, was traumatic for the Corps. Many military careers were wrecked. The Marines obviously wanted the tragedy to be forgotten as soon as possible.

Considering the Corps' sensitivity to the training disaster, Webb chose not to focus his film on the accident. Instead, Webb's 106-minute film centered on an obstinate and immature "Private Owens" who could harm his DI's unblemished reputation and negatively impact the morale and performance of his entire platoon. Jack would paint his motion picture using the backdrop of a sand flea.

The bothersome sand flea was always present at Parris Island. The ubiquitous insects, scientifically identified as *Culicoides*, have been called "sand fleas," "sand gnats," "biting midges," and "punkies." Recruits named them "no-see-ums" and "Flying Teeth." If a recruit in or out of ranks should kill a sand flea, a Drill Instructor was likely to view the act comparable to the murder of an archduke. In language that turned the air blue, a DI might scream, "Don't you eat to live? ...well, the sonofabitchin' sand fleas have to live too, don't they? ...those damn fleas were put here for a purpose. They're supposed to bother recruits. That's why they're here! And I won't have any of you knuckleheads smashing the damn life out of them!"

A recruit might then be ordered to furnish a small or match box-sized casket for the "murdered" insect. Next, the errant recruit was required to dig a regulation-sized grave in the presence of the entire platoon and bury the tiny sand flea. Such an event was never forgotten, nor was most of the distorted discipline and logic of Marine Corps boot camp.

The sand flea story became the framework for *The D.I.* The tale was the brainchild of James Lee Barrett, a screenwriter whose films included *Shenandoah, The Greatest Story Ever Told, Tick, Tick, Tick, The Undefeated, The Green Berets, Smoky And The Bandit, The Cheyenne Social Club*, and others. In 1950, Private Barrett was a Parris Island recruit who witnessed the murder of a sand flea, although he maintained that his story was not based on any one Marine or single incident. Later, at Penn State University, he recalled the annoying insect and made the sand flea the subject of a two-act play entitled *The Pine Box*. The piece was expanded into a one-hour Kraft Television Theater performance as *The Murder Of A Sand Flea*. Two aspiring cast actors were Lee Marvin and Hugh O'Brian, both former Marines. During World War II, Marvin went through Parris Island and was badly wounded on Saipan in the Pacific War while O'Brian was a San Diego DI. Webb recognized the story potential and purchased Barrett's play and its screen rights. The two eventually crafted the tale into

a motion picture that they named *The D.I.*

By mid-November 1956, Webb had sent letters to the Department of Defense and the Marine Corps seeking approval and cooperation for the production of *The Murder Of A Sand Flea* as a full-length motion picture. The Marines may have welcomed Jack's request, because Twentieth Century-Fox was considering making a film based on the tragic Ribbon Creek event. The Marine Corps, wanting to overshadow that misfortune, approved Webb's project. The Corps' Director of Information advised the Commandant that:

Sgt. Joseph Holmes was personally selected by Jack to play the part of Private Madison in *The D.I.*

Donated by Joseph Holmes —
Courtesy of Jack Webb Archives

> It is believed that some producer sooner or later will desire cooperation of a full length motion picture concerning recruit training at Parris Island. "Murder of a Sand Flea," which deals with the character building of an emotionally immature young man would be more advantageous to the Marine Corps than many other recruit training stories. Mr. Webb, with his particular emphasis on

authenticity, should produce, from the standpoint of the Marine Corps, at least as good a picture as and quite possibly a better picture, than most producers would.

The Marine Corps extended its full cooperation to Mark VII Productions for screenplay preparation by February 14, 1957, requiring only minor changes in the script. Other text alterations were made during the filming, which was completed on March 27, 1957.

In cooperation with Mark VII Productions, the Marine Corps dispatched Lieutenant Colonel Wyatt B. Carneal, Jr. to Hollywood as the picture technical advisor to insure that Marine Corps recruit training was portrayed accurately. The officer commanded the First Recruit Training Battalion, Parris Island, South Carolina. Mark VII Productions paid all of Carneal's expenses. In fact, Webb boasted *The D.I.* did not cost the taxpayer one cent. Major Richard Mample assisted Carneal by coordinating operations between the San Diego and Camp Pendleton Marine Corps bases and Mark VII. As the senior Marine with the Armed Forces Information Office in Los Angeles, Mample was highly praised by Carneal. Technical Sergeant and San Diego Drill Instructor Louis H. Lazarko was the noncommissioned officer in charge of the actual Marine cast and was equally praised.

The Marine Corps need not have worried about the story's accuracy. Because of Webb's fanatical quest for fact and realism, Mr. Barrett and George Stevens, Jr. visited Parris Island in mid-November 1956. They recorded barracks measurements for film sets, made voice tapes, and took photographs of the sights and sounds of boot camp for Webb and the professional actors to study. Barrett eventually wrote the film script and Mr. Stevens, whose father was a celebrated filmmaker, was Webb's production assistant. During filming, more emphasis was placed on the Drill Instructor role, so the story title was changed from *The Murder Of A Sand Flea* to *The D.I.*

During November and December 1956, Marine Corps Base San Diego and Camp Pendleton Marines were informed that a Jack Webb film was in the making, and that he was looking for Marines to fill story roles. Approximately 350 Leathernecks auditioned for the Mark VII casting staff during three days at the San Diego base's McDougal Hall. Seventeen permanent personnel and 36 recently graduated recruits made the final cut. Thus, male professional actors played very few parts before the Marines left Hollywood. Civilian "extras" were later filmed in portions of The Cotton Club scene.

On February 21, 1957, the Marine actors were billeted at the Hollywood Colonial Motor Hotel, then considered one of the best in the Hollywood area. All meals were served in an upscale Hollywood restaurant owned by former football great Elroy "Crazy Legs" Hirsch, a 1944 Parris

Island recruit. From February 21 to 25, the Marines were briefed, cleaned their equipment, received haircuts, and engaged in Close Order Drill to remain fit and disciplined.

The "Hollywood Marines" had little time to enjoy their unaccustomed luxuries, since the typical workday was from 6:00 A.M. to 6:00 P.M. or later. Taps, for most, was sounded at 10:00 P.M. Their enthusiasm was always apparent, and before the picture was completed, the Mark VII staff and others were using such Marine Corps jargon as, "On the double," "Squared away," and "Knock it off!" On one occasion, Major Mample and Jack were joking and the officer mentioned that Webb

The Cotton Club scene from the 1957 movie *The D.I.*, featuring Jack's future wife Jackie Loughery.

Donated by Joseph Holmes — Courtesy of Jack Webb Archives

"would not make a pimple on a Pfc's ass." Jack, in true form, wanted to put the comment in the film, but found no place to insert Mample's observation. Mample recalled that Webb always surrounded himself with excellent talent, was "a true character," and a "real American" patriot. The future Colonel Mample remained in contact with Jack until Webb's death.

Filming began on February 25. Office and barracks scenes were filmed until March 5. Outdoor scenes were shot at Warner Bros. on March 6-7. Clothing wash rack and rear of barracks shots were filmed March 8-11. Drill scenes were done at Camp Pendleton (Del Mar), California on March 12. With the exception of several major speaking parts, most of the Marines returned to their permanent military bases at that time. From

March 13-27, principal scenes were produced including the Dress Shop, The Cotton Club, the Armory, "Captain Anderson's" office, and the swamp area scene. The picture was finished in a stunning six weeks, ending on March 27, 1957. This remarkable production performance time was attributed to Webb's efficiency and the organization and discipline of the Marines.

The Motion Picture Guilds did not seriously object to Webb using Marines rather than professional personnel. However, Lieutenant Colonel Carneal recalled that the Guilds required "Mark VII Limited to make considerable reimbursement to the Actors' and Extras' Guilds. Mark VII saved nothing monetarily by the use of Marines in this production." The officer also noted that employing regular actors "would have been impractical if not impossible." Most professional actors would appear too mature, unwilling to submit to Marine hair styles, and did not know how to properly handle the standard military M1 Rifle.

At this time, several motion pictures were in progress or being filmed on the Warner Bros. lot. One was *Darby's Rangers* with James Garner. The meticulous Webb was delighted that his Marines were quick to detect errors regarding military equipment the actors used and wore in other productions. *Heaven Knows Mr. Allison* was another 1957 Marine-related film premiering in Los Angeles, starring Robert Mitchum and Deborah Kerr. For publicity, the studio requested that Webb's Marines don their dress blue uniforms and become a part of the film's premiere event.

In *The D.I.*, Jack played the part of "Technical Sergeant Jim Moore," the Senior Drill Instructor of Platoon 194. Webb's use of former associates' and acquaintances' names served him once more, as a real Jim Moore worked with Jack on *Pat Novak For Hire* at KGO radio in San Francisco. During the filming, Webb was concerned that he was showing a small amount of extra weight and might not appear as trim as a first rate DI. Leading lady Jackie Loughery suggested that Jack wear a skin-tight girdle under his military uniform until the weight disappeared. Webb's Junior (Assistant) Drill Instructor "Sergeant Braver" was played by Sergeant Paul E. Prutzman, Jr., a San Diego Marine Corps DI.

Corporal John R. Brown was assigned a major role in the movie as "Sergeant O'Neil." The Marine was not associated with any Parris Island platoon that Stevens and Barrett had taped originally. Yet, Brown possessed a unique marching cadence. After Webb heard Brown's distinctive marching chant, Jack immediately requested that the Marine Corps send the Korean War Purple Heart veteran to Hollywood to become the only Parris Island-cast Marine in California. Jack was so impressed with Brown that he appointed him a personal technical advisor. Later, Brown received fan mail and was a Parris Island celebrity when he returned to the base from Hollywood with his new French wife. [Editor's note: co-author Gene Alvarez was then Sergeant Alvarez and Corporal Brown's Senior Drill

Instructor. Sergeant Alvarez trained Platoon 351 in the same barracks visited by Stevens and Barrett.]

Actor Don Dubbins played "Private Owens," the problem recruit. Dubbins, one of the few professional actors, was a former Marine and a 1946 Parris Island recruit. The actor also appeared in films includ-

On the set of *The D.I.*, with Don Dubbins as "Private Owens," the problem recruit. Dubbins, one of the few professional actors, was a former Marine and a 1946 Parris Island recruit.

Courtesy of Jack Webb Archives

ing *From Here To Eternity* (1953), *The Caine Mutiny* (1954), *Mr. Roberts* (1955), and *Tribute To A Bad Man* (1956), starring James Cagney. Dubbins also worked with Webb in the second generation *Dragnet* series, 1967-1970. The third professional male actor in the cast was Lin McCarthy who played the part of "Captain Anderson."

The leading lady "Anne" was Jackie Loughery, who in 1952 was crowned the first "Miss U.S.A." Singer Monica Lewis also had a role and gave a charming performance of *(If'n You Don't) Somebody Else Will*, with music by Ray Conniff and lyrics by Fred Weismantel. David Buttolph wrote the score. Virginia Gregg played "Private Owens'" mother and Jeannie Beacham ("Miss Photoflash of 1957") appeared briefly in the Dress Shop scene. Jeanne Baird, Barbara Pepper, and Melody Gale were other actresses in the predominately male cast.

Technical Sergeant Charles A. Love, the first Marine selected for the cast, played the part of "Hillbilly." He also appeared on NBC-TV *Monitor* with Jack and served as a primary adviser to Webb. When Sergeant Love's family visited him while the production was in progress, Jack had him removed from the cast motel and rented a bungalow for the family near the studio gate. Webb paid for the rent and the family's food until the filming concluded. Such generosity was characteristic of Webb.

Sergeant Joseph C. Holmes revered his role of "Private Madison." One of many interesting experiences Holmes related was his being dressed down by actor Lee Marvin, who played "Private Madison" in television's *The Murder Of A Sand Flea.* On the day the two men met, Marvin is reported to have said, "I should have that part. You're just a candy-ass Marine. I was in World War II. I'm a real Marine." Holmes fortunately did not resent Marvin's bravura and later spent some friendly time with Marvin in Hollywood. Master Gunnery Sergeant Holmes retired from the Marine Corps as a Vietnam War combat veteran and remained in touch with Jack until Webb's death.

Though he had a reputation for sometimes being gruff on the set, Jack was respected by the Marines and was hailed as "a true Marine in every way!" His attention to detail and demand for perfection was congruent with the Marine Corps' standard operating procedures. In one case, Webb demanded 25 retakes of a scene in which a cup of coffee was being handed to him. Jack re-shot the scene until he was pleased with the way the actor spoke the lines and handled the cup. The scene involved a Marine Corps lieutenant portraying "Joey." Jack became so exasperated with the officer's performance that he replaced the lieutenant with Technical Sergeant Louis H. Lazarko.

Webb, Carneal, Brown, and the other Marines were so skillful at overseeing barracks sets that Marines not involved in the filmmaking swore the picture was produced at Parris Island — it was not. The film was shot primarily in California on a Mark VII Republic Studios set in Studio City and at Warner Bros. Two sequences were filmed at the Marines' Camp Del Mar (Pendleton) and at a USMCR (Reserve) Center in Pasadena. A most memorable scene was the platoon search for the "murdered" sand flea, which film critic Leonard Maltin called "priceless."

A cast banquet was held on the final filming day to celebrate completion of *The D.I.* Though none of the Marines were permitted to accept any remuneration for their efforts, Webb offered unauthorized recreational money. Each Marine actor was officially permitted to receive an expensive and engraved wristwatch presented by Webb. When the men left their motel, the manager was amazed that not a single item was missing. Jack later said of the Marines, "They were sensational and that's the 'weakest' word I could have used." Making *The D.I.* "was the greatest thrill of my life."

Lieutenant Colonel Carneal concluded his report to Commandant Randolph McCall Pate on April 2, 1957:

> This motion picture will be of immense value to the Marine Corps. As a unique type of production, never before attempted by a motion picture company, it is believed *The D. I.* will be well received and appreciated by the American public.

In other correspondence, Carneal reported that *The D.I.* was "a dynamic motion picture" that was so well done and realistic, "it stands as a relief from the usual 'Hollywood' military picture." Webb was praised as "a gentleman of extreme integrity who enjoys the respect of all who know him. Suffice to say that it has been a pleasure working with him."

In correspondence to Webb from the Pictorial Branch Chief, Office Of The Assistant Secretary Of Defense, Mr. Donald E. Baruch wrote on April 19, 1957:

> All those who saw the picture thought you had brought the story vividly to the screen. The Marine Corps especially is well pleased with the results and considers that all efforts of cooperation were justified. The Corps believes that the picture will be beneficial for recruiting. Therefore, it has indicated that full support will be granted within limitations of policies for premieres and subsequent local showings.

Commandant Pate praised Jack and the picture, "which realistically portrayed how, through its recruit training, the Marine Corps builds men." Warner Bros. scheduled a special screening and a cocktail party for the Commandant and his guests at the Motion Picture Association Building in Washington, D.C. The Assistant Commandant and a number of officers and their ladies enjoyed a sneak preview of the film at Marine Corps Headquarters, Washington, D. C. Jack, who had previously appeared on The Ed Sullivan Television Show as "Sergeant Friday," returned to Sullivan's top-rated program to promote *The D.I.* on May 26, 1957. The Commandant presented Jack with a Certificate Of Appreciation and appointed Webb as an honorary DI, complete with the swagger stick and a campaign hat.

In late May 1957, Parris Island Marines attended *The D.I.* premiere for two nights in the historic base Lyceum. A total of 2,238 Marines and their dependents were impressed with the story realism, though some ensuing professional reviews were tepid. The film premiered in Chicago on May 30 and in New York City on June 5. Today Marines consider *The D.I.* an outstanding film and a near accurate account of past recruit training. However, some civilians consider the story to be "high camp."

Following the 1956 Ribbon Creek tragedy, *The D.I.* served as a morale builder for Drill Instructors and a welcomed recruiting aid for the Marine Corps. Further, Webb may have attracted international attention to Parris Island, since 37-year-old producer Francois Reichtenback produced a French-made Parris Island documentary in 1957. Originally entitled *Le But*, the name was changed to *Les Marines* and was dedicated to all Leathernecks. The film won first prize at the Venice Film Festival, and in the French Film Academy, *Les Marines* was selected over 300 other entries in French film competition as the winner of the French "Oscar."

The D.I. story theme was resurrected in 1970, but with a different and anti-Vietnam War outcome in the television movie *Tribes*. In 1978, *The Boys In Company C* dealt with Vietnam War recruit training. *An Officer And A Gentleman* in 1982 had an Academy Award winning DI role for Lou Gossett, Jr. Actor Lee Ermey, who was once a San Diego Marine Corps DI, starred in the acclaimed *Full Metal Jacket* in 1987. Much of that story also involved Parris Island recruit training during the Vietnam War. However, Webb set the precedent for future Drill Instructor portrayals with his masterful characterization of a role that seemed tailor-made for him as "Technical Sergeant Jim Moore" in *The D.I.*

As successful, authentic, and precedent-setting as *The D.I.* was, the movie would have a more personal meaning for Jack than he could have imagined when he began the project. Ironically, the course of events began on Valentine's Day 1957 just before the filming of *The D.I.*

Jack with Jackie Loughery as "Anne" in *The D.I.*

Courtesy of Jack Webb Archives

"I was never
caught jaywalking again."

On Valentine's Day 1957, Herm Saunders arranged for Jack to meet with a possible new cast member for *The D.I.* Jack arrived wearing his red socks and a red sweater, obviously partial to the color red. He often wore his initials on his cuffs. This actress was destined to play the romantic female lead in the film and to become Jack's romantic companion off the set. Her name was Jackie Loughery. The couple fell in love while filming *The D.I.* During filming, Jack selfishly concluded in good humor that Jackie was wasting her time acting, when instead she could be caring for him: "I told her so in a sort of bumbling way."

Jack and Jackie were married on June 24, 1958. The civil ceremony

Jackie Loughery played Jack's romantic lead on and off the set of *The D.I.* They were married within 18 months of the day they met.

Courtesy of Jack Webb Archives

was performed in the den of Jack's apartment on Radford Avenue and included writers Jim Bacon and Jim Bishop, Jackie's friends, George Posty, Maid Of Honor Sylvia Posty, and Webb's friends Herm and Kae Saunders. Herm was the best man for a marriage of which Jack quipped, "Men dream about."

Though Webb had briefly dated Peggy Lee after he and Dorothy Towne divorced, he lost his heart to Jackie Loughery. Jackie was born in Brooklyn, New York on April 18, 1935, making her 15 years Jack's junior. Her father was a retired United States Navy Captain, and her mother (who ironically seldom wore makeup) encouraged Jackie to model and enter beauty pageants. Jackie won numerous beauty contests, including "Miss New York State," and in 1952, she took the top honors at the first "Miss USA" pageant held in Long Beach, California. She next participated in the "Miss Universe" Pageant won by "Miss Sweden," Armi Kuusela. Perhaps more importantly, she received a movie contract from Universal and pursued a career in Hollywood. In October 1953, she married singer Guy Mitchell, but the marriage lasted only one year.

Although Jack felt that Jackie could be "very explosive when the Irish comes out in her," she seems indeed to have been an understanding step-mother and a good wife. Jackie encouraged Stacy, as a child, to operate a lemonade stand (whose best customer was Jack) and to study ballet. Stacy saw herself only as a chubby little girl who, in her own words, looked like a "tomato in a Tu tu." Jackie and Stacy often visited Jack at work, but Jack's younger daughter Lisa was partial to her biological mother Julie London and Julie's future new husband Bobby Troup. In 1956, Stacy met her grandmother "Maggie" the only time in her life, when "Maggie" gave her a record player for Christmas.

Many times Jackie genuinely professed her love for Jack with these words, "I am only interested in Jack's happiness. Being a good wife to him, I will also be happy." She ensured that he took his vitamin pills, she purchased paints and brushes for him to sketch, had Jack wearing neckties, and even western garb at a Frank Sinatra costume party. Jackie shared with a *Saturday Evening Post* reporter that each night she endearingly told Jack at bedtime, "God bless you, Jack." Webb's reply to his beautiful wife was, "He already has."

Jackie helped bring Jack and his ex-wife Julie closer together in the interest of the children. Jackie was instrumental in enrolling Stacy and Lisa in the Louisville Catholic School. Jackie never met Jack's mother, but believed that "Maggie's" alcoholism may have contributed to any psychological problems Jack may have had. "Maggie" was relocated to numerous care homes, as her behavior was less than stellar. However, her public indiscretions were tolerated in deference to Jack. On those occasions when newspapers or the police did not recognize her, she was more than happy to inform them of her son's identity and notoriety.

Webb affectionately called Jackie "mouse." Once Jack even sent her a living gift that Jackie called "the cutest little white mice." To celebrate their first wedding anniversary, Jack had a large Palm Springs home built at 1255 Manzanita Avenue, staffed in part by Jack's house boy, Fred (formerly Amelia Earhart's house boy). Jackie recalls that the house "was fabulous." Every year Jack gave Fred a new Cadillac automobile, but the Filipino was embarrassed to be seen in the vehicle, since no one believed the car was actually his.

Frequent guests at the Manzanita Avenue home included Joan Crawford, Eva Gabor,

Engagement photo taken June 6, 1958 just 18 days before their wedding day.

Courtesy of Jack Webb Archives

Dick Van Dyke, and many others known in the entertainment industry. Jack and Jackie discussed having children, and the mansion included a large spare room which could be used for a nursery one day. The swimming pool had a large waterfall, which Stacy especially enjoyed. The Webb's Palm Springs residence was built just two doors down from Julie London's home, a site that Jackie believed Webb chose to be close to Stacy and Lisa. Jack often enjoyed taking Lisa, Stacy, and Jackie on a family outing to the Drive-In Theater where he showered them with armloads of candy, colas, and popcorn.

Jack and Jackie should have had an ideal marriage. Jackie seemed to have most, if not all, of the qualities one would want in a spouse, including respect and love for Jack. Having a family was important to her, but for Jack, his work became his family and his greatest concern. New babies never occupied the hopeful nursery in their Palm Springs home. This marriage, too, would end in divorce.

People who knew and frequently associated with Webb, such as "Riff" and Ann Rodgers, suggested that Jack did not know how to act as a married and family man, since his only family male role model as a child was an absent, unknown father. Locating Webb's mystery father created news when *Time* magazine reported in the mid-1950's that "their reportorial sleuths" had discovered one Sam Webb in a western state. Jack knew nothing about the investigation or the report, yet he received a "scorching" letter from Sam Webb's wife alleging that Jack was "guilty of an invasion of privacy." She informed Jack that her husband was not Jack's father, and Jack recalls that he was advised "to mind my own business." Jack questionably replied, "I never had any real curiosity about my father's whereabouts, and I always thought that if he were alive I would have had some word." Others would claim that Jack was their long-lost cousin or uncle. Jack even received letters asking him to have "Sergeant Friday" eliminate their traffic violations or other crimes.

By 1959, Webb was in his prime as a top producer, director, and actor. He was featured several times throughout the 1950's on the covers of and in articles and interviews appearing in *TV Guide*, *McCall's*, *Cosmopolitan*, *The Saturday Evening Post*, and *Time*. Jack also appeared as a celebrity guest on the television program *Place The Face*, a quiz show that challenged him to identify a mystery voice. Jack never guessed the identity of Jane Gibson, whom he had known since their Central Junior High School days. Nevertheless, the two did share a marvelous reunion after the program. Stacy appeared on television, too, as a guest with Julie London on a program called *Celebrity Moms*.

Unique situations became common for Jack, since "Sergeant Friday" had become synonymous with Jack Webb. During the summer of 1959 in New York, Jack began crossing a busy street and heard a whistle sound. A policeman quickly approached him and lectured, "Sergeant Friday, I'm surprised at you! You're a cop and you oughta know better." Jack had no idea what was bothering the officer and was bursting to tell the policeman that Jack was "Sergeant Friday" only one night a week. Webb instinctively wanted to enlighten the officer, "Actually, I couldn't solve a real crime if they gave me all the clues. I can't even find a tie pin when I lose it at home." Jack, feeling as if he were a small boy being spanked in public, vowed, "I was never caught jaywalking again."

On other occasions, Webb's name was signed to bad checks, and women he had never met accused him of fathering "their" children. Los Angeles citizens routinely telephoned "Sergeant Friday" at the LAPD and requested that he assist resolving domestic disturbances. The Desk Sergeant usually replied that "Friday" was not attached to their station. When pressed by the caller for "Friday's" station, the officer would typically reply that "Joe" was attached "to the Los Angeles station of the

Jackie and Jack enjoying the pool at their Encino home.

Donated by Jackie Loughery — Courtesy of Jack Webb Archives

National Broadcasting Company." Persons visiting the Los Angeles Police Department insisted on meeting "Friday," but after tiring from so many inquiries the LAPD would explain, "Sorry, it's Joe's day off." Whenever the LAPD Chief and his officers visited other cities, they were frequently asked, "How's Friday?"

Actual police officers often used "Joe's" laconic expression, "Just the facts, Ma'am," to break the ice of an investigation, while comedians and gag writers offered humorous variations of the nationally popular phrase. Durward Kirby performed numerous Webb skits using the language associated with *Dragnet*. In one routine, Kirby quips, "Frank, go to the P.D.C.L. and run a P.M.R.X. on the D.C.T. and make it P.D.Q. And, Frank—how's your bursitis?" Bands played the *Dragnet* musical motif at football games each time a referee walked off the penalty for a team. The theme was also interlaced into radio commercials, and at least one dance band had a swing version of *Dragnet's* score. Lawyers used "Friday's" clipped speech and his monologues in their closing arguments, while students composed papers or wrote theses regarding *Dragnet*.

Fan mail continued to be special to Jack, who personally wanted to sign every photo requested from him. However, Webb's long time and faithful secretary, Jean Miles, autographed some of his pictures, having

A 1955 Jack Webb "Safety Squad" coloring book was just one of the many merchandising items flooding the market during _Dragnet's_ peak.

Courtesy of Jack Webb Archives

mastered Jack's signature. Miles was devoutly loyal to Jack, often assisting him with his children. She remained with Jack until his death. _Dragnet_ and Jack received criticism, praise, and gifts in fan mail. One stamp collector forwarded Webb postmarks from _Jack_, Alabama; _Webb_, West Virginia; _Joe_, North Carolina, and _Friday_, Texas, which Jack proudly displayed. School principals requested his advice regarding troublesome situations, but the lies printed about his private life were most disturbing to him. He was accused of striking a drunk on Sunset Strip one night for calling a police officer a "cop." Another lie was that he was thrown out of New York's prestigious Stork Club because he was not wearing a necktie. Of course, Jack denied the gossip and often asked, "Who cares?" The truth was that, other than having dinner at his favorite restaurants, Webb mostly enjoyed staying home when he was not working, with little interest in Hollywood's party and glitzy social life.

With _Dragnet's_ popularity on radio, television, and in the movies, a merchandising industry emerged and generated numerous specialty items, some labeled as an "official" product of _Dragnet_ or Jack Webb. There was a Jack Webb toy police revolver and a _Dragnet_ target game. An "official" badge could be purchased, as could "The Game Of Dragnet" (for two to six players). Available were "Dragnet Badge 714 Crime Lab Kits" and a "Dragnet Badge 714 Flashlight Gun." The "Dragnet Badge 714 Puzzle" was advertised as "A brain teaser for everyone." A "Jack Webb's Safety Squad" coloring book was available that taught children safety practices while coloring _Dragnet_ and other scenes. The Kellogg Company packaged an "Official Jack Webb Dragnet Whistle" in their cereal boxes. There was also an "Official Dragnet Emblem," a "Deputy Junior Dragnet 714 Badge," an official member ID card, and secret "Dragnet" code. Children could drive the "Dragnet" pedal car as well as build the official model car kit. "Joe Friday" appeared in a cartoon strip based on *Dragnet* episodes.

There was adult *Dragnet* merchandising, too. Chesterfield cigarettes advertised, "You'll like Chesterfield regular — as Jack Webb does — or king-size, like Ben Alexander." The Chesterfield ad pictured "Sergeant Joe Friday" and "Officer Frank Smith." Jack was associated with *Hot Rod* magazine when he was producing the story about a "hot rod" hit and run driver. Jack once again worked to achieve script accuracy with the National Hot Rod Association, whose office was recreated on the set. In

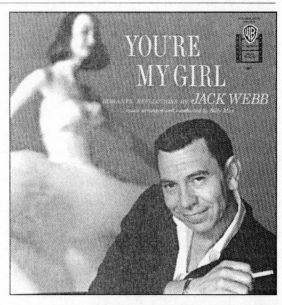

"Romantic Reflections", 1958

Courtesy of Jack Webb Archives

the "Big Rod" episode, "Friday" said to the villain driver, "You threw a ton and a half of metal at a hundred-and-one-pound woman, then ran away and left her in the gutter." Richard Deming wrote various hardback and paperback *Dragnet* books, offering a collection of case histories from the television episodes.

Dragnet was broadcast by NBC each Tuesday night but, by 1958, was slipping in the television ratings opposite *Sugarfoot* or *Cheyenne* on ABC and the *George Burns & Gracie Allen Show* on CBS. However, there was no evidence that Jack intended to abandon *Dragnet* or the Los Angeles Police Department. That year Webb published the book *The Badge*, which took two years to write. The book concerned the inner activities of the Los Angeles Police Department, revealing in depth how each department worked. The book was received well enough to demand a second printing.

Jack became active recording music following *Pete Kelly's Blues*. Conductor Billy May recalled that Webb truly enjoyed music, and even though Jack "had complete control," working with Jack was a pleasure. Webb attended all of the recording sessions and was meticulously selective for the music in his 1958 album *You're My Girl — Romantic Reflections By Jack Webb*. The Warner Bros. long playing album (WB-1207) featured Webb speaking, as noted on the cover by writer Jim Bishop: "He cannot sing a lick; he cannot run a riff on a balalaika. But he has a voice. It is deeply conversational and as intimate as a pair of big shoes or a pair of tiny ones under a bed. Jack Webb talks this album." The album featured sax solos by Murray McEachern and music arranged and conducted by Billy May, a music celebrity in his own right.

Dragnet-related music recordings included *Christmas Story* (RCA 0342/3; RCA 3199) from an episode of *Dragnet*. Stan Freburg recorded a 78rpm two-part record *Little Blue Riding Hood* satire on *Dragnet*. *TV Guide* assisted fans in learning the language of "Dragnetese" by suggesting: "The secret is all in the sound of the words and your facial expression. For practice, dip your face in paste (flour and water will do) and stand in front of a mirror while you utter the Dragnet words in perfect monotone." At times, the nation seemed to be *Dragnet*-mad.

By 1959, *Dragnet* had aired 278 half-hour episodes in eight years and posted over 500 radio shows. However, the show dropped to number 18 on the television charts and the ratings did not improve. Webb voluntarily aired the final *Dragnet* episode on September 6, 1959. Little fanfare was associated with the finale with the exception of "Joe" being promoted to "Lieutenant Friday." Webb reasoned that a new face in any following series might be refreshing, as Jack would only appear occasionally, permitting him more time for other endeavors. The episodes enjoyed numerous reruns as *Badge 714*, which at times drew greater audiences than the original series did. "Joe's" Badge 714 was retired in 1959, too.

Webb stated that *Dragnet* lasted four years longer than he thought it would. He attributed its television success to having a previous radio audience and no TV competition. The show brought Webb a substantial yearly income and built Mark VII Limited Productions. All *Dragnet* rights were sold to a subsidiary of the Music Corporation Of America (MCA) in 1956. Webb reported in 1959, "A few years ago we sold our interest in *Dragnet* in a package deal to Sherry Television Incorporated for $5,000,000, and this company is now distributing the films."

A 1959 series produced by Webb's Mark VII Productions was *The D.A.'s Man*, televised from January 3 until August 29. The half-hour NBC crime series was based on James B. Horan and Harold Danforth's book and starred John Compton as "Private Detective Shannon," who the New York District Attorney called upon for needed help.

One unsuccessful Webb venture was *The Black Cat*, which concerned a journalist who specialized in investigative work. The title was taken from a black cat statue created by Benamino Bufano, used by the San Francisco Press Club. If the statue was displayed on a table before a group of journalists, any confidential discussion was to remain off the record. The pilot, filmed in San Francisco, was in production no later than the fall of 1959 and scheduled for a winter release. Webb voiced, "This one is my baby," but only the pilot episode aired. Herm Saunders recalled, "We ended up with a black and white pilot that was finally scrapped."

Jack's fascination with the 1920's and jazz resurfaced when *Pete Kelly's Blues* appeared on NBC television. "Pete" was played by William

Reynolds, who had portrayed so-called "pretty boy" parts at Paramount and Universal-International for over eight years before landing the "Kelly" role. Reynolds was selected from over 50 other actors who competed for the part. "Pete's" actual trumpet playing was performed by Dick Cathcart off-camera, though Reynolds appeared comfortable in front of the camera with a horn in his hand. Webb noted, "If they like Reynolds, we've got a show." Singer Connie Boswell's played

Jack with Whitney Blake as Peggy Gatlin in the film -30-

Courtesy of Jack Webb Archives

"Savannah Brown," and Than Wyenn played "George Lupo."

The story, as on radio and in the motion picture, took place in Kansas City during the Prohibition years. "Pete" headed and played trumpet in "Pete Kelly's Original Big Seven Band." "Savannah Brown" was his romantic interest and "Kelly's" best friend was "Fred," who played piano in the band. The stories revolved around "Pete's" adventures, as he became involved in murders, tracking down missing people, and other non-musical exploits.

Trumpet player Dick Cathcart remained "Pete's" musical stand-in. Frank Comstock arranged the musical score for *Pete Kelly's Blues*. The show was received well by audiences, but remained unsponsored and lasted only from April 5 to September 4, 1959. Jack criticized those network executives whom he could not convince to retain a program with music as an integral part. Webb was informed, "You couldn't stop for music ... People wouldn't sit still for it."

Jack returned to the silver screen by filming -30- at Republic Studios in 1959. The designation -30- is one way journalists indicate "the end" of a written piece. The screenplay was written by William Bowers and Jack directed the 96-minute story that attempted to portray an eventful night in a big city newspaper office.

Jack played "Sam Gatlin," the night editor of a Los Angeles newspaper. The fictional staff included actors William Conrad, David Nelson, Joe

A scene from *-30-* featuring Webb's close friend, William Conrad

Courtesy of Jack Webb Archives

Flynn, Richard Deacon, Nancy Valentine, James Bell, and Louise Lorimer. "Sam's" wife "Peggy Gatlin," played by Whitney Blake, tries to convince "Sam" to go through with the adoption of a young boy. "Sam" was still grieving over the loss of his first wife and child, who were killed by a drunk driver. He has mixed feelings about an adoption until he sees the boy enter his office and ask, "Is Mrs. Gatlin in here, sir?" The film's climax concerns the rescue of a lost child who fell into one of the city storm drains during a torrential downpour. Saving the child is a race against the clock, as the waters are rising fast due to the heavy rains. The drama ends as the girl is rescued in a final effort, and "Gatlin's" newspaper is the first to report the story.

The film was, for critics and others, a disappointing effort on the part of Webb. Too many story lines were in progress at one time, and the picture was considered over-acted and poorly written. The music was forgettable, and the writers apparently could not decide if *-30-* was a comedy or a drama.

However, as the 1950's came to a close, Jack Webb could not be forgotten. In the 1960's, he would break new ground, again by marrying law enforcement and television.

"To Jack Webb,
The Best Reel Cop From LAPD,
The Best Real Cops."

Webb's portrayal of law and order in the 1960's became especially challenging. Civil rights, youth, and cultural revolutions erupted and questioned the morality and societal values existing since World War II. Pre-marital sex and use of the new birth control pill were practiced by many, as "Make love, not war!" became a familiar expression. A growing drug culture and disrespect for police officers and others in the "establishment" was in vogue, an environment that did not escape the attention of Webb. Assassinations included those of President John F. Kennedy, his brother Robert Kennedy, and Martin Luther King, Jr. A Cuban missile crisis and the Cold War posed frightening possibilities of nuclear war while objections to the war in Vietnam threatened to tear the country apart.

Jack had no sympathy for Communism. In 1961, he narrated two 30-minute black and white television productions for the Department Of Defense and the Armed Forces Information And Education Offices. *The Commies Are Coming (Red Nightmare)*, originally titled *Red Nightmare*, produced at Warner Bros., concerned a citizen who took for granted his liberty, freedom, and the quality of life his family enjoyed in the United States. The didactic theme of responsibility, duty, and a Communist attempt at world domination was revealed in a film nightmare that concluded with the citizen's execution by the local Communist regime. The story ended as the husband and father awakened from his dream to realize that liberty is not free and that taking his family for granted was a serious mistake. A young Robert Conrad had a brief part in the film.

The U. S. Fighting Man's Code Of Conduct was narrated by Jack portraying a professor in a lecture atmosphere. He stressed significant step-by-step lessons to remember should any American become a prisoner of war. The instructional film dwelled on discipline, faith, hope, and more. These characteristics were dramatized with stories extracted from American history, World War II, and the Korean War in which some American prisoners ("turncoats") refused to return to the United States.

A third Federally-funded military training film narrated by Webb was *USS V.D. — Ship Of Shame*. This film concerned the health dangers of venereal diseases and the crew of an American war ship that became an embarrassment to the fleet.

The Last Time I saw Archie was a 1961 Mark VII production in association with Manzanita and Talbot Productions, filmed at Republic Studios, and released through United Artists. Webb produced, directed, nar-

Robert Mitchum, Martha Hyer and France Nuyen with Jack in the 1961 film *The Last Time I Saw Archie.*

Courtesy of Jack Webb Archives

rated, and starred as "Private Bill Bowers," a Hollywood writer before World War II. The 98-minute black and white comedy mostly takes place in an "ill-fated outfit of the Army Air Corps." The script was written by Webb's true-life friend Bill Bowers and was based in part on Mr. Bowers' U. S. Army life. Robert Mitchum played "Private Archie Hall," a persuasive con man who eventually becomes President. The impressive cast also included Don Knotts, Richard Arlen, Martha Hyer, France Nuyen, and Louis Nye. Two cast athletes were baseball's Don Drysdale and football's Bill Kilmer. Mitchum's son James appeared in the film, as were numerous regulars associated with Webb. "Archie Hall" in the story was the true name of an irate or opportunistic person who sued, claiming an invasion of privacy.

In 1962-1963, Webb was the host and narrator of *General Electric True*, which was broadcast for numerous seasons at the same time as the *General Electric Theater*. The CBS half-hour anthology was a Mark VII production that aired each Sunday from 9:30 to 10:00 P.M. The episodes were based on actual stories which appeared in *True* magazine and which Webb presented "with as much fidelity to the original as possible."

Harold Jack Bloom wrote prolifically for *True*, whose tales chiefly had adventure-suspense or military themes. One episode that especially appealed to Jack was called *Little Richard*, which aired on February 3, 1963. The program concerned an adventurous hound dog named "Little Richard" that became trapped in a rock crevice while chasing a raccoon. Jack helped direct and narrate *Code-Name Christopher*, a two-part October 1962 episode. Webb played the leading role of an American agent who planned the sabotage of a Nazi factory during W.W.II. In the *True* series, Jack was the closest person to appear as the show's star. Others in the dramatic series were Jerry Van Dyke, Arte Johnson, Robert Vaughn, and Victor Buono. The producers were Webb and Mike Meshekoff.

General Electric True earned favorable reviews but experienced poor ratings. The series ran for only one season, September 30, 1962 to September 22, 1963. *TV Guide* claimed that the show lacked "the big thing *Dragnet* had — style." Webb explained that "the theory that you can follow one success with another is just not true."

Most of Webb's half of the $5,000,000 that MCA paid for *Dragnet* had disappeared by 1963. Jack credited his financial decline to capital-gains taxes, heavy and disappointing investments in his Mark VII Production Company, and divorces — all of which presented him with financial losses ranging between two and three million dollars.

In 1963, he began working for Warner Bros. as a Television Executive Producer to oversee such shows as *Surfside 6* and *Hawaiian Eye*. Another Warner Bros. assignment was to improve *77 Sunset Strip*. The popular story first aired on October 10, 1958. With the antics of "Kookie" played by Edd Byrnes, the series was one of television's top 10 shows and ranked favorably as late as 1963. When the show's appeal declined, William Conrad was brought in as the Director and Jack as the Producer in an effort to revive the show. Major changes were made, and all of the cast who had not quit were dismissed, except Efrem Zimbalist, Jr., who played "Stuart Bailey." Eight top writers were hired to produce quality scripts, but nothing saved the series, last telecast on September 9, 1964.

In the employment of Warner Bros., Webb saw himself as no more than a high-priced employee, whose creativity was stifled. Herm Saunders, who followed Jack to Warner Bros., recalled that Webb's tenure there was "a non productive time" in his life. With J. L. Warner in control, there was no way that Webb's ideas could flourish. As a creator and perfectionist, Jack reacted negatively to any threat to his control. In December 1963, after about 10 months at the Warner Studio, Jack was dismissed with three years remaining on his contract.

Webb and Warner Bros. obviously did not part on good terms, and a nasty legal battle ensued. The matter was eventually resolved when Warner agreed to pay Webb his contracted $3,000 weekly salary for the remainder of his contract. Bob Leeds and Ray Heindorf were laid-off by Warner Bros. at the same time. Heindorf, who had worked at the studio for 25 years, had a prior legal disagreement with Warner Bros. in 1954. After his dismissal, Heindorf was not even allowed to drive his automobile on to the lot. For Webb to work for Warner, or anyone who might restrain his creative vision, was a mistake. Those who knew Jack as an innovator and not as an organization man were puzzled as to why he would have accepted such a position.

When Webb and Warner Bros. fell into disfavor, Jack suggested that he had realized his ambitions and achieved his goals. He was quoted in 1963 saying that he was happier than ever, working 10 instead of 18 hours a day. Webb reported that he "never did want to be a big wheel" and was happy to have only two sports coats, two suits, a tuxedo, and a new car every year. However, he remained ambitious until his death and was unhappy unless he was in control.

The Webb-Conrad team also worked on *The Man From Galveston*. The 1963 motion picture was a 57-minute "unsatisfying little Western," according to Leonard Maltin. The cast included Jeffrey Hunter, Preston Foster, James Coburn, and Joanna Moore.

In 1965, Jack contemplated a return to *Dragnet*. Within a year, he produced an NBC two-hour color *Dragnet* television movie, which served as a pilot for a series to follow the next year. Lieutenant (Captain) Pierce R. Brooks of the LAPD Press Relations Office was assigned as Webb's technical advisor to assure that all of the information and scenes concerning the Department were accurate. Brooks actually worked in the Homicide Division for the case on which much of *Dragnet 1966* was based. As in the past, the new *Dragnet* had the full support and cooperation of Chief William Parker, who instructed Brooks to do everything the Department could to assist getting another edition of *Dragnet* on the air. Jack and *Dragnet* were excellent publicity for the LAPD.

Filmed at Universal Studios, Webb produced, directed, and starred in the 1966 television picture written by Richard L. "Dick" Breen. As in previous productions, the set atmosphere was charged with discipline and efficiency. Webb was so active that his stage crews often had difficulty keeping pace with him. Jack required that all details be accurate in every scene. As many as 15 LAPD officers reviewed scripts to detect any technical or libel slips. During the production, Webb occupied a comfortable, nearby studio bungalow. His Universal Studios office telephone number was, like "Friday's" badge, Extension 714.

Dan Cooke was also assigned to assist with *Dragnet*. The sergeant was in awe of Webb, although he had been forewarned of Jack's legendary devotion to detail. Yet, Cooke was astonished when Webb's art director dropped to his knees in a Department office to count the white flecks in the black floor tile which was to be reproduced on a set. Furniture used in earlier *Dragnet* productions was rescued from the LAPD Supply Division and transported to Universal Studios by truck. On one occasion, Cooke recalled that Webb was visibly upset to discover an incorrect office extension number on a set telephone. Jack picked up the phone and threw it down, though many in the room questioned if anyone would know the correct number or extension anyway. Even thermostat coverings were redone for accuracy. In another instance, Jack was upset for not being informed that the paint color in a Los Angeles Police Department office had been changed.

"Lieutenant Joe Friday" returned to his former rank of sergeant in the new production, since Webb voiced, "No, I'm not coming back as a Lieutenant. I'm coming back as a Sergeant. First of all, Sergeants do more work than Lieutenants, and sec-

Behind the scenes of *Dragnet 1966* with Harry Morgan "Joe Friday's" new partner "Bill Gannon."

Donated by Pierce Brooks — Courtesy of Jack Webb Archives

ondly, no one will remember it ["Joe's" promotion to lieutenant in 1959] anyway." "Friday's" LAPD Sergeant's Badge 714 was polished and returned to service once more.

The veteran actor Harry Morgan replaced Ben Alexander as "Friday's" new sidekick "Bill Gannon," since Alexander had signed to work in another production before the casting of *Dragnet 1966*. Morgan was born in Detroit as Harry Bratsburg on April 10, 1915 and enrolled at the University of Chicago as an aspiring lawyer. However, his speaking and acting classes interested him more than law. During the Great Depression, Morgan sold office equipment in Washington, D.C., where he received a small role in a civic theater production. Other larger and better parts followed in New York State and New York City where Morgan appeared in productions with Frances Farmer, Dan Duryea, and Henry Fonda. Harry recalled,

Jack's stand-in double, Marco Lopez and Harry Morgan

Courtesy of Jack Webb Archives

"I just fell into the acting game."

Other travels and productions followed for Morgan, including several Broadway failures, after which he journeyed to Hollywood. There he appeared with Jack in several movies and eventually acted in over 100 films. Yet, Morgan's fame largely rests with television's *Dragnet* and *M*A*S*H*. Vic Perrin, Herb Ellis, Sam Edwards, Virginia Gregg and Julie London's husband, Bobby Troup also appeared in *Dragnet 1966*.

Jack searched for and interviewed several actors for his stand-in and photo double. Webb's choice was Marco Lopez, who at the time was working for Paramount. Lopez had met Lisa, Stacy, and Julie when London was working on an earlier film. Once on the set, Jack discovered Marco solving a crossword puzzle and ordered Lopez to report to him immediately. The stand-in received a polite admonition as Webb informed Marco that if he wanted to excel in the industry, Lopez must pay attention to everything occurring on the set. Marco recalled, "I respected him for that" and "it was the greatest learning lesson in my life." Lopez later appeared in numerous episodes of *Adam-12*, *Emergency*, and Webb's pilot films.

Dragnet 1966 opened with the familiar music and dialogue as "Joe Friday" returned from a vacation to witness a Russian-American diplomatic crisis. He and "Bill Gannon" escaped that touchy assignment and were reassigned to a case that concerned the eventual murder of four beautiful young women. Much of the story investigation occurred at the "Adam & Eve Lonely Hearts Club," operated by "Mrs. Kruger" played by actress Virginia Gregg. The picture was well produced and at times humorous, especially concerning "Gannon's" bothersome toothache. Slightly veiled messages were offered between the lines, as when "Friday" was questioned by

134

a civilian, "Sergeant, you don't pay this man too much, do you?" "Joe" replied, "No, ma'am, he's only a police officer." For realism, police codes and procedures were evident in the story that dealt with murder, racism, child molestation, and "Gannon's" imminent retirement. The murderer was finally captured in a literal cliffhanger. "Gannon" briefly retires but returns to active service.

When the filming of *Dragnet 1966* was finished, Webb treated the cast to dinner to say "thank you." Pierce Brooks recalled Jack's thoughtfulness: "He was very generous to all of us who helped on that picture," and "I thought the world of him." Others did, too. When Brooks was in need of transportation, Webb furnished him with a Mark VII car.

The ensuing weekly *Dragnet 1967* was produced by Webb's Mark VII Productions in association with Universal. The series aired on January 12, 1967 and ran for nearly three years on NBC. The network dropped the show on September 10, 1970 — the final airing date of *Dragnet*. The date was included in the later episode titles to avoid any confusion with *Dragnet* reruns. *Dragnet* made history again, as the first major television program to come out of retirement and enjoy a successful comeback.

As in the past, the Los Angeles Police Department assisted Jack. He again rewarded officers $50.00 for a story submission, while either the case detective or his partner received $150.00 for the day or two required to film an episode during the officer's off-duty hours. The Police Academy received six percent of the program profits, an arrangement that was sealed only by a firm handshake. Webb assisted the Department in other ways, too. When he learned that an Academy building was in need of repair, he unhesitatingly offered a $7,000 check, asking only if the amount was sufficient. Dan Cooke recalled that Jack was "as tough as nails, but had a heart of gold."

Dragnet 1967 included "Joe Friday's" dry wit and an injection of humor by "Officer Gannon." "Bill Gannon" had a voracious and bizarre appetite that astonished "Friday." For example, two of his favorites dishes were "Garlic Nut Butter Sandwiches" and a mixture of ice cream and barbecue sauce. "Gannon" also raised pigeons and engaged in other unusual endeavors. His *Dragnet* wife "Eileen," played by Randy Stuart, appeared in only two episodes. As Webb had used his Uncle Frank and Aunt Faye's names for the 1950's episodes, he used actor Morgan's wife's name "Eileen" for the character's name. "Friday's" and "Bill's" detective car was a gold 1966 Ford Fairlane. "Joe's" private car, seen in some episodes, was a light blue 1964 Ford Fairlane.

Webb wanted to examine more of the inner-workings of the Department in many episodes. Jack stressed more community involvement and personal assistance by the police and less of a focus on outright crime fighting, as in the earlier *Dragnet* series. For instance, episodes dealt with such contemporary problems as racial prejudice and the growing use of marijuana and LSD. In fact, the color premier was titled *The Big LSD*, though the production is popularly referred to as the *Blueboy* episode. Webb wrote the script under his pseudonym of John Randolph. Michael Burns acted the body-painted and "freaked-out" young man on drugs, whom his doting parents refused to accept until "Blueboy" ("Benji Carver") died from an overdose of the drug LSD. Burns found Jack humorous and patient. (Burns later earned a Ph.D. in Modern European History from Yale University in 1981.)

One *Dragnet 1968* episode that troubled the NBC "Continuity Acceptance," commonly known as "censors," raised the suggestion of police misconduct by depicting a shooting on "prime time" TV. In the story, "Sergeant Friday" entered an all-night Laundromat to buy a pack of cigarettes and witnessed a robbery. The robber shot at "Friday," who returned the fire, wounding the suspect who escaped through a back door to a waiting convertible automobile driven by his girlfriend. The thief died, and "Joe" was accused of murder by the girlfriend. Much of the episode centered on locating the projectile fired from "Friday's" revolver. Finding the spent bullet and verifying its trajectory supported "Friday's" contention that he shot in self-defense. The on-screen shoot-out was considered shocking at the time, even though television cameras were bringing the Vietnam war into the nation's homes each night. Jack did not yield to the censors' sensitivity regarding a TV show shooting and the episode did air. The program later served as an instructional film for the LAPD.

The reading of rights to persons placed under arrest by police officers became overly conspicuous in *Dragnet 67* and following episodes. Though legally accurate, the repetition could become tiring. In *Miranda v. Arizona*, the 1966 United States Supreme Court ruled 5-4 that, prior to any questioning, criminal suspects must be informed of their rights.

At other times, Webb's new *Dragnet* raised eyebrows in episodes concerning alcohol, unmarried and communal living, cultism, and sex crimes. One program addressed the riots following Martin Luther King's assassination, and another addressed security in Los Angeles for a presidential visit. One episode included actual film footage from an astronaut spacewalk. Though Jack never used *Dragnet* for political gain, he did stress the need for law and order during the 1960's when police officers were being spit on and called "pigs" and other demeaning names. Webb observed and cautioned:

> Today, being a policeman is a distasteful, almost tragic, way to make a living. The abuse he takes is ridiculous. If the public doesn't begin to loudly support their policemen, I'm afraid we're heading for a bleak period in urban history. We hope, in some way, we make the policeman's job easier for him.

Dan Cooke once asked Jack if he knew what "Pig" meant. Jack replied

On the set of _Dragnet 1967_ with L.A.P.D. Technical Advisor Dan Cooke (center) and Mark VII Producer Bob Cinader

Donated by Dan Cooke —
Courtesy of Jack Webb Archives

that he did not, and Dan hurriedly made-up, "Personality, Integrity and Good Looks." Webb grasped the idea, but suggested, "Let's give it a little more meaning." Cooke answered with "Pride, Integrity, And Guts." Jack embraced the idea on the spot and used the acronym's translation in an episode. Dan recalled: "When the show aired, and Lord knows how many police officers around the nation heard that quote, we began thanking people for calling us PIGS."

Dragnet and Webb created female police officer roles far in advance of other television shows doing so, because Jack was concerned about prejudice on all accounts. In one _Dragnet 1969_ episode, the story focused on a retreat meeting of the LAPD to discuss racial understanding and the pitfalls of stereotyping people.

In the best of times, Jack could turn out a TV program in one week, using a three-day filming schedule, which Harry Morgan described as "pretty remarkable." Morgan recalled that people often kidded him about the semi-monotone voice that he and Jack used, but explained that Webb used the technique so that his officers would appear as unemotional in their roles as most doctors did with patients. His intent was also to focus the audience on the story details and not on "the flash of the storyteller." The practice was difficult for Harry. Morgan shared, "As an actor, you're used to trying to make every line interesting, and then you have to flatten things out like that — that's a damned tough acting job!"

Jack's words for the end of a workday were "Let's call it a wrap," meaning that the cast could then join him in his office. The social gathering became known as "holding court." Webb, cast members, and others from the Mark VII staff would socialize and occasionally partake in shots of his Crown Royal. Webb explained, "I never have a drink while I am working," and no one recalls that he ever did.

Webb believed that the new *Dragnet* was successful because the timing was right, and people in the late 1960's no longer wanted to malign police officers. *Dragnet* ranked Number 20 in the 1967-1968 television season. *Rowan And Martin's Laugh-In* was first, followed by *Gomer Pyle, U.S.M.C.* Dragnet's ratings were higher among youth. For example, in November 1967, *Dragnet* was ranked Number nine among the Top 10 TV programs most viewed by teenagers from the age of 12 to 17. Webb later said, "Of all the benefits I have reaped from *Dragnet*, the most pleasing is to be accepted by the toughest critics of all — the young."

In February 1967, Jack and Julie lost their close friend Richard "Dick" Breen. From his hospital bed, Dick advised Jack to slow down and to take more vacations. Dick's condition soon became so serious that only a few visitors were permitted to enter his room. Shortly before his death, Julie surreptitiously climbed a hospital fire escape to visit the writer who had been so important in her and Jack's life.

Webb and an overflow crowd of more than 250 reporters and friends met on February 28, 1967 at the Los Angeles Press Club to honor and "roast" Inspector Ed Walker of the LAPD. Walker was Chief Parker's number one assistant and was credited by the Chief as a person who was greatly instrumental in making Parker's career successful. Though Walker was actually the LAPD Press Relations Officer, he retired with the title of "Inspector." Beginning in 1954, Ed worked with Webb as a Technical Advisor for the original *Dragnet*, *Adam-12*, and the later *Dragnets*. As the master of ceremonies for the dinner, Jack kept the festivities moving along with humor reminiscent of his Belmont High School and Army days. For example, he asked, "Is there a cop in the house? Somebody just stole my speech!" Regarding Walker, Jack joked, "I don't know why I tell you about Walker, because he gets on TV more than I do." In other gatherings, even among professional comedians, few could match Webb's "zingers."

Stacy and Lisa reached their teens during the 1960's, and as celebrity children, they knew such luminaries as Walt Disney, Lorne Greene, Ray Charles, Ella Fitzgerald, Count Basie, Jack Jones, and Rick Nelson. The teenage girls were ecstatic when they briefly met Elvis Presley and The Beatles. Sometimes Lisa and Stacy accompanied their mom Julie London when she performed at the Tropicana in Las Vegas. Jack allowed the children to visit the set or permitted them to ride their bikes in studio lots, but he could be a strict parent who monitored the girls' conduct and demeanor. Yet, he did not believe in spanking Lisa or Stacy. Instead, he disciplined them with words, and did so skillfully. Bob Leeds remembered, "The best thing to do when Jack got mad was to walk away. It was senseless to argue with him. He had a way with words, and he could out talk anyone."

A rare shot of Jack in his reading glasses speaking at Inspector Ed Walker's retirement party

Donated by Ed Walker —
Courtesy of Jack Webb Archives

Stacy recalled her father's penetrating words once at age 13, when she was placing curlers in her hair while sitting on her bed. Webb entered the room and admonished, "We don't use the bedroom to curl our hair. We use the bathroom; that's what it's for." On another occasion, the girls were lectured not to place water on their bedroom nightstand. They learned that the moist glass could stain the furniture, and, according to Jack, people were to drink water in the kitchen. Stacy related, "You had to sit there and take it." At the dinner table, the girls were encouraged to sit properly. They also read etiquette books to learn how to act politely in public.

Once, when Stacy reported for work on the *Adam-12* set wearing shorts, Jack took one look at her and sternly said, "We don't wear shorts in this office or anywhere else around here!" She was ordered to go home and return to work in a dress. Sometimes the girls would tell little white lies to spare them the wrath of a Webb lecture. Even when the adult Stacy broke her leg while sky diving, she explained to her father that the accident occurred while dancing.

For most parents, the time arrives when children ask questions about sex and babies. When Stacy questioned her father about the origin of babies, Jack replied, "What did your mother [Julie] say?" Stacy answered, "She told me to ask you." Jack suddenly became pensive and awkwardly tried to explain the act of conception but completely avoided a discussion of the sex act. When Stacy inquired further, Jack once more instructed her, "Go ask your mother!"

Sensitive to his childhood poverty, Jack once taught Stacy and Lisa a lesson regarding their good fortune in life. The two children were invited to his home one evening, assuming they would be dining out at some elaborate restaurant, such as the Cock 'N Bull, Monte's Steak House, or perhaps the Lido Pizza Parlor in Van Nuys. When the girls arrived at Jack's Encino home, they noticed that the kitchen was filled with the scent of beans. Jack said, "I hope you're hungry, girls," and to their amazement he had prepared an entire supper of pink beans. Stacy asked, "What are you doing?" Jack replied, "I just wanted to show you what I had to go through, having to eat beans for 18 years!"

At times, Jack seemed not to understand that he embarrassed the girls or that his sense of humor might offend them or Jackie. While in the company of William Conrad and Jackie at the El Torito Restaurant in 1963, Webb criticized twelve-year-old Stacy for being slightly overweight: "Stacy, you know I would take you to Chasen's [Restaurant], but the *maitre d'* would seat you for two." Jackie left the table crying. Webb could also be critical of the girls' dress and even their poetry choices. At the China Trader Restaurant, Stacy commented that she enjoyed reading the poetry of Rod McKuen and Rudyard Kipling. In the presence of Bob Forward, who was then working on *The D.A.*, Jack quickly lectured her never to place the poetry of McKuen in the same company of Kipling's.

Typical of young women in the 1960's, Stacy went through a "Twiggy" phase of wearing clothes associated with the emaciated-appearing British model and the "hippie" style. Jack often disapproved of Stacy's musical taste and once suggested that the LAPD should place a ban on alleged words in "The Kingsmen's" controversial *Louie, Louie*, a youth culture song. Nevertheless, Jack was considered "hip" among the teenage youth. Stacy recalled one of her father's favorite recordings was The Beatles 1967 album *Sergeant Pepper's*, which Jack enjoyed playing repeatedly. Webb's LAPD friends were instructed that if any rumors were discovered concerning his daughters' drinking or use of drugs, he was to be informed at once.

Though strict, Jack was a compassionate person capable of experiencing tender moments. In 1965, Stacy had her first boy-girl party at Bobby and Julie's home. Jack was present, as were many of Stacy's friends. One friend accidentally backed a car over "Honeybee," the girls' Lhasa Apso dog. The tragedy caused one of the few instances when Stacy saw her father cry. The following day, Jack purchased another puppy for the girls. On another occasion, he was nearly moved to tears when Stacy presented him a copy of the song *Color Him Father* for Father's Day. For her birth-

day, he frequently sur-
prised Stacy with roses
attached to one or more
$100 bills. On her 16th
birthday, Jack presented
her with a sparkling new
dark blue Volkswagen
automobile, though
Stacy's poor coordination
failed to impress her
father when she shifted
gears. The two girls
received their respective
trust funds when each
reached age 25.

Stacy graduated from
Louisville High School in
1968. In her senior year,
she toured the world for
three months by ship.
Her conduct caused Jack
some concern when she
missed her sailing time in
Mexico and used his
American Express Card
without permission and
ran up a substantial bal-
ance. Jack required that
she work-off the entire
debt.

Stacy, unaware of her
father's wishes, enrolled
in a private San Francisco

"To Jack Webb, The Best Reel Cop from L.A.P.D., The Best Real Cops" reads the inscription on the plaque.

Donated by Dan Cooke —
Courtesy of Jack Webb Archives

college. Not until her high school graduation party did Webb reveal, "I
always wanted you to drive a yellow Camaro convertible and go to USC."
Stacy told her father, "Dad, I would have enrolled at USC if I had known
you wanted me to."

While in San Francisco, Stacy met her Uncle Frank and Aunt Faye,
whose names Jack used on *Dragnet*. The couple had a beautiful home on
Nob Hill near the Fairmont Theater where Julie London once performed.
On her first visit, Stacy found them to be wonderful and kind people, but
she was surprised at how much Frank's skin and his impressive ears
reminded her of Jack. When Stacy phoned her father from the Smith residence, he joked, "What do you think of Uncle Frank's ears? They are even

bigger than mine. If he stood atop Nob Hill on a windy day, he would be blown away." Stacy also enrolled in Chapman College in Orange, California where Dick Breen's children were students, and in UCLA, where she attended film classes.

In August 1969, Jack received a phone call from Stacy explaining that she was at a music concert with her friends in New York. Webb casually told her to be careful and to have a good time. Later, while watching the national news he became frantic to learn that Stacy failed to mention she was at the famous 1969 Woodstock Rock Festival in New York.

Though a veteran in his craft by 1970, Jack occasionally consulted the *Farmers' Almanac* to determine when to film outdoors. He always compared and measured himself to the famous director, screenwriter, and producer Billy Wilder, who learned much of his trade from a long and fruitful collaboration with screenwriter Charles Bracket. Webb taught his associates never to film a person yawning, since the audience might be infected by the yawn, "grab their coats, and go home." He also advised never to make a scene longer than five pages of script. Jack instructed Stacy, "The best way to be a good producer is to know each aspect of pre and post production, and know that what you are asking for can be done."

Over the years, the Los Angeles Police Department received many inquiries from law enforcement agencies and others concerning the relationship between Jack and the LAPD. Some police units even timed their musters so as not to miss watching "Sergeant Friday's" television adventures and how the Los Angeles Police Department did things. Dan Cooke related that Webb's "impact on law enforcement was tremendous, not to mention the many young people who joined us," inspired by *Dragnet*.

In 1967, Sergeant Cooke reminded Chief Tom Reddin about Jack's many contributions to the Department, and that the LAPD had done little to recognize Webb for his efforts. The Chief informed Cooke, "That's your problem." The sergeant searched a number of trophy shops for the appropriate recognition item, but a commercial trophy did not convey the admiration and respect the Department had for Jack. Cooke then had the idea to extract "Joe Friday's" Badge 714 from a capsule in the Police Academy building cornerstone, to encase it in lucite, and to imprint an inscription written by Captain Tom Hays of the Academy on a wooden base, which read:

"To Jack Webb, The Best Reel Cop From LAPD, The Best Real Cops."

Chief Reddin was puzzled how the Department could circumvent a City Ordinance which prohibited persons other than active officers from having a badge, to which Cooke bravely echoed, "That's your problem." At the badge presentation, Chief Reddin spoke, "The voice of Jack Webb and the contributions of *Dragnet* have been one of the greatest assets to the reputation of the Los Angeles Police Department." Dan Cooke remembered that Webb was so moved, "that filming for the day was stopped. Jack could hardly say a word and choked up when he did."

On the *Dragnet 1967* colorcast of February 9, Webb, as "Sergeant Friday," offered a well-received speech to a rookie police officer. The rookie had become disgusted with the LAPD after he was mistakenly suspected of armed robbery and of being a bad cop. "Friday's" lecture to the rookie is titled "What Is A Cop" and was written by Webb and Richard L. Breen (shortly before Breen's death). Kent McCord played the undercover rookie officer, "Paul R. Culver." Four House Representatives and one United States Senator introduced the 1967 recitation into the *Congressional Record,* and numerous police departments have used the dialogue.

"What Is A Cop?"

It's awkward having a policeman around the house. Friends drop in. A man with a badge answers the door. The temperature drops 20 degrees.

Throw a party and that badge gets in the way. All of a sudden, there isn't a straight man in the crowd. Everybody's a comedian. "Don't drink too much," somebody says, "or the man with the badge will run you in."

Or, "How's it goin', Dick Tracy? How many jaywalkers did you pinch today?" And there's always the one who wants to know how many apples you stole.

All at once, you've lost your first name. You're a "cop," a "flatfoot," a "bull," a "dick," "John Law"; you're "the fuzz," "the heat" ... you're poison, you're trouble ... you're bad news.

They call you everything, but never a policeman. It's not much of a life ... unless you don't mind missing a Dodger [baseball] game because the hotshot phone rings ... unless you like working Saturdays, Sundays, holidays ... at a job that doesn't pay overtime.

Oh, the pay is adequate. If you count your pennies, you can put your kid through college. But you'd better plan on seeing Europe on your television set.

Then there's your first night on the beat. When you try to arrest a drunken prostitute in a Main Street bar and she rips your new uniform to shreds. You'll buy another one ... out of your own pocket.

You'll rub elbows with all the elite: pimps, addicts, thieves, bums, winos, girls who can't keep an address and men who don't care.

Liars, cheats, con men, the class of Skid Row.

And the heartbreak: underfed kids, beaten kids, molested kids, crying kids, homeless kids, hit-and-run kids, broken arm kids, broken-leg kids, broken-head kids, sick kids, dying kids, dead kids.

The old people that nobody wants, the reliefers, the pensioners, the ones who walk the street cold and those who tried to keep warm and died in a three-dollar room with an unvented gas heater. You'll walk the beat and pick up the pieces.

Do you have real adventure in your soul? You'd better have. You'll do time in a prowl car. It'll be a thrill-a-minute when you get an "unknown trouble" call and hit a backyard at two in the morning, never knowing who you'll meet ... a kid with a knife ... a pill-head with a gun, or two ex-cons with nothing to lose.

And you'll have plenty of time to think. You'll draw duty in a "lonely car" ... with nobody to talk to but your radio. Four years in uniform and you'll have the ability, the experience and maybe the desire to be a detective.

If you like to fly by the seat of your pants, this is where you belong.

For every crime that's committed, you've got three million suspects to choose from. Most of the time you'll have few facts and a lot of hunches. You'll run down leads that dead-end on you.

You'll work all-night stake outs that could last a week. You'll do leg work until you're sure you've talked to everybody in California ... people who saw it happen, but really didn't. People who insist they did it, but really didn't. People who don't remember, those who try to forget. Those who tell the truth, those who lie.

You'll run the files until your eyes ache. And paperwork ... you'll fill out a report when you're right, you'll fill out a report when you're wrong, you'll fill one out when you're not sure, you'll fill one out listing your leads, you'll fill one out when you have no leads, you'll make out a report on the reports you've made.

You'll write enough words in your lifetime to stock a library. You'll learn to live with doubt, anxiety, frustration, court decisions that tend to hinder rather than help you.

You'll learn to live with the district attorney, testifying in court. Defense attorneys, prosecuting attorneys, judges, juries, witnesses.

And sometimes you won't be happy with the outcome. But there's also this:

There are over 5,000 men in this city who know that being a policeman is an endless, glamorless, thankless job that must be done. I know it, too. And I'm damned glad to be one of them.

In contrast to "What Is A Cop," Webb and Johnny Carson performed a comical routine on Carson's *The Tonight Show* in 1968, which nearly had the two laughing out loud. The *Dragnet* spoof is often repeated on Johnny's *Tonight Show* anniversary specials. The sketch should be seen to appreciate its humor fully.

"The Clapper Caper"

WEBB: "My name's Friday. I'm a cop. I was working day watch out of Robbery when I got a call from the Acme School Bell Company. There'd been a robbery."

CARSON: "There's been a robbery."

WEBB: "Yes sir. What was it?"

CARSON: "My clappers."

WEBB: "Your clappers?"

CARSON: "Yeah, you know the things inside a bell that make them clang."

WEBB: "The clangers."

CARSON: "That's right. We call them clappers in the business."

WEBB: "A clapper caper."

CARSON: "What's that?"

WEBB: "Nothing, sir. Now can I have the facts? What kind of clappers were stolen on this caper?"

CARSON: "They were copper clappers."

WEBB: "And where were they kept?"

CARSON: "In the closet."

WEBB: "Uh, huh. Do you have any ideas who might have taken the copper clappers from the closet?"

CARSON: "Well, just one. I fired a man he swore he'd get even."

WEBB: "What was his name?"

CARSON: "Claude Cooper."

WEBB: "You think he ...?"

CARSON: "That's right. I think Claude Cooper copped my copper clappers kept in the closet."

WEBB: "You know where this Claude Cooper is from?"

CARSON: "Yeah, Cleveland."

WEBB: "That figures, that figures."

CARSON: "What makes it worse, they were clean."

WEBB: "Clean copper clappers."

CARSON: "That's right."

WEBB: "Why do you think Cleveland's Claude Cooper would cop your clean copper clappers kept in your closet?"

CARSON: "Only one reason."

WEBB: "What's that?"

CARSON: "He's a kleptomaniac."

WEBB: Who first discovered the copper clappers were copped?"

CARSON: "My cleaning woman — Clara Clifford."

WEBB: "That figures. Now let me see if I've got the facts straight here. Cleaning woman Clara Clifford discovered your clean copper clappers kept in a closet were copped by Claude Cooper, the kleptomaniac from Cleveland. Now is that about it?"

CARSON: "One other thing."

WEBB: "What's that?"

CARSON: "If I ever catch kleptomaniac Claude Cooper from Cleveland who copped my clean copper clappers that were kept in the closet —

WEBB: "Yes?"

CARSON: "I'll clobber him."

In the late 1960's, Jack lost many of his loved ones. His Uncle Frank and Aunt Faye died in 1968. "Maggie," Jack's mother, passed on in 1969, as did his friend and *Dragnet* sidekick Ben Alexander. Stacy recalled that she first learned about Ben's death on the radio. Ben's wife and children found Alexander dead when they returned home from a camping trip.

Nearing age 50, Webb was showing some midriff weight gain despite his daily 20 push-ups and 20 sit-ups. He had astigmatism requiring prescription reading glasses. He was bothered by a peptic disorder and consumed large quantities of Alka-Seltzer. Ignoring his health, he drank and smoked two packs of cigarettes each day. He should not have been surprised by his self-evaluation: "I no longer have much spiz left. Age slows me down."

Following *Dragnet's* two-decade success story with another innovative program would not be an easy task for anyone. A less motivated person might not have bothered. Webb was mature. *Dragnet* was mature. However, Jack could not sit idle. Jack's next offering was called by *TV Guide*, "an ostensibly new police show ... which easily could have been dubbed 'Son Of Dragnet'." Instead, Jack choose to christen the new series *Adam-12*.

Adam-12 was a R. A. Cinader and Webb creation, produced by Mark VII Productions in association with Universal Studio Television. The 30-minute NBC police story was rated in the top 10 TV programs and ran from September 21, 1968 to August 26, 1975. *Adam-12* eventually aired 174 episodes, not including syndication airings. Herman S. Saunders produced *Adam-12* from 1968 to 1974, and Tom Williams produced the show from 1974-1975, when Jack promoted Saunders to Executive Producer. Dennis Donnelly was the Director for most of the series.

Bob Forward, who first met Webb when Jack was doing *Johnny Madero*, had worked as the Director of Programs and Production at KABC (Channel 7) in Los Angeles. The Stanford graduate wrote scripts for the 1968 season of *Adam-12*. Saunders briefly hired a young Stephen J. Cannell to write and edit the show. Cannell later established an impressive television career with such shows as *The Rockford Files*. Webb declined an invitation to join Cannell's series. Herm Saunders recalled, "I think one of Jack's biggest mistakes was turning down *The Rockford Files*."

Frank Comstock wrote the music for *Adam-12*, with music supervision by Stanley Wilson. Webb again listed the name John Randolph as his own pseudonym and may have fabricated other production member names. *Adam-12* was filmed around Los Angeles and in the studios of Universal City. The arm and hammer Mark VII logo appeared as in *Dragnet* but was eventually redesigned as a more direct Mark VII statement, which no longer included Jack's hands.

Captain Pierce Brooks and Dan Cooke served as LAPD Technical Advisors to *Adam-12*. Stacy worked with the series until her father fired her as a Production Assistant for not being punctual for work. Webb's mandate, even for his daughter, was: "I don't like to wait, and I don't like to keep people waiting."

Violence, in the form of gun shootings, appeared in *Adam-12* in contrast to very little violence in *Dragnet*. Webb resorted to story repetition, a technique that he had previously criticized regarding TV. Yet, Jack maintained his realistic style of showing the day-to-day police duties and hazards confronting officers, and he portrayed them as normal hard-working human beings. While *Dragnet* focused on what *TV Guide* termed "the elite of law enforcement — the detective," *Adam-12* concentrated on the rank-and-file officer, his sundry assignments, and his reliance on teamwork. Further, Jack wanted to reveal in *Adam-12* that officers frequently respond to more than one call at a time.

The Los Angeles Police Department demanded, "This series of programs will adhere strictly to the problems encountered by the man in uniform and will 'tell it like it is.'" Jack guaranteed the same realism and attention to detail as in *Dragnet*. Technical credits were posted for the office of LAPD Chief Thomas Reddin and his successors.

The *Adam-12* switchboard operator was a female officer from the Los Angeles Police Department Valley Division, who was auditioned and selected by Webb from among four other women recommended by their supervisors. However, male voices were also used. The opening scene and the story dispatcher's succinct calls captured the viewers' attention with, "One Adam-12. One Adam-12. A 415 Man With A Gun. One Adam-12. One Adam-12. Bikers With Chains And Knives. One Adam-12. One Adam-12. Grand Theft, Horse." The officers would reply with "One Adam-12, Roger." Similar to *Dragnet*, each *Adam-12* story concluded with "The incidents you have seen are true. The names are changed to protect the innocent."

The series begins soon after "Officer Pete Malloy's" partner is killed in a gun battle. The loss leaves him bitter and disillusioned, and he is teamed with an over-eager rookie, "Officer Jim Reed." "Malloy" feels responsible for "Reed's" well-being and is determined to keep his younger partner unharmed as the two men engage in their duties in a "black and white" LAPD patrol cruiser, identified as "Adam-12."

Several explanations are offered concerning the vehicle's designation. Webb's childhood friend Marion Fitzsimmons remembered that in the 1930's, the first LAPD radio patrol cars cruised Jack's boyhood vicinity of Third & Flower Streets, which was then District 12. Most who lived in the District had little difficulty hearing the cruiser radio, especially while the car was stopped at traffic lights, or when they were walking along sidewalks as the police drove by. Marion recalled, "I think this is where he got '12' for 'Adam-12.'"

Sergeant Dan Cooke offered that Jack had some trouble selecting a title for a series about two officers in a police cruiser, so Cooke suggested, "1-Adam-81." Webb asked, "What in the hell does that meant?" Cooke

Kent McCord and Martin Milner on tour in Pittsburgh promoting *Adam-12*. For this series, Jack created the now standard vehicle "Tow Shots" filming technique.

Donated by Pierce Brooks –
Courtesy of Jack Webb Archives

explained that the first number stood for the LAPD division and that "Adam" designated a two-man car. The numerals "81" were the area number within the division. Webb was at first unimpressed with Cooke's idea. The sergeant next suggested "Adam-48." Jack was more impressed with that title and began counting aloud the numbers one to twelve. When he reached "12," Webb said, "That's it!" For the series title, they decided to omit the first number, as in "1-Adam-12," since story episodes could be gleaned from any LAPD Division files (and not just Division "1"). At the time the series launched there was no Adam-12 for the LAPD, but several officers in Pacific Palisades (the West Los Angeles Division) requested permission to change their cruiser number to 12.

Kent McCord and Martin Milner starred in *Adam-12*. Both had previously appeared on television and in motion picture films. McCord was in the *Dragnet 1967* episode *The Big Interrogation*, which set him up for *Adam-12*. Producer Bob Cinader recalled that casting McCord took only seconds, as Webb "had a real thing" about using Kent to play "Officer Jim Reed." The audition consisted of no more than McCord reading several newspaper lines, whereupon Jack said, "You've got the job, kid!" McCord also got Badge 744 for his character "Officer Jim Reed" to use.

McCord grew up in a tough and predominately Mexican-American neighborhood, where kids imprinted a small tattoo on their hand, using a needle and a thread dipped in ink. In his private life, McCord cared little for the police, claiming, "They always seemed to be rousting people for no good reason." However, as he came to know, work, and ride with real patrol officers, McCord realized that their actions were justified.

Kent declined a football scholarship from the University of Utah and dropped about 50 pounds before attending the University of Southern California. Ideas of pursuing a career as a physical education instructor were abandoned when McCord was befriended by Rick Nelson, which led to bit parts in the Nelson Family's *Ozzie And Harriet* TV show.

McCord described Webb as "a hard man to work for," who had "such definite ideas and he makes such large demands of a performer." The patriotic Webb may have harbored some animosity towards Kent, since McCord vowed that he would go to prison rather than serve in the Vietnam War.

Martin Milner received the lead billing and played the part of veteran "Officer Pete Malloy," who carried Badge 2430. The Detroit native began acting at a young age, though he suffered with polio. Having overcome the crippling disease, he appeared in the 1947 movie *Life With Father*, starring William Powell and Irene Dunne. Milner played other roles in *Sands Of Iwo Jima* (1949) and *Halls Of Montezuma* (1950), in which Webb also appeared.

The two became cast friends on the *Halls Of Montezuma* set. Milner once won $150 from Jack in a gin rummy game, but Webb did not immediately pay the debt. Milner's father suggested that Marty forget about the $150. Several months later, Webb invited Marty to "come down to NBC Radio and pick up your check." At that meeting, Jack asked Marty if he had done radio, and Marty had not. Webb replied, "What difference does it make? We've got a lot of parts for you here." Soon Milner appeared in *Dragnet* radio and television programs, even after he was drafted into the Army and directed Korean War era military training films.

Jack continued to assist Marty with finding roles after Marty left the Army. Milner appeared in *The Long Gray Line* (1955), Webb's *Pete Kelly's Blues* (1955), *Sweet Smell Of Success* (1957), *Marjorie Morningstar* (1958), *Valley Of The Dolls* (1967), *Sullivan's Empire* (1967), and other films. Milner was also a star in the successful television series *Route 66*. When the TV show was canceled, Webb invited Marty to play a major role in Webb and Bob Cinader's latest series, *Adam-12*. Marty received much of the credit for the success of *Adam-12*. Producer Herm Saunders said that Milner was "the cement" that held the show together. Marty later worked briefly with Webb in a 1978 Mark VII production called *Little Mo*.

Webb again became a film innovator by creating, what are referred to today as, "Tow Shots." They were unquestionably one of Jack's most ingenious filming innovations and saved enormously on *Adam-12* production costs. Before the development of Webb's Tow Shots, a car would remain stationary and motion pictures would be projected in the background to simulate, unrealistically, a moving vehicle. Webb's Tow Shots required that three cameras be mounted on the front of the patrol car, each camera facing the officers inside the vehicle. The driver's-side-mounted "A" camera filmed the driver; the center-mounted "B" camera filmed both occupants; and the passenger's-side-mounted "C" camera filmed the passenger. Later, with three camera views, any combination of pictures could be achieved during editing, eliminating more filming or preventing costly retakes.

After the cameras were set, the *Adam-12* unit was towed by a leading vehicle to provide the realism of a moving car. A director and a cameraman observed while riding in the leading or tow vehicle, and a script prompter was hidden in the following patrol car on the rear floor to assist Milner or McCord with their lines. At other times, the *Adam-12* unit was driven around Los Angeles and followed by a camera truck to film background buildings and locales that appeared on the show. There was no need for Marty and Kent to be in the car during the filming of the exterior shots.

The series boasted a cast of numerous luminaries, some who were already established stars and others who became leading actors in later years. For example, Jodie Foster, June Lockhart, Sharon Gless, Karen Black, Cloris Leachman, Jayne Meadows, Jo Ann Worley, and Lindsay Wagner played female roles. Stacy Harris, Art Gilmore, Ozzie Nelson, David Cassidy, Ed Begley, Jr., Trini Lopez, Scatman Crothers, Edd Byrnes, and Leo V. Gordon (who also wrote for *Adam-12*) played male roles. The list could be greatly expanded.

While the show was in its initial production, LAPD Deputy Chief Bob Rock questioned, "How in the world is Jack going to sustain a show about two radio car officers? It gets dull after a while." Seven years later, when Lieutenant Dan Cooke reminded Bob Rock of his remark, Rock responded, "Who would have thought it possible?" The unspoken reply was, of course, "Jack Webb."

In later years, Cooke proclaimed that *Adam-12* had a "tremendous beneficial effect, not only to this Department, but to police agencies nationally, by humanizing the radio car officers and presenting their story in a factual and dramatic way." The Los Angeles Police Academy used *Dragnet*, *Adam-12*, and *Emergency* in the 1970's for training police recruits. In one *Dragnet* television episode, O.J. Simpson appeared as a potential recruit. The *Adam-12* cast included a number of other black actors, since Afro-American and other minority police officers served (and serve) in the LAPD.

As much as Webb's writers endeavored to portray police officers' lives realistically, certain Police Chiefs argued that television personalities remained "less than real." Former Beverly Hills Police Chief and national crime authority, Joseph Paul Kimble argued that "the American public has long clung to at least two major fantasies; one about sex, and the other about police." Kimble pointed out that most police stories never mention officers working overtime, appearing in court, or that criminals are sometimes freed or willingly submit to arrest. Other real-life situations included police making erroneous arrests, fighting the political system, and an occasional hostile public. "All in all, one is led to believe that the patrolman's role is a simplistic one," according to Chief Kimble. Overall, however, Chief Kimble spoke highly of *Adam-12* and the efforts of Webb and his staff:

> In spite of some reservations about the program, most policemen (including myself) feel that *Adam-12's* merits far exceed its omissions. They appreciate the acting excellence of the two principal characters. They are impressed by the good scripts and technical accuracy. Regardless of whether or not they work an "eight-year day," the characters in *Adam-12* are doing what the American public, too often, does not. They acknowledge the existence of good policemen and their undeniable influence for the public good. When John Q. Citizen clicks off his TV, and make-believe fades to a fleeting pinpoint of light on the screen, I wonder if he realizes how badly he needs a real *Adam-12* in his town.

Jack would later show that Kimble's "John Q. Citizen," in addition to needing "a real *Adam-12* in his town," also needed something more. However, the California Legislature would have to pass the Wedworth-Townsend Act in 1972 before Webb could bring this new message to the TV screen.

"Without Emergency, who knows how long it would have taken for this country to realize the benefits it derived?"

In the 1970's, Jack was a celebrity who never fully grasped his public status. For example, when Webb, Bob Forward, LAPD Chief Daryl Gates, and Inspector Ed Walker dined in Perino's Restaurant — an upscale bistro where one could lunch at the bar sans a tie — Muhammad Ali entered and immediately recognized Webb. Ignoring the others, including *Los Angeles Times* sports columnist Jim Murray (who had written numerous columns about Ali), the boxer approached Jack in awe, exclaiming, "Wow! Jack Webb, I grew up on you! Would you please say, 'This is the city?'" At 165 pounds, Webb was not one to refuse the heavyweight boxing champion of the world and happily fulfilled this and additional requests. Ali, still entranced, replied, "I can't thank you enough. I used to listen to you on the radio as a kid and I've been a fan of yours ever since." After Ali departed, Jack truly appreciated the flattering encounter and commented to his friends, "Do you believe that?"

In the early 1970's, Webb made several guest television appearances and last played "Sergeant Joe Friday" on Jack Benny's special farewell television show. Webb honored and admired the venerable comedian and refused payment for his appearance. However, Benny insisted, "Come on, Jack, I have to give you something." Webb finally accepted a gold money clip featuring Benny's profile and the inscription: "From Jack To Jack." When Frank Sinatra, Jr. admired the clip, Jack gave it to him. After Webb's death, Sinatra returned the clip to Jack's daughter Stacy.

Jack remained a staunch friend and supporter of the Los Angeles Police Department. On August 21, 1970, he donated an "Academy Trust Building" to the Department. The year was also significant, as the final *Dragnet* episode was televised on September 10, 1970. Jack further supported law enforcement by traveling by train from Los Angeles via Chicago to Washington, D. C. to assist President Richard Nixon at the White House concerning a national anti-drug campaign in the early 1970's.

Jack created or assisted with a number of new themes and ideas throughout the 1970's. A spin-off of *Adam-12*, entitled *Fraud*, cast Frank Sinatra, Jr., Ed Nelson, Sharon Gless, and Maureen Reagan. Stacy also worked on the short-lived *Fraud*, which ended in August 1975. *The D.A.*, a Mark VII produced half-hour NBC series, was conceived and produced by Bob Forward, who approached the Los Angeles County District Attorney Evelle Younger at a social dinner and asked, "How would you like to give me access of the records in your files?" When Younger inquired why, Forward replied that he wanted to take them to Jack Webb, who might be interested in their content for a new television show. Younger answered, "You're on!"

The following day, Bob met with Webb who joked, "Forward, you son-of-a-bitch! I should have thought of the idea myself. I can't believe I didn't think of that. Here we have the officers on *Adam-12*, we have the detectives in *Dragnet*, now we've got the prosecutors in *The D.A.*"

Jack and Bob visited Burbank to sell *The D.A.* to NBC's Program Vice-President Herb Schlosser. Webb's presentation displayed Jack's salesmanship at its best. The group was mesmerized as Jack dramatically played each part. After finishing his sales pitch with the appropriate histrionics, the room was silent. The NBC executive surveyed the assembly and asked, "What do you think?" Their answer was a resounding, "Yes!"

In two months, a two-hour pilot was in progress called *The D.A. Murder One*. Directed by Webb and produced by Bob Forward, the crime drama concerned a mystery that involved an insulin overdose. The cast included Robert Conrad, Howard Duff, Diane Baker, and J. D. Cannon. The 120-minute pilot aired on December 8, 1969 on NBC's *Monday Night At The Movies* and received such excellent ratings that a second pilot followed. *The D.A. Conspiracy To Kill* concerned the prosecution of a crime syndicate boss and was telecast January 11, 1971. The show was directed by Paul Krasny, produced by Bob Forward, and listed Robert Conrad, William Conrad, and Belinda Montgomery in the cast.

The ensuing half-hour series was produced by Mark VII Productions and was first televised on September 17, 1971. Since most of the story occurred in a courtroom, Webb's studio set builders recreated one of the chambers in every detail. The true-to-life story judge and his legal clerk remarked that they felt as if they were in their actual courtroom. The judge chided the clerk that if his real desk was as messy as the set desk, perhaps the clerk should catch up on his paperwork.

Robert Conrad played Los Angeles Deputy District Attorney "Paul Ryan," Harry Morgan played Chief Deputy District Attorney "H.M. 'Staff' Stafford," Ned Romero played investigator "Bob Ramirez," and Julie Cobb played the Deputy Public Defender "Katy Benson" in *The D.A.* Since the program was in the time slot opposite the popular *The Brady Bunch*, the series survived only for 15 episodes, last appearing on January 7, 1972. However, the series was honored by The American Bar Association, which presented *The D.A.* with "The Gavel Award" for the best television depiction of a District Attorney's office. Jack and Bob each received the additional honor of being appointed an "Honorary D.A."

Webb also produced *O'Hara: U. S. Treasury*. The pilot, a one-hour CBS movie, was made to launch a weekly show introduced on September 17, 1971. The program last aired on September 8, 1972. The story depicted the life and duties of government narcotic agents and starred David Janssen as "Treasury Agent Jim O'Hara." *Operation Cobra* was one story in many episodes. The cast included William Conrad, Lana Wood, Jerome Thor, Gary Crosby, and Charles McGraw. Webb explained that *O'Hara* aired for only one year because the show was assigned a time slot associated with children viewers. *O'Hara's* competition was *The Partridge Family* and *The Brady Bunch*. Moreover, Jack believed that David Janssen should have had a series sidekick, as few shows were successful "with just one continuing character."

One other Mark VII project, in which Webb invested a considerable amount of money, was called *Black Pearl*. The two-hour story, filmed for television at Universal and off the coast of Mexico, concerned the adventures of a man whose grandfather bequeathed him a ship.

None of these productions, despite their various levels of success, was the next groundbreaking series that Jack was to launch. To find that hot Hollywood property, Jack would have to turn to the Los Angeles County Fire Department. While *The D.A.* was in production, Sid Shineberg, President of Universal Television, called Jack to suggest that he might consider producing a *Dragnet* format, semi-documentary type series about Fire Department paramedics. Webb immediately accepted the challenge.

Jack knew, of course, that Fire Departments had engaged in rescue work for years. However, he discovered that by 1969, as many as 175,000 Americans died each year because there was no specifically trained organization to care for accident and other victims injured or dying on the scene. To reduce those deaths in California, rescue squads employed a team of highly trained and skilled firemen-paramedics. Candidates received three month's of medical classroom training and field duty with physicians and nurses learning how to check vital body signs and manage emergencies from minor mishaps to disasters. Some students had medical military combat experience learned in Vietnam.

However, since the paramedics were not *licensed* to practice medicine, the law required that a registered nurse accompany these paramedics during the program's first year. This mandate prevented paramedics from saving lives, when a registered nurse was not available to join the paramedic in the field. In 1972, to eliminate this restriction, legislation was introduced to the California Legislature to create paramedic teams *licensed* to practice immediate emergency medicine at an accident or a disaster scene without a registered nurse or other medical professional present. The passage of the Wedworth-Townsend Act in California created the legal basis for paramedical practice. Other states soon passed similar legislation.

Though Webb did not create the show out of an emergency, he dubbed the series *Emergency*. The show, produced "in a straightforward dramatic style" (per *TV Guide*), ran from January 15, 1972 to September 3, 1977. The one-hour series recorded the adventures of paramedics in the Los Angeles County Fire Department Rescue Division, "Squad 51" and their association with the doctors, nurses, and staff of "Rampart Hospital." As in the past, Jack and his associates insisted on accuracy. Authentic hospital and paramedic equipment was donated by fire department rescue units, though only Los Angeles Fire Department personnel were permitted to drive *Emergency* fire trucks. Department paramedic technical advisers saved the lives of people on the story set on at least two occasions.

When filming a 1978 two-hour *Emergency* special, motorists passing by an abandoned part of Compton, California, believed an actual tragedy had occurred concerning the midair collision of a chartered DC-8 passenger plane and a private aircraft. Jack's demand for realism had the remains of a DC-8 obtained from an aviation junkyard placed atop a demolished house. Fires were set to have it appear that a disaster had just occurred. The scene appeared so real that nearby radio station mobile units reported a major disaster. On another occasion, the *Emergency* script called for an unoccupied residential house to be burned while filmed. About half way through filming the burning, the crew discovered that the structure in flames was the wrong one. Luckily, the building was unoccupied, but the Long Beach community "politely" asked the crew to film burning houses elsewhere.

The original story, created by Harold Jack Bloom and Robert A. Cinader, was to appear as a television movie "pilot" followed by a series on NBC. Webb was sometimes a Director and an Executive Producer with Cinader, but Jack was not always listed in the credits. The Producers were Edwin Self and Robert Cinader. Nelson Riddle and Billy May directed the music.

Emergency listed five stars: Robert Fuller, Randolph Mantooth, Kevin Tighe, Julie London, and Bobby Troup. Fuller played the role of "Dr. Kelly Brackett." Fuller, a known outdoorsman, was always interested in acting. Originally from Troy, New York, Fuller served in Korea with the 24th Infantry Division as a Sergeant First Class, and, after being discharged from the Army, he had the opportunity to be an extra in *Friendly Persuasion* (1956). The Quaker story starred Gary Cooper and Dorothy McGuire. The music by Dimitri Tiomkin gave singer Pat Boone a great hit with the film's lead song. Fuller was one of the most successful and awarded western stars of the 1960's, appearing in such TV shows as *Laramie* and *Wagon Train*.

However, the two most popular *Emergency* actors were Randolph Mantooth and Kevin Tighe. Randolph Mantooth, born on September 19, 1945, hailed from Sacramento, California. Having moved to Santa Barbara, he took a drama course in high school and decided that he wanted to be

Kevin Tighe, Robert Fuller, Julie London, Bobby Troup, and Randolph Mantooth of *Emergency*. The show ran from 1972 to 1977.

Courtesy of Jack Webb Archives

an actor. More theater work followed in college, at community theaters, and the American Academy of Dramatic Arts in New York. There he received the "best actor" award and was lured by Universal Studios to come to Hollywood. During only his second day in Los Angeles, he appeared in *Marcus Welby, M.D.* In *Emergency*, he played "Fireman John Gage."

Kevin Tighe played "Fireman Roy DeSoto." Tighe, born Kevin Fishburn on August 13, 1944, hailed from Los Angeles. He first studied drama through his actor father. Tighe's acting debut, while yet a youngster, was at the Pasadena Playhouse. Kevin received a Master's Degree from the University of Southern California, where he taught contemporary theater for one year. Following two years in the Army and studying law in Europe, Tighe decided he wanted an acting career and returned to Hollywood. He had an obscure 1967 role in all-but-obscure *The Graduate* and he acted in *Yours, Mine And Ours* in 1968. Universal was attracted to Tighe when he appeared in *Design For Living* at the Ahmanson Theater in Los Angeles. With Webb's support, Tighe achieved a star role in the 1971 *Emergency* "pilot," and, later while acting in the series, Kevin directed several episodes.

Jack's decision to cast Tighe was made in haste. He needed an actor, most any agreeable and appealing actor, and hired Tighe. Kevin recalled, "Mr. Webb got me through it all. Without him, I wouldn't have had the job." However, Tighe and Mantooth soon demanded and received salary increases to $4,500 a week.

Before long, Tighe became critical of Jack's directorial style. Kevin observed:

> Mr. Webb knows an awful lot about television, but I don't think he knows how to work with actors. There's no room for any sort of variability or idiosyncrasy. A mold is established that you work in, without time taken to find out who you are. That's been worrying me since the day I took this job.

In October 1971, Jack invited his ex-wife Julie London and her husband Bobby Troup to join his newly created series called *Emergency*. Both accepted and received significant parts. Julie played "Nurse Dixie McCall," often called "Dix." However, according to daughter Stacy, Julie was initially apprehensive about working for Jack. Nor was she flattered with the rumor that her story name "Dixie" was possibly from Jack's recollection of an old goat. When approached about her feelings to be working with her former husband, she replied that *Emergency* was merely a "business relationship ... not embarrassing at all. The divorce happened years ago. That part of my life is all behind."

There is no question that Julie London could have had a long and successful musical career. However, by her choice, much of Julie's entertainment life was then, in fact, behind her. Though London occasionally sang at supper clubs, her aversion to performing before live audiences persisted, and she became increasingly more uncomfortable in front of the motion picture camera, despite her inherent natural beauty. Julie admitted that she could loose five or so pounds from the stress of just contemplating a singing engagement. London was known sometimes to enjoy a stiff drink of gin and tonic and, if she stumbled with her lines on recorded television, could let fly with a string of four-lettered words that might turn the air blue. She remarked:

> A picture is different. The psychology is different. You know that, if you goof up, there's another take. You can do it again. And, in a picture, you're not performing before a lot of people who are loaded — hopefully.

Julie obviously preferred her conservative home life with Bobby and their maturing kids. At home, if one of her old movies appeared on television, she admits that she wanted to "crawl under a chair." London seems to have enjoyed her *Emergency* role, however. She received praise for her perfor-

Webb directing former wife, Julie London, on the set of *Emergency*.

Courtesy of Jack Webb Archives

mance by being nominated for a Golden Globe award as the best actress in a television drama in 1974.

TV Guide characterized Julie as "a very earthy woman." *Los Angeles Times* TV critic Cecil Smith disagreed with those who said that *Emergency* was all about watching Julie breathe. Yet, Smith added, "the way she fills out a uniform, those young firemen must be gung-ho for her." Producer Bob Cinader saw Julie's role as adding "basic femininity" to the series. Unquestionably, her famous sensuous voice pleased everyone.

Julie's husband Bobby Troup briefly sang and played the piano on the premier episode and was a regular in the cast. As neurosurgeon "Dr. Joe Early," Bobby was known more for reciting such lines as, "Let's try plasma," than for his excellent music. He joked that his *Emergency* part seemed secure as long as people watched stories about paramedics and fire trucks. During the *Emergency* production, Troup and Tighe became close business and social friends. Robert Fuller believed that he and Bobby were selected for their roles as doctors because of Jack's "penchant for off-beat casting."

There is no question that Jack respected Bobby, whom he considered an excellent stepfather to Stacy and Lisa. Webb was not one to meddle in

159

Julie's life. By offering her and Bobby *Emergency* roles together, Webb felt that he contributed to a stable home life for the couple and increased their family income. One Webb associate recalled, "Jack did so many good things for his friends that most people don't know about." More than once, Webb expressed that Bobby had provided a warm and wonderful home for Stacy and Lisa, who enjoyed their music records, gifts, a coyote, and many dogs. Webb mused, "I sometimes think they love him as much as their old man. 'I'll be grateful to him as long as I live.'"

The first hour long *Emergency* episode, following the January 15 two-hour premiere, aired on January 22, 1972. The short clipped sentences were an obvious Webb signature, though Jack did not act in the series. Jack received innumerable letters requesting paramedic team information. One letter writer wondered that without *Emergency*, "who knows how long it would have taken for this country to realize the benefits derived?" In only a few years, most larger cities had paramedics, whom Jack afforded the same respect that he did police.

In five-and-one-half years, *Emergency* placed in television's top 35 listing and for several seasons attracted a substantial audience opposite *All In The Family*, the top-ranked television show. Webb's series went into syndication as *Emergency One*, and four two-hour productions were televised by NBC from January 7 to December 31, 1978. A revised two–episode *Emergency* aired in June-July 1979 concerning "Gage" and "DeSoto" visiting the "87th Rescue Unit" of the San Francisco Fire Department. A 30-minute *Emergency Plus Four* animated series for children was carried by NBC from September 8, 1973 to September 4, 1976. Tighe and Mantooth acted their roles for the sound track assisted by four youths — the "Plus Four." Webb had nothing to do with the animated or 1979 versions.

Emergency spawned such memorabilia as comic books, bubble gum cards, board games, View Master reels, lunch boxes, and more. *Emergency* paperback novels with more adventures of "Squad 51" were published. "Autographed Kiss Portraits" of Kevin were available to gullible and anxious young females for one dollar as was a "Kev Lover's Kit," which supposedly included "Intimate Handwritten Notes" from Kevin himself. Mantooth received over 12,000 fan letters each week, and an "All-Star Private Address Book" was published containing fictitious Tighe telephone numbers. "Boots," "Squad 51's" canine mascot, did not receive the same notoriety as the dog's human counterparts.

Numerous projects by Webb and Mark VII Productions followed. *905 Wild* was an unsuccessful pilot spin-off of *Emergency* and aired on March 1, 1975. The story portrays the Los Angeles Animal Control Department responding to animal emergencies, such as removing a tiger from a store and saving the life of a kid goat rescued from a forest fire. Webb directed the series, created by Harold Jack Bloom and R. A. Cinader. Members of

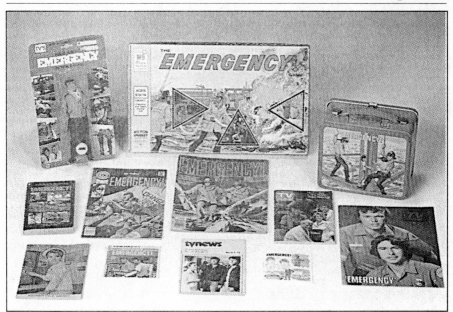

the impressive cast included Mark Harmon, Gary Crosby, Virginia Gregg, and stars from *Emergency* and *Adam-12*.

A sampling of *Emergency* merchandise

Courtesy of Jack Webb Archives

Calvin And Clyde was a Laurel And Hardy type comedy "pilot" produced by Mark VII and directed by Webb. The story began as the two main characters drove through the desert in an antique automobile and parked for a nap under what they recognized as the wing of an abandoned airplane. The two were unaware that they were parked under the wing of a large rocket about to be launched into outer space and only awakened as the launch countdown proceeded to "3-2-1!" Other scenes in the comedy included slapstick pie throwing skits that had Jack laughing aloud as he watched dozens of cream pies flying on the set. However, the "pilot" did not sell and *Calvin And Clyde* was shelved.

Hec Ramsey aired on NBC from October 8, 1972 to August 25, 1974. The story starred Richard Boone as former gunslinger *Hec Ramsey*, who at the turn of the century became a deputy police officer in New Prospect, Oklahoma. Rick Lenz played "Olive B. Stamp" and Harry Morgan was the town barber "Doc Amos B. Coogan." Morgan was also a Director and the series narrator. Douglas Benton produced the series for Webb's Mark VII Productions.

Jack narrated the short-lived NBC *Escape* episodes. The television series was a string of adventure stories about man-made and natural disasters. The show aired from February 11 to September 9, 1973.

Jackie Cooper and Julie Gregg in *Mobile One*, a Mark VII production aired on ABC-TV from September to December 1975.

Courtesy of Jack Webb Archives

The pilot for another series entitled *Chase* aired on March 24, 1973, and the show's episodes were broadcast from September 11, 1973 to September 4, 1974. Webb was a Producer and Director for the 24 *Chase* episodes created by Stephen J. Cannell. *Chase* concerned a special Los Angeles Police Department undercover unit that investigated unsolved cases or ones that no one else wanted. Mitchell Ryan played the special plain clothes unit "Captain Chase Reddick," Wayne Maunder played "Detective Sergeant Sam MacCray," and Reid Smith played helicopter pilot "Officer Norm Hamilton." Other roles added to the program were Gary Crosby as "Officer Ed Rice," Craig Gardner as "Officer Tom Wilson," Albert Reed as "Officer Frank Dawson," Michael Richardson as "Officer Steve Baker," and Brian Fong as motorcyclist "Fred Sing." Smith, Richardson, and Fong were later dropped from the cast.

Jack's frenetic activity continued in 1974, when *Sierra* was first aired for television on September 12 in a 60-minute debut. The Mark VII production was partly filmed in the Yosemite National Park, though the story locale was the "Sierra National Park." The series concerned a dedicated group of National Park Service Rangers, the likes of the *Emergency* team. Some sources list the production as *The Rangers*. Featured were James C. Richardson, Ernest Thompson, Susan Foster, Mike Warren, and Jack Hogan. The Executive Producer was Robert A. Cinader, and the Producer was Bruce Johnson. The NBC hour-long adventure, airing opposite *The Waltons* on CBS, lasted for only about six episodes. *Sierra* awakened the ire of environmentalists when an over zealous "prop" man painted a rock for effect. The stone was believed to be over a million years old. Rather than risk confrontation with environmentalists, and considering the popularity of *The Waltons*, NBC Executives passed down orders in the midst of filming to immediately end the show.

A 1975 Universal production by Herm Saunders was *Houston, We've Got Problems* starring Sandra Dee and Robert Culp. The program, filmed in Houston in only 11 days, was similar to the later motion picture *Apollo 13* with Tom Hanks. Webb was not heavily involved in the picture, though his daughter Stacy worked on the film.

Kent McCord, Executive Producer Herman Saunders and Martin Milner on the set of *Adam-12* at Universal Studios

Donated by Herman Saunders - Courtesy of Jack Webb Archives

Mark VII's production of *Mobile One* was briefly broadcast on ABC from September 12 to December 29, 1975. Jackie Cooper had the lead part as "Peter Campbell," Julie Gregg played "Maggie Spencer," and Mark Wheeler played "Dough McKnight." Cooper first acted as a member of the famous *Our Gang* comedy series in 1925 at age three. On *Mobile One,* he portrayed a veteran KONE-TV news reporter covering events in a large city while working out of "Mobile Unit One." The city was not specified as Los Angeles, but the program was filmed in and around LA. Webb was the Executive Producer, and William Bowers was the Producer. Nelson Riddle did the music.

By 1977, Mark VII's offices moved from Universal Studios to the Sam

163

Goldwyn lot at 1041 North Formosa Street. By then, Webb's associates noticed that his frenzied pace had slowed. Moreover, the film and television business had changed so much that Jack was lectured by some friends that many of his methods and techniques were outdated. Unstoppable, on May 24, 1977, his pilot for *Sam* aired, which concerned a police officer and his police dog. Webb had a close attachment to the project and performed the Prologue of each episode. The show was his first venture away from Universal. He had teamed-up with Worldvision to distribute his Mark VII films.

Dan Cooke first approached Webb about a dog series, and Jack searched for a name. Cooke suggested "Barney," his uncle's name, but that name was rejected to avoid confusion with the *Barney Miller* television show. Cooke mentioned his other Uncle Sam and this name for a dog appealed to Jack. Lieutenant Cooke wrote some scripts during his off-hours and was given some of the rights to *Sam*. However, on the advice of LAPD Chief Davis, credits to Dan were listed under the last name of Noble, Cooke's middle name.

To sell the program, Jack and associate Hal Graham took the yellow Labrador retriever to meet Bill Self in the television programming executive office. Graham started with Webb in the early *Dragnet* days, when he worked with an advertising agency representing Chesterfield cigarettes. Hal was later employed with Worldvision, Jack's foreign distributor, and he eventually retired from the Cadillac Motors Division.

Police canine "Sam" could detect drugs or explosives. As the dog began "sniffing out" the entire TV executive offices, his loud barking caused a major disturbance near a particular Chinese figurine standing on a desk. Bill Self explained that the item belonged to the previous inhabitant, who had recently vacated the office under suspicious circumstances. With Jack's remarkable sales pitch, and "Sam's" marvelous demonstration of what wonderful work police dogs could do, Webb had a new show.

Jack was *Sam's* creator, Executive Producer, and a Director along with Bob Leeds. Len Wayland as "Officer Clagett" found Jack to be a "fabulous" and a "truly amazing" friendly person, but a demanding producer, who fired whoever did not meet his expectations. Webb and the older actors seemed to get along well and were typically invited to his Friday night after-work parties. However, several of the younger actors said they would never work with Jack again.

Mark Harmon played "Officer Mike Breen" (possibly named for Richard "Dick" Breen), and Gary Crosby was "Captain Gene Cody." The music was scored by Billy May. The CBS half-hour crime series survived only from March 14 to April 18, 1978. Webb, an animal lover, was disappointed that the show was canceled so quickly and believed that if *Sam* had been given more time, the program would have succeeded. Jack's associate Hal Graham recalls that Jack "was really disappointed on this one because he loved animals and loved the idea."

Not having much luck portraying non-human life forms from this planet, Webb looked to the skies for inspiration. Jack was always fascinated with the possibility of other life in the universe. He was particularly curious about the first 1947 reported sightings of Unidentified Flying Objects (UFO's). Jack spent eight months examining over 13,000 civilian sightings recorded in United States Air Force files, officially known as the *Project Blue Book,* for his new concept *Project U.F.O.* Most of the UFO's sighted were erroneously reported or fraudulent, but approxi-

Glynnis O'Connor (r) and Anne Baxter (l) in *Little Mo.* Jack sold the show to TV executives over lunch.

Courtesy of Jack Webb Archives

mately 30% were unexplained — and these were the stories that Webb edited and dramatized. He also explained possible reasons for mistaken sightings in the show. In true Webb style, he had a 10-foot diameter UFO assembled and displayed in the middle of his office floor. When people visited the office and exclaimed how remarkably real the object looked, Jack took great delight asking, "How the hell would you know what a UFO looks like? Have you ever seen one?" He would then break into laughter.

Project U.F.O. was a Mark VII Production born from the public's and Jack's interest in UFO's and The Freedom Of Information Act. The one-hour show appeared about one year after Steven Speilberg's *Close Encoun-*

A scene from one of the final episodes of *Dragnet 1970*.

Courtesy of Jack Webb Archives

ters Of The Third Kind (1977) and aired 23 episodes on NBC-TV from February 19, 1978 to January 4, 1979. The show returned with three more programs airing from July 5 to August 30, 1979. The story was also known as *Project Blue Book.*

The cast included William Jordan as "Major Jake Gatlin" and Caskey Swaim as "Staff Sergeant Harry Fitz." Jordan was replaced later by Edward Winter as "Captain Ben Ryan." Aldine King was cast as the secretary "Libby." Jack was the program narrator and, with Gene Levitt, an Executive Producer. Other producers included Colonel W. Coleman, USAF (Ret.), Levitt, and Robert Blees. Coleman claimed that he actually saw a UFO, a sighting verified by his aircraft crew. Other Directors with Webb were Richard Quince and Robert Leeds. Nelson Riddle scored the music.

In the 1970's, Jack may have felt that UFO's were not the only things that were not grounded on this earth. Stacy remained perplexing to her father, as she accumulated large numbers of parking tickets at the Universal lot, where she briefly worked as a Universal studio tour guide. She learned more about television production once she began assisting with *Adam-12, Emergency,* and *Project UFO.* During *Adam-12's* and *Emergency's* cast baseball games, she was the batgirl for both teams. Outside show business, she taught handicapped children and worked with deaf mutes, which Jack certainly must have felt was a grounding experience for her. Lisa also worked on various Mark VII productions.

Stacy and her father often enjoyed having lunch at "Mel's Meatloaf Stand." However, on each Friday, Webb preferred spaghetti at the Farmer's Market. Jack always ate what he considered a "quality" dinner. His favorite restaurants included El Torito, Tony Roma's for ribs, the Scandia Restaurant, and the Cock 'N Bull, where Jack sat at his favorite table, number nine, enjoying his Crown Royal. Some of his favorite plates were steak, Salisbury steak, and Welsh Rabbit. Though Webb was an immaculate dresser, in his recreational hours, he preferred visiting restaurants that did not require wearing a coat and a tie.

Jack was a punctual man. He disliked people who made others wait. He did not like to be kept waiting himself. Stacy learned that her father did not tolerate anyone being late for work, and when she arrived tardy, Jack sternly looked at her and then his watch. To be certain she was punctual, Stacy, for a while, lived nearby the studio at the Roosevelt Hotel, which consumed her $200 per week salary. When she was as much as an hour early, Jack mildly rebuked her with, "Hey, you're early." Stacy became so paranoid that when she drove through the studio gate and saw a guard answering his telephone, she thought her father was being informed of her arrival time.

Another production called *Little Mo* aired on September 5, 1978. Produced and distributed by Mark VII Limited and Worldvision, the story was brought to Jack by Director George Sherman. Webb sold the show to executives over lunch. Jack was the Executive Producer and worked with Hal Graham. *Little Mo* praised San Diego's marvelous tennis champion Maureen Connolly, who was nicknamed after the U. S. Navy battleship *USS Missouri*, popularly called "The Big Mo." Connolly, a powerful female athlete, was affectionately addressed as "Little Mo." The three-hour television special portrayed the tragic story of Connolly's early death at the peak of her career. John McGrievy wrote the film. Glynnis O'Connor played "Little Mo," and Anne Baxter portrayed "Little Mo's" mother. Billy May scored the music. As always, Jack abided by the facts. He demanded that May use Irving Gorden's song *Unforgettable*, Maureen's favorite piece. Billy agreed, and Jack bought the rights to use the song in the film.

An opportunity Jack missed was producing a program concerning female homicide detectives and police. Dan Cooke approached him about such a series, but Webb did not seem enthused, even after meeting two likely staff officers who would assist in such a show. When Webb asked, "What could we call the show?" Cooke responded, "Let's use their real names — 'Kidder & York.'" Jack did not pursue the theme, but in March 1982, a very successful series based on the same premise aired called *Cagney & Lacy*.

Jack showed that he could be the butt of a joke as well as author one.

On one occasion, when he walked past his star on the "Hollywood Walk Of Fame," Jack noticed that a dog had left a large "calling card" situated exactly in the center of his star. Webb found the situation so humorous, that he took several pictures of the soiled spot and placed an enlarged photograph of the embarrassing moment on his Mark VII Productions office wall.

By the 1970's, Webb frequently used the word "Paly," which he learned from Jackie Gleason, who addressed people as "Pal." Gleason apparently relied on the expression, as he was not very good at remembering names. Conversely, Webb had an excellent memory but enjoyed using the expression. Once when Jackie Gleason was making a movie in Hollywood, Jack leased him a house including the service of Fred, Jack's longtime Filipino house boy and cook. Gleason boasted that Fred made the best chili he had ever eaten. When Gleason vacated the house and Webb inspected the premises, Jack noticed about 50 empty Hormel chili cans in a garbage dumpster. Gleason was never told about Fred's "secret" ingredients, and Jack enjoyed a good laugh.

Despite ongoing challenges, Jack was able to maintain a successful career in the entertainment industry for over three decades. However, the 1980's would deliver a challenge to Webb that he would not be able to overcome.

Jack in his convertible

Courtesy of Jack Webb Archives

chapter header

....CHAPTER 17

"Such recognition and honors for Jack would surely have been the crowning achievement of his life."

In the 1980's, the United States endured a lengthy capture of Americans in the Iran hostage crisis, a stalemate in part responsible for President Jimmy Carter's re-election defeat. Former Beatle John Lennon was senselessly assassinated. An attempted slaying of Webb's longtime friend President Ronald Reagan gratefully failed, but not without injury to the President and his cabinet member Mr. Brady. MTV replaced disco music, and playing video games became a popular pastime. Programs such as *Hill Street Blues*, *Cheers*, and *Magnum P. I.* dominated television screens. And, in 1980, Jack Webb celebrated his 60th birthday.

As with many pre-World War II Americans, Jack had reservations about the direction of the nation and the disturbing socio-political events that had occurred in recent years. Although never politically active, Jack professed the following opinions, as early as 1968, on issues that are still debated today:

Patriotism:

Flag has become the dirtiest four-letter word in our language. Our world image has shrunk to virtually Lilliputian size, because we don't seem to voice pride in flag and country. We seem to have lost all the [Patriotic songwriter George M.] Cohanisms. We feel our flag is corny, and that's why we're in trouble.

Violence on television:

When you look at the aggregate of one night's television fare, it [violence] is pretty strong, particularly as far as the young viewer is concerned. But let's not put all the blame on the television industry. We would have a little more normalcy in our programming if many of the more violent old movies were eliminated.

Gun-control legislation:

All weapons should be banned from sale on an interstate basis. All new gun purchases should be registered. Whatever must be done to stem the flow of weapons, we damn well ought to try it. This Nation is bleeding openly and profusely from a valve it never knew it had. If nothing else, regulation will be a significant psychological aid.

169

Contemporary society:

There is a hell of a parallel between this generation and the decay of Roman civilization, the absolute crumbling of Pompeii, just before they went under. The very foundations of our culture come from the very people that went under. What makes us think that we are better equipped than they were?

In 1981, Webb completed production of a TV pilot called *Jake*, directed by Bob Leeds and produced by Jack assisted by Bob Forward. The pilot was videotaped rather than filmed to save money. The story was partially financed by Bing Crosby Productions and by former screen cowboy and business entrepreneur Gene Autry. KTLA-TV in Los Angeles would broadcast the program. Webb's acceptance of using new talent surfaced once more. *Jake's* lead role was given to a bartender that Jack discovered in the Bel Air Hotel (California) while waiting for his wife to have her hair done. Pat Buttram, Autry's radio sidekick on Gene's *Melody Ranch,* also appeared in the cast. Bob Forward, who had previously worked with Autry's productions, played a minor role, though his son landed the second lead in *Jake*. The story name derived from Jack's attorney, Jacob "Jake" Shearer. The half-hour programs were to feature two policemen, as in *Adam-12*, and a third officer with his police dog, as in *Sam*. However, *Jake* never aired and still remains a pilot in the Mark VII archives.

Jack completed other *Sam* pilots in 1981 and 1982. Even though the show had been dropped in 1978, Jack still believed in the canine series. The March 24, 1982 *Sam* pilot was Jack's last completed production.

Another Webb project was *The Corps*. This story concerned the United States Military Academy at West Point, New York and was associated with the late General Douglas MacArthur's life. Jack invested much of his money into the project, as he was enthusiastic about the story and its patriotic theme. Like with *The D.I.*, Webb dispatched crews to study the Academy campus, to acquire information to assist the actors, and to contribute to the story's realism. Webb took the story to the networks, whose executives included younger men with no idea of the significance of this famous five- star general known as "The American Caesar." One reply was, "Who would want to watch a story about him? No way!" Jack was astonished that the executives scarcely knew anything about World War I, World War II, or Korea, in which MacArthur played such a pivotal role. The experience devastated Jack beyond the loss of the series. Jack was disappointed at the apparent lack of patriotic perspective in the young people that he met.

Two other Webb projects that never materialized concerned music and sports. *Swing* was envisioned as a story about the big band era, while a second Webb possibility concerned professional football's Jim Plunkett. The

Webb (r) attending the L.A.P.D.'s 1979 "Medal of Valor" awards ceremony honoring Detective Richard E. Kalk (3rd from left)

Donated by Richard Kalk -
Courtesy of Jack Webb Archives

Stanford University All-American quarterback received the Heisman Trophy in 1970 and eventually found his way to the Oakland Raiders football team. Under Plunkett's leadership, the Oakland Raiders defeated the Minnesota Vikings in Super Bowl XI in 1977 and won a second Super Bowl XV in 1981. Several companies courted Plunkett to sell his life story for an entertainment production, but Jim refused them all.

Regarding his personal life, Jack confided to friends that he would never marry again. Webb's three divorces cost him nearly a million dollars in alimony and financial settlements. In 1968, he quipped that it was always nice to place ladies "back in circulation a little better than you found them." After his and Jackie's 1964 divorce, Webb remained single for 16 years.

Yet, Jack always appreciated and enjoyed the company of the women who appealed to him. Stacy recalled that her father sometimes "had strange tastes in women, and sometimes they were very poor tastes. What he liked about his ladies was that they did not interfere with his work. But he was used a lot." In the early 1970's, Jack had an apartment where Stacy played on the tennis courts, and she discovered that Webb's romantic dinners occurred at that residence. He commented that he never cared to date more than one woman at a time, and he was primarily a "one-woman man."

Jack never cared to be alone. As a bachelor, he socialized with a number of prominent women. For example, when Bob Forward and Webb were invited to Governor Ronald Reagan's family Christmas gathering, Jack was reacquainted with Dee Dee Davis (Nancy Reagan's mother). Jack and Dee Dee shared a friendship that existed for many years. Others in attendance included James Cagney and his wife. Jack and Ronald Reagan's daughter, Maureen, worked together on a NBC pilot show *The Specialist* with Robert Urich. The program concerned the Los Angeles County Health Department with Maureen playing the part of a doctor and Urich as an Epidemic Intelligence Service Officer trained by the Centers For Disease Control. In his quest for realism, Webb and his actors spent hours at the Los Angeles Health Department studying such topics as "morbidity reports" and "communicable diseases."

Jack also dated actress Luana Patten, who appeared in various late 1960's *Dragnet* episodes. He also dated Robin Grace of the Grace Shipping Lines. From about 1967 to 1971, he dated Sandra "Sandy" Quinn, an executive secretary at Universal. She was considered Jack's main girl friend. Sandy, an avid Minnesota Vikings football fan, had always wanted to meet Viking quarterback Fran Tarkenton. So, Webb invited the quarterback and much of the Viking team to join Jack and Sandy for dinner. Sandy was ecstatic!

A woman only identified as "Pam" was Jack's girlfriend from 1971 to 1972. Stacy recalled, "She cracked me up." The lady wore braces and, what Stacy termed, "goofy stockings." When Jack heard that Pam reportedly boasted having all "but the ring" to marry Jack; he ended the relationship. As a parting gesture, Jack had Pam's lawn landscaped, though no one is sure if the gift had any symbolic significance.

From 1975 to 1979, Julie's friend, Jane Sherman, dated Jack, and they may have considered marriage. Stacy recalled that Jane was "a very nice lady who had class."

By 1980, Webb was attracted to the widowed Opal Gates, who worked in his Warner Hollywood Studio (formerly Goldwyn) office as a bookkeeper and accountant. Opal's husband Virgil had owned a stereo shop and installed Webb's many television and sound systems in Jack's Encino home. The Gates', Jack, and Ray Heindorf often gathered as friends in the shop and at Webb's home to enjoy listening to music together. Following Virgil's death, Jack and Opal dated briefly. Webb called her "Little O."

However, when marriage was discussed, Opal was concerned about how Jack's drinking, his late dinner hours, and prolonged time at work would impact their relationship. The extent of his drinking is arguable, but Webb was recalled by some friends as an "ultimate social drinker." Jack himself joked that he "had a hollow leg." Several of Jack's associates warned Opal that he could be a "handful" of a husband, and she should not marry him. Jack was less kind, calling himself a "lousy husband." However, the couple seemed to work out any anticipated problems, as Webb first informed Bob Forward that he and Opal planned to wed. Jack told him, "I'm getting married and I want you to meet her."

The marriage was also a surprise to Bob Leeds. On the morning of the ceremony, Jack approached Leeds and commented, "You're not dressed up." Bob asked what the occasion was, and was surprised when Jack announced to his staff, "I'm getting married today." He pointed to Leeds and Jean Miles, appointing them as "the best man, and the best woman."

Jack with Chief Parker on the set of *Dragnet 1966*

Courtesy of Jack Webb Archives

When Bob mentioned that he was not dressed for the occasion, Jack replied that neither was he. Both of them would have to change clothes. Since Leeds and Webb wore the same-sized clothing, Jack offered Bob the use of his wardrobe. After changing clothes in Jack's Sierra Towers apartment and picking up best woman Jean Miles, the group drove to the Courthouse for the wedding ceremony.

Dan Cooke remembered that Jack telephoned him and said, "I'm getting married and I want you to arrange it at the Courthouse downtown." Cooke seemed surprised and replied, "What the devil have you done now? Hello, hello! I must have a bad connection!" Jack confirmed his plans and requested that Dan arrange for an after-hours ceremony at the Courthouse on the night of December 30, 1980. Dan phoned Opal to tell her that the LAPD wanted to do something special for Jack. She responded that they preferred a quiet service. Dan honored their privacy, saying, "It's the least we could do."

Cooke made the necessary arrangements through a sergeant friend who Dan said "knew everyone, and he made it possible to go through an unlocked side door, up the stairs and into an office where the judge and a few others were gathered." Cooke was Jack's official wedding photographer, using a borrowed camera to take an entire roll of film, which he later gave to Jack. Following the intimate ceremony, Webb treated some of the guests to dinner at Perino's Restaurant, before the newlyweds honeymooned at the Hotel Del Coronado in San Diego.

The two truly wanted their marriage to succeed. Opal noticed that Jack reduced his drinking. Though he rarely spoke of his other marriages, Opal sensed that Jack still had a special place in his heart for Julie London. Opal and Jack were tidy people, and he was always gentlemanly in "the old style" towards her. For example, once Webb and Bob Forward were sitting in the posh lounge of the Bel Air Hotel waiting for Opal to have her hair done in the hotel salon. If she seemed to be running as much as five minutes late, Jack inquired of her and always sat in the bar where he could see Opal's approach. When no one was present to hold the door open for her, he bolted from his chair to extend the courtesy.

According to Opal, Jack was a generous man with a big heart and "a wonderful husband. I found him to be a 'handful of love,' and we truly had a wonderful home." Once, she and Jack shopped for shoes at the very expensive Charles Rodun's. Webb asked the saleswoman in what colors Opal's shoe style was available. When the clerk presented the shoes in multiple colors, Webb asked Opal to pick the pair that pleased her most. She, in turn, asked Jack to pick the shoes that pleased him most. Jack said, "We'll take them all," and bought the lot with bags to match. The bill came to over $5,000. Regarding Jack's lavish purchase, the sales lady commented to Opal about her husband, "I want one of those!"

Jack's opened his Malibu beach condo, a weekend retreat for him and Opal, to only a few close friends, such as Bob Forward and Jean Miles. Since Opal did not drink, the only alcohol present was wine. A huge rock was in front of the oceanfront condo, and Webb enjoyed watching the waves crash over the boulder. He was also fond of cooking at the ocean retreat, walking on the beach, and feeding the sea gulls.

Stacy's favorite photo of her father.

Courtesy of Jack Webb Archives

The couple went on several vacation cruises. In 1982, they traveled to Texas to visit General Omar Bradley and his wife Kitty to assist her in writing a book. Since Bradley was the last surviving five-star general, Jack was delighted to be in the presence of the famous World War II veteran, who died soon after Webb's visit. Jack had always been a genuinely patriotic man. When he and Opal visited the Lincoln Memorial in Washington, D. C., Jack was moved to tears.

In December 1982, Opal and Jack were living in Apartment 2604 at 9255 Doheny at Sunset Boulevard, atop the impressive Sierra Towers. Webb created the spacious apartment by joining two top floor condos with a large spiral staircase, which he referred to as his "stairway to heaven." The feat required drilling through massive reinforced concrete. One level was the living area, and the other was primarily private quarters. The floor was covered in red carpeting, and a movie screen dropped down out of the ceiling for viewing. The spacious kitchen had a restaurant appearance with its stainless steel cabinets. The master bathroom was appointed with an all black toilet, basin, tub, and elaborate mirrors. Bob Forward described the setting as "Chinese modern. It was fascinating!" Conveniently, the Cock 'N Bull Restaurant was near enough for Jack to enjoy a leisurely walk there.

By Christmas 1982, Jack had completed scripts for his most current project, *Dragnet 1983*. The initial broadcast, produced by Mark VII Productions, would contain clips from *Dragnet* episodes of the 1950's and 1960's. Jack considered Kent McCord to be his new on-screen partner, since Harry Morgan was then appearing as "Colonel Sherman Potter" in the very successful *M*A*S*H* and was unavailable for *Dragnet's* 1983 projected return.

Webb was still smoking two or more packs of Chesterfield and L&M cigarettes daily and indulging in large-sized indigestible meals of red meat, fried foods, rich sauces, and chocolate deserts. However, Opal recalled that, after they were married, Jack mostly curtailed his drinking to a nightly glass of wine. A more serious issue was that Webb unwisely ignored reporting to a doctor that he experienced chest and arm pains — warnings of a possible or impending heart attack. Such a cavalier attitude may be attributed to his philosophy that quality was more important than quantity of life. In other words, he practiced a lifestyle that included thick steaks, abundant alcohol, and attractive women — a lifestyle he had no desire to change. He did not care if his food and drink were purportedly killing him. He never thought much about old age or going to the doctor. He believed that doctors were for other people, not for him. He wanted to enjoy his life fully in the moment.

Herm Saunders was concerned with Webb's health habits, although the two had professionally parted around the year 1976. In 1982, Herm was producing substance abuse training films for the FBI, prisons, and others. Particularly sensitive to Webb was an episode concerning alcohol abuse, as Herm and Jack had previously talked about Webb's drinking. Their discussion may have been one of perspective. Jack rebuked any criticism, which Herm attributed to what he called Jack's "macho image," apparent at Jack's private studio late afternoon and evening happy hours.

By 1980, Webb was showing his age, and his dark hair was slightly graying on the sides. Jack did not use hair coloring, even in his last years. Dick "Moe" Turner remained in touch with Jack, and in November 1982, he met Webb at Monte's Steak house. Turner sensed his friend was not healthy and suspected that Jack had heart problems and might need bypass surgery. Dick shared how he had undergone heart surgery, and if a doctor recommended the procedure, Jack should have the operation.

Webb's doctor had, in fact, recommended surgery, but Jack, as Turner would recall, "had a fear of someone cutting him open." Jean Miles also suggested that Webb visit his doctor. Stacy expressed concern that during the 1982 pre-Christmas week, her dad had complained about pains in his arms and chest. Had Webb heeded just one person's warnings, Turner concluded, "he would still be with us today."

In the recording studio

Courtesy of Jack Webb Archives

TV Guide Magazine
Reprinted with permission from TV Guide Magazine Group, Inc., publisher of TV Guide Magazine, Copyright TV Guide, Inc., TV Guide is a trademark of TV Guide Magazine Group, Inc.

Daughter Stacy wondered what to purchase her father for a 1982 Christmas gift: "What do you get a dad who already has every latest gadget?" Then she remembered how much he enjoyed visiting the beach and being in the sun, and how he had recently praised the movie *E.T.* Before the film's release, Jack pre-screened the picture. Given Jack's fascination with extra-terrestrial life, *E.T.* is perhaps fitting as the last film Webb would pre-screen. The movie brought Jack to tears and moved him to purchase additional MCA/Universal stock and Steven Speilberg offerings.

So, for Christmas, Stacy purchased her father a large "E.T." beach towel that she presented to him on December 22. Jack was pleased, and replied, "Thank you, Stacy. I love it." His last words to her would be, "Stacy, I love you." Later that day Jack continued planning for *Dragnet 1983*, as he pondered over 1952 film clips from *The Big Mother* and other episodes to incorporate into the new series.

Opal and Jack cared little about large parties and gatherings, preferring to remain at home. Friends who visited the couple at their home were usually limited to Jack's secretary, Jean Miles, and Bob Forward. Several days before Christmas, Jack and Opal considered spending the holiday with the family, at the beach, or at home. The couple decided to spend most of the holiday at home. There, Webb enjoyed testing his history knowledge against television quiz programs. He also enjoyed listening to his record collection through his state-of-the-art sound system. Johnny Carson once remarked on *The Tonight Show* that he did not care to drop names, but he heard one of the most superb music systems he ever experienced when he visited Jack's home.

During the afternoon of December 22, Jack visited Tiffany's and purchased Opal a large jewelry piece as a Christmas gift. When he arrived home he reported, "I have your Christmas present. Do you want it now or do you want to wait till we go to the beach tomorrow?" Opal replied, "I want it now." That night as the two were about to retire, he kissed Opal and said, "You've been a wonderful wife to me," and he soon fell asleep. He woke around three o'clock on the morning of December 23, complaining of severe stomach pains. Webb then went to the kitchen for some toast and milk and lapsed into unconsciousness. Opal summoned the Los Angeles County Fire Department paramedics, who tried valiantly, but in vain, to revive the man responsible for portraying their life-saving efforts in *Emergency*. Jack died peacefully. He was pronounced dead at 3:23 A.M. on December 23, 1982. The cause of death was recorded as "Occlusive Coronary Artery Disease" and the obituary was reported in *The Los Angeles Times* on December 24. The burial was on December 28.

Stacy, then 32, had become much closer to her father. She received her Christmas present from him the day before his passing. At that time, she was working on *The Twilight Zone — The Movie*. On the morning Jack died, she was casually listening to her car radio while driving to work about 5:00 A.M. An announcer reported, "Paramedics tried to save the life of actor/director ... [unintelligible]." Stacy thought she might know who had died. She turned up the radio volume to hear the person's name more clearly and heard the words "Jack Webb." Stacy became hysterical. She turned her car around and into oncoming traffic on a freeway ramp to reach her mom Julie London's Encino home. There she ran into the house shouting, "Mom, Dad died! Dad Died!" Julie told her that Stacy must have dreamed such a story, since they both had just seen Jack the previous day. Stacy replied, "No, I just heard it on the radio!"

The two women remained glued to a radio as the news was announced again and again. The telephone calls started shortly thereafter. Stacy later retired to her room where she wept while watching *It's A Wonderful Life* on television. To honor Jack at Bobby and Julie's Christmas Eve family gathering, a bottle of Crown Royal was placed on the counter upside down alongside a crystal glass at the place where Jack usually sat.

Hal Graham and Jack's attorney Jake Shearer learned of Webb's death that morning. They met for lunch at the Cock 'N Bull Restaurant, sitting at a table adjacent to Jack's and staring at his empty table which the restaurant reserved for the day in Jack's honor. A flower was placed on the table with a bottle of Crown Royal in front of Jack's favorite chair. James Bacon, also at the restaurant, worked with Jack on several *Dragnet* productions and wrote for the *Los Angeles Herald Examiner*. Bacon found it to be a sad 1982 Christmas not to receive a cheerful "hello" from Jack sitting at his

A MEMORIAL TRIBUTE TO JACK WEBB

December 30, 1982

LOS ANGELES POLICE ACADEMY

favorite corner table, just off the bar, at the Cock 'N Bull Restaurant.

The memorial program from the Los Angeles Police Department

Donated by Ed Walker
- Courtesy of Jack Webb Archives

Webb's friends and associates flew to California from all over the country to join those already in Los Angeles to pay their respects. Peggy Webber had penned a letter to Jack about a week before he died to thank him for all that he had done for her, but she never mailed the letter. Webber flew to Los Angeles from Texas for the memorial service, where she recalls that Julie London "was really upset" when she threw her arms around Peggy and wept:

> She grabbed me and hugged me and began to cry. "I don't know what I should feel," she said, knowing that I *knew* what she meant — that she had been very hurt emotionally by Jack, yet she felt bereft at his death.

"Moe" Turner was more direct regarding the loss of his friend. He stated that Jack knew he was dying of congestive heart failure for several years but "didn't want to go under the knife."

Jack was interred in the Forest Lawn Of Hollywood Hills Memorial

Park, 6300 Forest Lawn Drive. Julie, Stacy, and Lisa were taken to the funeral in a police cruiser driven by Dave Paulsen, who was a young rookie officer in the 1970's when Jack first met him. The funeral procession was lengthy and impressive and included many Los Angeles Police Department cars.

All LAPD flags were ordered to be flown at half-mast. The Los Angeles Police Department recognized Jack's burial with *full* Departmental honors, awarding him the distinction of being the *only* civilian at that time to receive funeral services reserved for police officers killed in the line of duty. Such recognition and honors for Jack would surely have been the crowning achievement of his life.

Webb's Memorial Service was covered extensively by the media. Those who spoke included actor and friend William Conrad, LAPD Assistant Chief Robert L. Vernon, and LAPD Commander Joseph A. Gunn (Retired). Bill Stout read the eulogy. The famous "What Is A Cop?" monologue from the February 9, 1967 *Dragnet* episode was delivered by William Conrad on that very windy winter day.

Tributes to Webb poured in from all over the nation. Police Chief Daryl F. Gates lamented at the service that the Department had lost a family member, who projected the image "we all wished we could project." The Chief retired "Joe Friday's" Badge 714 on the day that Jack died. The badge is now on permanent display at the LAPD. Lieutenant Dan Cooke privately expressed his respect for Webb and added, "No public relations campaign could ever have been so successful as his shows were for us."

The Department Scottish Pipe Major John Massie played *Amazing Grace*, and the Police Color Guard discharged a Memorial Rifle Volley. The LAPD Air Support Division performed an Airborne Salute. The ceremony ended as a bugler played taps. Webb was buried in a suit similar to the one he wore on *Dragnet*, and Stacy ensured that her Dad was laid to rest wearing his signature red socks.

Despite Jack's rise from poverty to fame, his many accomplishments, influence, and honors, only a small and unimpressive ground-level metal plaque identifies his grave. The marker bears a simple inscription that states just the facts:

JACK WEBB
1920—1982

"Jack Webb: He Tried."

Jack was not forgotten following his death. His reputation and film contributions remain today. Although *Dragnet 1983* was never released due to Jack's premature death, in 1987 Tom Mankiewicz (with the encouragement of Dan Aykroyd) directed a *Dragnet* parody based on Webb's radio, film, and television work. "Sergeant Joe Friday" was absent from the film, but Aykroyd portrayed "Joe's" somewhat naive but dedicated nephew in the lead role.

Dan Aykroyd informed Stacy that he did not intend to mimic "Friday," and he admired Webb as an actor, creator, writer, and scenartist. In preparation for the comedy, Aykroyd viewed about 100 *Dragnet* episodes and read selected scripts as Jack had written them. Aykroyd asked Stacy to serve as an advisor and frequently asked her opinion on how Jack would play a certain scene. When Stacy shared that Jack wore red socks

Dan Aykroyd played Joe Friday's nephew in this 1987 parody of *Dragnet*. Tom Hanks was his partner and Harry Morgan, Joe's former partner on *Dragnet*, is now a Captain of the L.A.P.D.

Courtesy of Jack Webb Archives

181

to work, on the following day Aykroyd reported to the set wearing red socks. The celebrated actor Tom Hanks played Aykroyd's partner "Pep Streebek." "Friday's" former sidekick "Officer Bill Gannon," played by Harry Morgan, was promoted to the august rank of LAPD Captain. Others in the cast included Christopher Plummer, Alexandra Paul, Jack O'Halloran, Elizabeth Ashley, and Dabney Coleman.

A syndicated 30-minute *Dragnet* revival aired with 52 episodes from 1989-1990. Jeff Osterhage as "Detective Vic Daniels" narrated the series, based on Webb's Dragnet. His partner was "Carl Molina," played by Bernard White. However, the program failed to capture the following Webb had enjoyed in earlier years. In 1990, a new version of *Adam-12* appeared in syndication as *The New Adam-12*.

In televised 1993 ceremonies held at Disney World, Florida, Webb was inducted into the Television Academy Of Arts And Sciences Hall Of Fame. Stacy and Lisa, accompanied by Marty Milner and Kent McCord, accepted the award and bronze statue on their father's behalf. They also placed a full-page photograph of Jack in the program signed, "We miss you, Stacy and Lisa." Others honored at the 1993 event were Agnes Nixon, Phil Donahue, Dick Clark, Bob Newhart, John Chancellor, and Mark Goodson.

Also in 1993, the Los Angeles Police Department launched the annual Jack Webb Awards. This event is attended yearly by celebrities, government officials, the business community, and members of the LAPD. The annual event recognizes citizens who serve Los Angeles in as positive a spirit as Webb did, especially in the areas of law enforcement and children. The fundraising program includes silent and live auctions that benefit the LAPD's Historical Society, founded by Retired Detective Sergeant Richard Kalk.

Following Jack's death, Stacy began preparing this biography of her father with the authors, but a tragic automobile accident claimed her life on September 27, 1996. Stacy Webb was remembered by many of her friends and associates as a warm and loving person with a great sense of humor like her dad. She was briefly married, but she was widowed and had no children. Lisa Webb Breen married and has a daughter Ryan Kelly Breen, Jack Webb's only grandchild. Julie London lost her second husband of nearly 40 years when Bobby Troup died at the age of 80 in Sherman Oaks, California on February 7, 1999.

Several television commercials used Jack's perennial popularity to help companies deliver their messages to the world. In 1996, a television commercial appeared for Lotus computer software featuring Actor/Comedian Dennis Leary talking to Jack by means of computer editing. The commercial began with Leary speaking, "You want to talk about the web? Let's talk about Jack Webb!" Other commercials in 1996 and 1997 featured "Sergeant Friday" and "Bill Gannon" shopping at a Service Merchandise department store. The commercials were a clever composite of spliced film clips from *Dragnet* episodes to create the illusion of "Joe" and "Bill" shopping for exercise equipment. A long-running Tums antacid commercial also aired in the 1990's using Schuman's recognizable *Dragnet* theme "Tumm— tum-tum-tum." A 1998 Cadillac Seville television commercial portrayed a motorist detained by a traffic officer, asking, "Who are you, Jack Webb?" The officer replied, "No, but he was a god to me."

As recently as 1998, Webb and *Dragnet* came to the nation's attention during the controversial Judge Kenneth Starr investigation of President William J. "Bill" Clinton. Judge Starr likened himself to "Joe Friday," who only wanted "Just the facts, Ma'am." However, widow Opal Webb claimed that Jack would have never supported an investigation into someone's personal life and certainly not that of a President of the United States. Harry Morgan agreed that Jack was never interested in politics and said that the entire investigation would probably have bored Webb.

The 1995 release of The Beatles *Anthology* included the song *Searchin'* in which "Sergeant Friday" was recognized. In 1998, by popular demand, Matchbox Toy Company released an *Adam-12* miniature Plymouth Grand Fury police car simultaneous with the "Johnny Lightning" issue of "Joe Friday's" 1966 Ford Fairlane 500. *Dragnet, Adam-12* and *Emergency's* popularity on television continues today via reruns in syndication.

Jack thrived on worry, and his work was his life. One of his fears was that he would not live long enough to realize all of his ambitions, a fear that made him work even more. Hollywood's nightlife and social glitter never appealed to him. Since Jack did not rely on press agents, he was unlisted in some actor directories. Yet, he attracted and received the respect of people inside and outside of Hollywood, never acting superior to anyone. For example, "Scotty" the guard on the Universal lot recalled that Webb always acknowledged and spoke "with kindness" to him: "He was a very nice man."

Webb matured early due to his impoverished youth, but never forgot his humble beginnings. Though recognized internationally, Jack freely participated in Stacy's local high school charity drive. The event included his sitting on a dunking board and being repeatedly doused in a pool of water.

A booksigning event in a Los Angeles department store featuring Webb autographing copies of *The Badge* clearly reveals Jack's humility and appreciation for his fans. When a little gray-haired woman placed a bag into his hands, Webb asked, "What's this?" The elderly lady told Jack that she had made a bag of candy for him. As Jack retold the story to a *Saturday Evening Post* reporter:

I was fumbling for something nice to say, when she pulled some crumpled bills from her purse. "Mr. Webb," she said, "I'm going to buy a copy of your book, but don't give me any change. I want you to have that for cigarettes, and I think you ought to have a cup of coffee and —" She suddenly began to cry, and I took her hands and held them tightly and leaned down and kissed her on the cheek. She took the book and wiped her eyes and melted into the crowd and I never did get her name. There were so many things I wanted to say, and I couldn't get the words out, but every time some writer calls me a tough s.o.b., I remember this sweet little woman, and cruel words don't seem to matter.

Though Webb did not consider himself a great actor, he was teased by his friends that he would probably never win an Academy Award. Dick Turner once joked with Jack, after viewing *Sunset Boulevard*, that Webb was a "lousy actor," but after seeing *The D.I.,* Turner admitted that Jack's role of "Sergeant Moore" was some of the best acting Webb had done. Jack recalled that he never had any "illusions about my place in the scheme of things." He added, "I was an itinerant radio actor and I got lucky. I enjoyed acting, but I am not enamored of it. I was no threat to Gregory Peck or Jack Lemmon."

During several interviews Webb confessed, "I was never really very deeply involved in acting. I've had a great love for the production side of the business." Yet he added that he derived great satisfaction from performing a role well and that it was "immensely flattering" to have people pay to see and applaud his work. On another occasion, Webb commented, "If anything, I am probably a better director than actor, but then I don't consider myself a good actor." Concerning his multiple functions in radio, television, and motion pictures, Webb explained that "Acting and directing in the same show is a little like learning to pat your stomach and rub your head at the same time."

Regarding his appearance, women usually considered Jack handsome, but he joked, "My ugly Irish mug has no good camera angle, so the boys don't need to worry which way to shoot me." Few would be so candid of their screen image.

After his *Dragnet* success in the 1950's, Jack lamented that "everyone was trying to get in my pocket." He was understandably sensitive to unfair reporting, criticism, and unkind words spoken about him. Dick Turner recognized his sensitivity, recalling, "Jack was a very thin skinned person, not like 'Sergeant Friday' that you saw on the screen. He was a very sensitive individual. It didn't take much to hurt him." One person observed that Webb was not the most popular person in Hollywood and that "his road to success is paved with the bodies of old pals." Others accused him of being "as savage as a wildcat," a "slave driver," and a "tough s.o.b." Bob Leeds remembered that Jack could be overbearing at times. Jack would argue, "Don't fight with me because you're not going to win." However, Leeds felt that Webb "was way ahead of his time with everything," though "we had our ups and downs."

Writer Jim Doherty saw Jack as one of those rare people one meets in a lifetime. Jim admired Webb for keeping his productions clean of smut. Yet, he described Webb as "an ogre on stage — very tough on actors, very tough on crews. You could hear a pin drop. There was no fooling around like on other shows." Once Jack invited Dan Cooke to come work with him. The LAPD Lieutenant refused. When Webb asked why, Dan replied, "I can tell you to go to hell now and get away with it. If I worked for you, I would be fired." Jack agreed.

Jack believed that few people really knew him, perhaps because, as Bob Forward observed, Webb was "a very private man." Ben Alexander agreed that Webb was not an easy man to understand but explained that most people did not make an effort to understand Jack. Webb seldom remained angry, and he often recalled dismissed people back to work with him following a dispute.

Following his death, Jack's friends and others paid him a level of respect that may have embarrassed him in life. Most praised the man and his work, remembering him as a generous person. Harry Morgan called Jack "a gregarious, congenial associate" with "kind of a dour expression and laconic speech" that did not make him appear to be a "terribly affectionate man on *Dragnet*." Morgan argued that, in reality, Jack was just the opposite and "a man of great warmth, generosity and affection." Others conveyed that, contrary to Webb's film image, he could "roar with laughter," had a great sense of humor, and was excellent at composing comical limericks.

Still others observed Webb to be warm, sympathetic, modest, and one who admired talented people. Bob Forward characterized Jack as "a loner who never wanted to be alone," yet not a public person. According to Forward, Jack was a "true genius" and a "wonderful, generous human being." Jack was more comfortable one-on-one with a person and with his close friends.

Webb approached every project with intensity. He frequently tapped his pen or pencil while working on the set, but when the tapping ceased, everyone knew to be quiet. Herm Saunders, associated with Jack from 1944 until his death in 1982, said, "Jack was one of the most talented and complex individuals I've known. His good qualities far outweighed his bad and I miss him and still dream about him."

Others praising Webb included Ben Alexander, who noted that Jack had everything required to make him "one of the finest directors the film business ever had. This young guy is the closest thing to a genius Hollywood has seen in years." As early as 1955, *TV Guide* labeled Webb as "one of the truly brilliant young talents in this business" and an excellent film-editor. Michael Burns recalled that Jack was "a lovely man with intelligence, humor, and the fanciest gold-trimmed Cadillac ever."

Peggy Webber remembered Jack as a "workaholic," who so badly wanted to remain free of the poverty he had known in his youth. Still, she admired him and stated, "I will always love Jack."

Colonel Richard Mample, who witnessed Jack's good humor, patriotism, and generosity while working with him on the film *The D.I.*, related:

> He was a dedicated, thoughtful and considerate man. Many times, I was aware of or knew about his generosity to someone in need for one reason or another; yet he would do it without any thought of repayment by any means. Jack was also a very patriotic American, a side of him that very few people ever saw. He had a deep respect for those involved in law enforcement and the members of the Armed Forces of the United States. Another side of Jack — seldom in evidence — was his great sense of humor; very wry, always with wit.

Jack's generosity was also evident by the many and expensive presents he gave. He also enjoyed entertaining associates in his office and treating them to lunch or dinner at his Encino home. On dinner occasions at restaurants, he insisted on paying for all of the food and entertainment, and if another offered to accept the bill, Webb could become angry in a polite way. His secretary Jean Miles received Cadillac's and a Hawaiian vacation throughout her 30 years of employment with Mark VII. Jack gave countless coffee mugs, key chains, 714 lapel badges, ashtrays, and other small gifts, often appearing with the insignia of Mark VII, to all on the set. Most of his "quiet contributions" to the Los Angeles Police Department went unpublicized. Hal Graham, who worked with Jack on numerous projects, found him "one of the most generous men I ever knew." Jack's contributions to the fame and image of the LAPD were so overwhelming that one official remarked, "No one can ever touch him. Not any TV series before or after him — None!"

Though Webb's productions were known to be filmed as realistically as possible, his ability to write, to rewrite compulsively, and to place his feelings on paper are often overlooked. Bob Forward believed that Jack would rewrite *The Lord's Prayer*, if he could do so respectfully. On one occasion, when Webb, Bob, and Jim Moser were dinning at Monte's Steak House, Jack turned the conversation to the subject of death, questioning Forward, "How do we know we're really alive and not already dead? How do you know you're alive?" Webb had no answers to his own inquiry, but he said that on his tombstone he wanted the inscription "Jack Webb: He Tried." Moser, knowing Jack's compulsion to rewrite, asked facetiously,

"Wouldn't it be better to write 'He Really Tried'?" Forward, recognizing the joke, immediately responded, "How about — 'Jack Webb: He Tried Real Hard'." Totally unaware of the kidding, Jack replied, "You sons-of-bitches are trying to rewrite my tombstone." When Webb finally picked-up on the gag, all three of the men enjoyed a good laugh.

In addition to his terse, punctuated writing style, Jack Webb's major contributions to the film industry included his development of the teleprompter, tow shots, and emphasizing close camera angles. He is credited as the person who pioneered the television police drama that remains a popular genre today. Further, Jack always demanded accuracy, realism, and "an economy of dialogue," "a clean script." He would have strongly objected to today's level of violence on TV.

His quest for realism approached semi-documentary style with techniques perfected in Webb's most enduring legacy, *Dragnet*. As NBC's first long-running hit and America's first successful police TV series, *Dragnet* delivered a reality-based entertainment experience to the public. Jack did not romanticize law enforcement. Instead, Webb portrayed the police in nonviolent settings and as lowly paid men and women performing real-life police work. In 1982, *TV Guide* reported that Jack had a "commitment to good television," a positive image for law enforcement that never wavered, "and for those things he should be fondly remembered." Webb, portraying one of the most famous fictional detectives of all time, felt that *Dragnet's* acceptance was one of the greatest accomplishments of his life.

Law enforcement agencies timed their roll calls to be able to view *Dragnet* and to compare their operations with the LAPD's. Civic meetings were often rescheduled so as not to conflict with any episode's airing. Television critic R. D. Heldenfels wrote that other entertainment law officers have been able to walk the mean streets, because "'Joe Friday' had walked there ahead of them."

However, Jack's critics argued that his officers were antiseptic and that *Dragnet* and *Adam-12* did not explore the psychological aspects of police work as later programs did. Yet, these critics may fail to realize that much of what is seen on television today would have been, in Webb's early career, grounds for significant viewer protest.

Actor Harry Bartell, who worked with Webb from the early days of radio *Dragnet* and through many of Jack's later productions including *Adam-12*, explained:

> I had the greatest respect for the man and he did things in tele-vision that revolutionized the whole industry. He was the father of the big head close-up, and of course, there was a reason for that because of the teleprompter. He really changed television overnight. He had an idea that he stuck with and he did it well. He was a wonderful producer and director.

Mark Harmon found that Jack could be as caustic as a frustrated football coach. Yet, Webb is also remembered for his "acts of great kindness." Both Harmon and prime-time series king Aaron Spelling are among those who credit Webb for helping to start their careers. In the 1950's, Spelling played four *Dragnet* roles over three years, ranging from what he called "every kind of pyromaniac, dipsomaniac, and sex maniac you can think of." Spelling recalled that *Dragnet's* set, as compared with *I Love Lucy's*, was "a very controlled and calm set; on *Lucy* everyone talked at the top of their lungs and had outrageous fun with each other." Moreover, Spelling always remembered that Jack directed the young Aaron to forget his memorized script and only to read from the teleprompter in front of him. Webb instructed, "Don't act, Aaron. Just read. That's the kind of reality I want on the show." Jack called it "dramatic monotone." Spelling related, "Webb was my first great mentor and that I started going to the set every day to watch one of the great TV Pioneers at work doing his craft, and I learned an awful lot."

Several significant producers and directors wanted their sons to work with Jack and a small company such as Mark VII to learn the business. One was the celebrated George Stevens, who requested that Webb hire and train his son George. Webb did so in *The D.I.* Others who paid tribute to Jack include Dick Wolf, Stephen J. Cannell, Steven Bochco, and Steven Spielberg, who was influenced by *Adam-12*.

Excerpts from the Academy of Television Arts & Sciences *Hall of Fame* magazine put much of Jack's career in perspective:

Jack was a visionary ...

The first glimmerings of shows like *Hill Street Blues* can be seen in *Dragnet's* workmanlike attitude ...

His idea was simply to turn the camera on a couple of 'cops' as they went about their lives ... very simple style of storytelling, directing, and acting ... real in every sense of the word ...

Instead of the cops-and-robbers, shoot-'em-up shows of his day, Webb, ahead of his time, was producing a more realistic and complex crime-fighting series. Universal-MCA President Sidney Shineberg credits Webb "with path finding the trail for contemporary reality-based programs." For Shineberg, Webb was "a slightly unusual character in that he was a strong and loyal friend in a business where strong and loyal friends are not necessarily the rule."

In many ways, Jack was the personification of "The American Dream." Born into poverty and sickly during his childhood, he proved that with belief and effort, one could succeed, despite the odds. Upon achieving fame and wealth, Jack shared his prosperity with others. For many, in a very tough business, he remained a true friend. "Sergeant Joe

Friday's" place in radio and television police drama is assured, as is Jack Webb's reputation. Perhaps the words of Jack's high school classmate Marion Fitzsimmons are most fitting to his memory, as she recalled:

"Jack contributed so much to

humanity and the entertainment industry,

he shouldn't be forgotten."

Jack Webb was named to the Television Academy "Hall of Fame" in 1992. The actual ceremony wasn't held until 1993 at Universal Studios in Florida.

Courtesy of Jack Webb Archives

189

Glossary of "**DRAGNET**ese"

AID Accident Investigation Division.

APB All Points Bulletin.

BIA Bureau of Internal Affairs.

Big Time Has served time in any state pen.

Booster Shoplifter.

Bunco A crime where money or other valuables are taken from victim under misrepresentation.

Caper A crime.

Carry Away Carry safe away before working on it.

Code 3 Emergency call using siren and red light.

Dip Pickpocket.

DR Number Division record number.

FBI Kickback—In all arrests, fingerprints were sent to Washington and checked to see if they were on record from another state.

Fish New man in prison.

Grifter Con man.

Hang-On Citation Parking citation issued without signature of driver.

Heavy Squad Robbery Squad.

Heel and Toe Job Hitting a cash register.

High Power Tank Where prisoners under heavy bond were kept.

I Sheet Identification sheet which gives suspect's physical description.

ID Card Identification of police officers.

Jail Prowler An officer who makes jail rounds checking prisoners.

KMA 367 Radio identification.

Make Identification of suspect or car.

Muscle Happy Guy who belongs to the gym team in prison.

MWA Male, White, American.

Oddity File Special file maintained of physical oddities.

Package Criminal record.

Paper Hanger Check forger.

P&F Ward Police and Fire Ward.

Punch Job Punch dial out of safe.

R and I Records and identification.

Rip Job Rip safe or peel.

SD Scientific investigation.

Small Fry Pushers Narcotic peddlers.

Soup Job Use of nitroglycerine on a safe.

Statts Office Statisticians' office compiles crime reports on solved and unsolved crimes.

Steer Steer victim to confidence man.

Vag Charge Vagrancy.

To Qualify Police officers must qualify shooting each month.

F car Felony car.

K car Night detective car.

T car Traffic car.

R car—Radio car.

TT Teletype.

WIC Welfare & Institution Code.

32 S&W 32-caliber Smith & Wesson revolver.

211 Robbery, penal code section.

311 Lewd conduct.

390 Drunk.

390 W Drunk woman.

415 Disturbing the Peace.

459 — Burglary.

484 — Theft.

484 PS—Purse Theft.

510 — Authorization form filled in by investigating officers (also called mama sheet).

4127A LAMC—A drunk.

A Jack Webb Chronology

This chronology is intended as a quick reference.
Complete and related information can be found in the text.

Important Personal Dates

1920   Born in Santa Monica, California, April 2.

1926-32   Student at Fremont Grade School and Central Jr. High School, Los Angeles.

1932   A child "extra" in his first movie, *Three On A Match.*

1935   Graduated from Central Junior High School January 31.

1938   Graduated Belmont High School, Los Angeles. His mother "Maggie" was engaged, later married.

1941   First met Julie London in Los Angeles.

1942-45   Served in the U.S. Army Air Corps, November 24, 1942 to January 4, 1945.

1944   Julie London appeared in her first films.

1947   Jack and Julie London were married in July.

1950   Daughter Stacy Webb was born on January 11.

1952   Daughter Lisa was born on November 29.

1953   Julie London Webb filed for a divorce. It was finalized in 1954.

1955   Webb married Dorothy Towne January 11. The marriage lasted about one year.

1958   Jack and Jackie Loughery married on June 24. Divorced in 1964.

1959   Julie London married musician Bobby Troup on December 31.

1980   Webb married Opal Gates on December 30.

1982   Jack Webb died on December 23.

1993   The first Annual Jack Webb Awards are held.

1996   Stacy Webb died in an automobile accident, September 27.

1999   Bobby Troup died February 7.

1999   *Just the Facts, Ma'am*, an authorized biography of Jack Webb's life is published.

Radio

1945-47   San Francisco station KGO: *The Coffee Club, One Out Of Seven, Pat Novak For Hire.*

1947   Other Radio: *Johnny Madero, Pier 23 (*April 24 to September 4, 1947).Webb may have appeared in *Murder And Mr. Malone* at this time. Parts were also awarded in *The Whistler* and *This Is Your FBI. Escape*, July 7, 1947 until about 1950.

1948-49   *Jeff Reagan, Investigator.*

1949-50   *Dragnet*, June 3, 1949 radio debut. The program captures the number one spot on radio in 1950. *Dr. Kildare* bit parts 1949 to 1950.

1951   *Pete Kelly's Blues*, July 4 to September 19.

Motion Pictures

1948   *Hollow Triumph* and *He Walked By Night.*

1949   *Sword In The Desert.*

1950   *The Men, Dark City, Sunset Boulevard., Halls Of Montezuma.*

1951   *You're In The Navy Now, Appointment With Danger.*

1954   *Dragnet.*

1955   *Pete Kelly's Blues.*

1957   *The D.I.*

1959   *-30-.*

1961   *The Last Time I Saw Archie.* For The Department Of Defense: *The Commies Are Coming (Red Nightmare), The U. S. Fighting Man's Code Of Conduct, USS V.D. — Ship Of Shame.*

Television

1951   *Dragnet* television debut December 16. Went off of the air September 6, 1959. Later reran as *Badge 714.*

1956   *Noah's Ark,* September 18, 1956 to February 26, 1957. Reruns June-October 1958.

1959   *The D.A.'s Man,* January 3 to August 29. *Pete Kelly's Blues* April 5 to September 4. *The Black Cat* did not air.

1962   *General Electric True,* September 30, 1962 to September 22, 1963. *Code-Name Christopher,* a two part October 1962 episode.

1963   Jack Webb worked as Television Executive Producer for Warner Bros. He was involved with television series including, *77 Sunset Strip.* He also served as the Television Executive for *Temple Houston* and *The Man From Galveston series.*

1966   *Dragnet 1966* television pilot.

1967   *Dragnet 1967* airs regularly on television, beginning January 12.

1968   *Dragnet 1968. Adam-12* ran from September 21, to August 26, 1975.

1969   *Dragnet 1969. The D.A.* premiers on December 8, from September 17, 1971 to January 7, 1972.

1970   *Dragnet 1970.* The final episode aired on September 10.

1971   *O'Hara: United States Treasury,* September 17, 1971 to September 8, 1972.

1972   *Emergency* premiered on January 15. The series aired January 22, 1972 to September 3, 1977. *Emergency One* from January 7 to February 25, 1978. *Emergency Plus Four* aired from September 8, 1973 to September 4, 1976. *Hec Ramsey* was televised from October 8, 1972 to August 25, 1974.

1973   *Escape* was broadcast from February 11 to September 9. *Chase* pilot aired on March 24. The series ran from September 11, 1973, to September 4, 1974.

1974.   *Sierra,* September 12 to December 12.

1975   *905 Wild* aired on March 1 for a short run. *Mobile One* was televised from September 12 to December 29. At some time in the mid-1970's, Webb produced *Calvin And Clyde* and *The Black Pearl,* but neither program sold.

1977   *Sam.* The pilot aired on May 24. The series ran March 14, 1978 to April 18, 1978.

1978   *Little Mo.* A television movie. *Project UFO* ran Feb. 19, 1978 to Jan. 4, 1979.

1981   *Jake* was a Webb production which did not air. Other unfilmed projects were *The Corps,* and *Swing.*

1983   *Dragnet 1983* was being considered at the time of Webb's death, Dec. 23, 1982.

1987   *Dragnet.* A motion picture parody.

1992   Jack Webb was inducted into the Academy Of Television Arts And Sciences Hall Of Fame. His work is rerun on television, and into the new century.

Authors' Research Notes by Chapter

ONE — "WE WERE UNBELIEVABLY POOR."

Much of Webb's early life is recorded in "The Cops' Favorite Make-Believe Cop," by Richard Tregaskis, the *Saturday Evening Post*, September 26, 1953, and in a trilogy by Dean Jennings, "Facts About Me," *Saturday Evening Post*, September 5, 12, 19, 1959. Also see, "Jack, Be Nimble," *Time*, March 15, 1954, cover picture and story on Jack Webb. Excellent articles with photographs representing Webb's early life are "The Jack Webb Story," *Cosmopolitan*, May 1954, and "Behind The Scenes With Webb," *Screen Stories* Magazine, September 1955.

Webb's obituary appeared in Eric Malnic's, "Jack Webb, Sgt. Friday of TV Dies," *Los Angeles Times*, December 24, 1982. The obituary listed his birthday as April 3. It also stated his mother was a widow. Daughter Stacy Webb recalled that her father seldom mentioned his early life. County of Los Angeles Registrar-Recorder/County Clerk, January 21, 1999: Investigation of documents from January 1920 to December 1920 did not reveal a birth certificate for Jack Randolph Webb. Also, Office of State Registrar of Vital Statistics (California) has no birth certificate.

Leon "Bix" Beiderbecke died during an alcoholic seizure. He performed with the famous Paul Whiteman Orchestra and many other bands. Davenport, Iowa, is the site of the Bix Beiderbecke Jazz Festival to honor his memory.

Webb's Certificate Of Death #0190-058248 lists both parents were from Idaho. Webb's secretary Jean Miles recalled that she was informed "Maggie's" parents were named Smith, and that her father may have been a judge. A Los Angeles Unified School District Record, microfilmed January 5, 1996, does not give a father's name. Jackie Loughery [Webb] recalled Jack mentioned the name "Goldstein," and that Jack was in and out of foster homes and in a juvenile home for two years. Jack informed Loughery that his mother confirmed the Webb name. Daniel Moyer (hereafter Moyer) and Webb's daughter Stacy could not locate a Jack Randolph Webb birth certificate.

For Webb's father being an "Egyptologist," see Dean Jennings, "The Facts About Me," *Saturday Evening Post*, September 5, 1959. Stacy Webb was told by her mother Julie London that when she and Jack first married Webb mentioned wanting to go to Washington, D. C. to visit his father. Jack's mother informed Roy Knight that she was married in San Pedro. Other hearsay includes rumors that Jack's father was a soldier who fathered Webb during a one night affair with Margaret and Jack may have later chosen the Webb name. One person related that his mother was part Jewish, and they said Jack may have had Indian blood in him. Webb seemed to fantasize about his father at times, and much of the above is speculation and should be cautiously received as such.

Margaret's alcoholism is mentioned by several people, including in correspondence between Moyer and Charles B. Anderson and Gus Stamos and Moyer interview of Roy Knight . See Isabella Taves, "Nobody's Man Friday," *McCall's*, September 1953.

Stories and accounts differ in Jack Webb's life, possibly from poor reporting or a result of the passage of time. For example, it is stated in a July 23, 1959 *TV Guide* interview that Jack purchased Beiderbecke's recordings of *At The Jazz Band Ball* and *Jazz Me Blues* at an Elk's Hall for "two bits" as a teenager.

TWO — "NO, MA'AM, I'M JEWISH AND IRISH."

Webb must have made an error when he stated that he was nine years old before "I got into any school." See, Dean Jennings, "Facts About Me," *Saturday Evening Post*, September 5, 12, 19, 1959. Both Fremont Elementary and Central Junior High Schools no longer exist. See Moyer interview of Gus Stamos. Webb's classmate Dorothy Randles stated that Central Junior High School was the first High School in Los Angeles but was later converted to a Junior High School.

For Penner see, Sam J. Slate and Joe Cook, *It Sounds Impossible: The Hilarious Story Of Radio Broadcasting From The Beginning To The Future* (1963). Webb's Penner imitation and his being in *Three On A Match* were recalled by Marion Fitzsimmons.

Webb's childhood poverty was remembered by many of his classmates interviewed by Moyer and Stacy Webb and in correspondence of Moyer to Webb Junior High and High School classmates Dorothy Randles, Gus Stamos and Jane Gibson. Classmate Marion Fitzsimmons recalled the insensitive teacher story. Dorothy Randles remembered that Jack was one of "the most likable people you would ever hope to meet, but that he had difficulty truly trusting people because of the way his mother treated him ... She let him down so many times as a child that he must of thought everyone was that way, but this is from my perspective of the situation. I am only speculating" (from Moyer interview of Dorothy Randles).

THREE — "A WELL-FAVOURED MAN IS THE GIFT OF FORTUNE."

The malt shop and ice cream stories were recorded in correspondence of Marion Fitzsimmons and Gus Stamos to Moyer. Fitzsimmons first met Webb when she was age 12. Memories of Belmont High School were recalled during a Los Angeles reunion of alumni arranged and interviewed by Stacy Webb and Moyer. All present at the reunion praised their teachers at the Central and Belmont schools.

The string bass story was reported in correspondence of Moyer to Webb's school classmate Charles B. "Chuck" Anderson. The "big head" comment is in "Campus Miscellany," *Belmont Life*, January 1938. Webb's ambitions are cited in, "On The Campus," *Belmont Life*, January 1938, pp. 3-4. The school newspaper was *The Belmont Sentinel*. Cf. correspondence of Moyer to Webb's school classmates Dorothy Randles, Charles B. Anderson, Margaret MacGregor and Gus Stamos.

Baylor Maynard was a Belmont football player and a champion pole vaulter. Gus worked as a bus boy at the Brown Derby restaurant in high school. Jack was a stickler for getting permission to use things and perform plays, as in *Pennies From Heaven*.

Roy Knight recorded Webb had several girlfriends, and he said that Roberta Sadler graduated from Belmont High School in the summer of 1938. See Isabella Taves, "Nobody's Man Friday," *McCall's*, September 1953. The *Saturday Evening Post* trilogy notes that Webb was offered an art scholarship at the Los Angeles "Chouinard Art Institute," which was not a part of the university and was founded in 1921. The Institute produced Chuck Jones who drew "Bugs Bunny," and the school remains in service today. George Wells and Dick "Moe" Turner recalled Webb was 16 to 17 years old when he collected light bulbs. See Moyer interview of Dorothy Randles.

FOUR — "MY HEART DID NOT BELONG TO HART, SCHAFFNER & MARX."

Correspondence and interviews conducted by Moyer and Stacy Webb with Harry Reder, Dick "Moe" Turner, Roy Knight, Charles Anderson, and Gus Stamos. Webb also bought a cashmere sweater for one of his girlfriends. It is mentioned that Jack "found time away from work [at Silverwoods] to appear on various radio programs over local stations" at this time. No listing of programs was found. See Marjorie Dent Candee, "Jack (Randolph) Webb," *Current Biography Yearbook 1955*.

FIVE — "I WENT IN WITH A DREAM. I CAME OUT WITH A BLANK PAGE."

See Moyer interview of Roy Knight. Much of Webb's military life was offered in correspondence of Lloyd W. Whitlow to Moyer. A Class 44-D listing of barracks, squadrons and students is found in Detachment Order Number 229, Headquarters Aviation Cadet Detachment 4th AAF Flying Training Detachment Office Of The Commandant Of Cadets, Tulare, California November 1, 1943. Copy courtesy of Mr. Al Gentry. The documents lists 413 students and six officers for Squadrons A through D. Dick Turner recalled that Webb was "a sucker for a beautiful girl," and once convinced his Commander at St. John's to permit him to do training or theatrical work in the St. Cloud hotel where women were present.

For a sketch of Webb's early life and military service, see "Jack, Be Nimble," *Time*, March 15, 1954, cover story on Jack Webb. See also Military Discharge Of Jack R. Webb, Military Personnel Records, St. Louis, Missouri, September 5, 1995 copy.

Marion Fitzsimmons recalled Jack never resorted to cruel humor. Webb's variety shows were recalled by Dick Turner. The Tex Rankin Academy was named after a famous stunt pilot of the time. See Moyer interview of Herm Saunders. Saunders worked with Webb in *Dragnet* television and movies, *Pete Kelly's Blues*, *The D.I.*, *-30-*, *The Last Time I Saw Archie* and, among other accomplishments, was the Executive Producer for *Adam-12*. Saunders was also an excellent musician. Vocalist Anita O'Day was a jazz legend who sang with the big bands of Gene Krupa and Stan Kenton.

See, Douglas L. Waide, *How The United States Won World War II In Spite Of Douglas L. Waide* (1997) for discussions of training at Santa Ana, Tulare, and Gardner Field. He was in Class 44-D and billeted in the same quarters as Webb. Several excellent group photos are in the private publication.

"We had no problems picking up girlfriends since Austin had the University of Texas," Roy Knight in correspondence to Moyer. See correspondence and interviews by Moyer with Dick Turner, Lloyd Lavine, Ken Sealy, Herm Saunders and Bob Forward and telephone conversation of Bob Forward and Eugene Alvarez (hereafter

Alvarez).
The United States Air Force (USAF) supplanted the U. S. Army Air Corps and Army Air Force following World War II. The USAF was created by the Department of Defense on September 18, 1947 as "a single executive department."

Webb's service number cited above is recorded on his U. S. Army discharge. However, in Jack's narration of The U. S. Fighting Man's Code Of Conduct, he states that his military serial number was 1646872. Social Security numbers replaced service numbers in later years.

"Washing-out," and being relocated to other barracks was not necessarily disheartening. Mr. Forward offered the student drop-out rate was "approximately a very low three percent."

Among Webb's friends, "Moe" Turner had an impressive war record, too. Dick flew 31 combat missions in P-38's near and over New Guinea in the Pacific war. He later piloted experimental aircraft for military and civilian manufacturers. He flew over 119 different aircraft overall, and his most notable passenger was President Nixon.

SIX — "FOR EIGHT OR NINE WEEKS I WAS EVERYBODY'S HOT CAKE."
See Moyer interviews of Herm Saunders and Frank Comstock; Dean Jennings, "Facts About Me," Saturday Evening Post, September 5, 12, 19, 1959; "Jack, Be Nimble," Time, March 15, 1954. For radio programs see John Dunning, Tune In Yesterday: The Ultimate Encyclopedia Of Old-Time Radio, 1925-1976. (1976); Isabella Taves, "Nobody's Man Friday," McCall's, September 1953.

Wilder and Brackett both won Oscar's for Sunset Boulevard, in which Webb appeared. Charles Anderson recalled that Jack took some of his music records after Webb left the military service and prior to Anderson's discharge, and he was not "very cooperative when I asked for them back." Ken Ackerman, when interviewed by Moyer stated, "I worked with Jack on a [unspecified] documentary program at KCBS in 1945. He was great to work with." Current Biography 1955, reports Webb also appeared on radio in The Whistler, and This Is Your FBI.

The actors listed for the respective radio shows in this book are those who worked with Webb. Moreover, programs and actors experienced broken broadcast times. Some conflicts or vague information is found in radio sources.

SEVEN — "THE MAGIC CARPET UNRAVELED AND I COULDN'T GET A JOB."
Gus Stamos stated that Jack lived on Marathon Street when he met Julie London, and meeting accounts are numerous. For example, they met on a bus that the two took to work; or they met in a "jazz joint," since both worshiped Bix Beiderbecke, Billy Butterfield, Johnny Hodges, Benny Goodman and other musical giants. The Julie London meeting at a "jazz joint" is recorded in Richard Tregaskis', "The Cops' Favorite Make-Believe Cop," Saturday Evening Post, September 26, 1953.

Much of Webb's story is recorded in Dean Jennings, "Facts About Me," Saturday Evening Post, September 5, 12, 19, 1959; "Jack, Be Nimble," Time, March 15, 1954. Dick Turner recalled Julie's personality. Pete Martin, "I Call On Julie London," Saturday Evening Post, August 17, 1957 states the two met before Julie began working. Conflicts regarding Miss London are found in Leonard Maltin, Movie And Video Guide 1993 and in Ephraim Katz's, The Film Encyclopedia (1990). Jean Miles stated that Julie worked at Brooks Brothers.

Peggy Webber knew Jack and Julie prior to their marriage and remained a friend and one of Jack's leading actresses until Webb's death. Some sources record that while he was working in San Francisco, Julie called and asked him for a date. She had just finished The Red House at this time and had listened to Jack broadcast. A Webb friend suggests that Jack may have been more interested in Julie's accompanying stepsister, until Webb, while with Roy Knight at the San Francisco airport, saw how much Julie had matured. One source described her as "a tiny little thing, devastatingly pretty." Roy Knight went for the stepsister. Isabella Taves, "Nobody's Man Friday," McCall's, September 1953, reports that Julie lived in Los Angeles while Jack was in San Francisco, and the two commuted for awhile. Julie said, "It was fun, but it was more like a love affair than being married." An excellent 1972 article on London is found in, Arnold Hano, "She's On Hand To Provide The Basic Femininity," TV Guide, June 17, 1972.

Sources regarding Julie London conflict. For example, her birth name is listed as Julie and Gail. The name Julie may have been assumed early in her life, since classmates interviewed used Julie rather than Gail. Yet, this could be attributed to London's fame. The stage name Julie London may have been assumed just before her very first film, which is also unclear. There are also conflicts about her birthplace, and Julie's mother was cited in some sources as a singer and a pianist. The family first moved from Santa Rosa to San Bernardino and then to Hollywood. Not all of London's films and television appearances are listed in this work.

Peggy Webber knew Jack and Julie before they were married, when she and Julie were young radio actresses doing an audience comedy show at KHJ for the Mutual Network entitled *That Brewster Boy*. Julie also wore Oxfords with bobby socks and an Angora sweater with a white shirt and collar opened at the neck, "looking very young and boyish and happy." Jack visited and the couple reportedly "necked" during rehearsal breaks.

EIGHT — RADIO DRAGNET — "DON'T CHANGE A THING. KEEP IT JUST AS IT IS."

"For Dragnet's Jack Webb Crime Pays Off," *Look*, September 8, 1953, states Webb "liked to hang around with policemen" as a boy. Also see *TV Guide*, July 22, 1972; Moyer interview of Roy Knight. Other sources state that Webb approached Wynn about doing a radio program based on actual police file cases. Another source offers that Webb got the "idea of dramatizing actual police stories" from *He Walked By Night*. See, *Los Angeles Police Department Heritage Book*, Los Angeles Police Department, Los Angeles, California, "The Hall Of Fame" — *Academy Of Television Arts & Sciences Hall Of Fame Magazine*, 1993. The publication was available to those attending the Hall Of Fame induction ceremonies held at Disney World, Florida.

In "Jack Be Nimble," *Time*, March 15, 1954, Webb was described as "a dark-haired, jug-eared hero of "Dragnet."" Rex Miller wrote there were at least two American films named *Dragnet*, one from "the early days of the talkies, and one from the '40s," and a British title. "None are remotely related to 'Sergeant. Friday.'" See Rex Miller, "Just The Facts, Ma'am." About Sergeant Friday & Sergeant Preston," see *The Antique Trader Weekly*, February 2, 1994. Mention was made of Webb being "slapped with a million-dollar suit for invasion of privacy after one too-literal account of a crime." See, *Newsweek*, January 14, 1952. George Fenneman was also an announcer on the *Groucho Marx Show*. For early *Dragnet* radio, see Patrick Luciano, <u>Sperdvac Radiogram</u> (June 1999).

For information on Chief Parker, see Dean Jennings, "Portrait Of A Police Chief," *Saturday Evening Post*, May 7, 1960; Daryl F. Gates with Diane K. Shah, *Chief: My Life In The LAPD*. (1992); Moyer interview of Peggy Webber. Webber continued acting, writing, directing and producing, and said "the spirit of Jack is leaning over my shoulder all of the time." See Charles B. Anderson correspondence to Moyer regarding Schumann and Webb's famous music. Mr. Schumann also assisted high school students to write music for school productions, and he knew Jack and his grandmother "Emma." Margaret MacGregor recalled a person named "Mad Man Munty" who made a fortune in the auto business and "bank-rolled what became *Dragnet*." No other research supports this. Jack was "as poor as he could be" in 1949.

The "Friday" name is mentioned in Isabella Taves, "Nobody's Man Friday, *McCall's*, September 1953. The *New York World-Telegram And Sun* quote is found in Marjorie Dent Candee, "Webb, Jack (Randolph)," *Current Biography 1955*.

See Margaret MacGregor interview by Moyer. See "Dragnet," John Dunning, *Tune In Yesterday. The Ultimate Encyclopedia Of Old-Time Radio, 1925-1976*.(1976). Dunning incorrectly lists *Dragnet* first aired on July 7, 1949. See Dan Cooke, "Jack Webb Tribute," *The Link: News Magazine of the Los Angeles Police Historical Society*, February 1995 and Donald F. Glut and Jim Harmon, *The Great Television Heroes* (1975). For the Rosenberg story see, Richard Tregaskis', "The Cops' Favorite Make-Believe Cop," *Saturday Evening Post*, September 26, 1953. The extended quote and John Crosby information appears in *TV Guide*, February 2-8, 1963. Also see, *New York Herald Tribune*, June 13, 1949. Connie Bates', "Now He Wants To Be A Cowboy," *TV Fan*, December 1954.

Los Angeles was founded by the Spanish in 1781. The Modern Police Department was formed in 1869 with six officers in a town with gunslingers, gamblers, and con artists. Out of 285 businesses, 110 were saloons, serving 6,000 inhabitants.

LAPD Chiefs in office during the production of radio and television *Dragnet*, and interims were: Clarence B. Horrall , 1941-1949; William A. Worton, 1949-1950; William H. Parker, 1950-1966; Thad F. Brown, 1966-1967; Thomas Reddin 1967-1969; Roger E. Murdock, 1969; Edward M. Davis, 1969-1978; Robert F. Rock, 1978; Daryl F. Gates (in office at the time of Webb's death).

Webb was known internationally by the mid-1950's. It was reported in 1954 that a Chinese Ambassador and his wife visited the Warner Bros. studio and enjoyed a red carpet tour. The official was truly impressed but, near the end of his visit, inquired, "This is all so wonderful. Now, is it possible to see Mr. Jack Webb?"

NINE — "I CAN'T STOP WORKING."

Jack was working on a *Dragnet* radio program the night that Stacy was born. Peggy Webber recalls he was worried because Julie was late and having difficulties birthing the child. The couple was then living on Serrano Street. (Moyer interview of Gus Stamos.)

Lewis Milestone directed *All Quiet On The Western Front* and directed *Halls Of Montezuma*. Film information was taken from Leonard Maltin, *Movie And Video Guide 1993* (1992). See, *TV Guide* September 19, 1992, John Dunning, *Tune In Yesterday, The Ultimate Encyclopedia Of Old-Time Radio, 1925-1976* (1976).

Jackie Loughery [Webb] suggests Jack may have had his "Jewish trumpet player father" in mind when he produced *Pete Kelly's Blues*. Fred Zinnemann produced and directed numerous significant films including *High Noon* and *Oklahoma*. For Webb's interest in the 1920's quote see, "Jack Webb's Blues," *TV Guide*, May 2-8, 1959.

Other movies, but not all in which Julie appeared were, *Saddle The Wind, Night Of The Quarter Moon, A Question Of Adultery, Wonderful Country,* and *The Third Voice*. One work concerning London is by Joseph Lanza, *The Cocktail: The Influence Of Spirits On The American Psyche. TV Guide,* February 2-8, 1963, reports that Julie received a settlement of $500,000, $1500 monthly alimony, and $250 a month child support for the two daughters. See, Helen Gould, "Jack Webb Talks About Women," *TV Star Parade,* August 1954. Much of Webb's story is recorded in Dean Jennings, "Facts About Me," *Saturday Evening Post,* September 5, 12, 19, 1959, "Jack, Be Nimble," *Time,* March 15, 1954, and James Bacon's, "Just The Facts, Only This Time The Truth Hurts," *Los Angeles Herald Examiner*, December 24, 1982.

Webb quote is from Isabella Taves, "Nobody's Man Friday," *McCall's,* September 1953. Troup source: Spencer Crump, *Route 66 — America's First Main Street.* (1995). See Stacy Webb interview of Bobby Troup; Bill O'Hallaren, "Let's Try Plasma," *TV Guide,* August 16, 1975; Moyer interview of Margaret MacGregor and Peggy Webber. Margaret and Julie remained friends after the Webb's were married. The Bobby Troup information was in part taken from the Internet and a telephone conversation between Alvarez with Bobby Troup. See "The Loves In Their Lives," *TV Fan,* January 1955. An excellent London article was written by Arnold Hano, "She's On Hand To Provide The Basic Femininity," *TV Guide,* June 17, 1972. However, a number of contradictions appear. A tribute was written for Troup soon after his demise by James O. Goldsborough in the *San Diego Union-Tribune*.

Morgan chose to be identified as "Harry" rather than "Henry," since a well-known comedian at that time was named Henry Morgan.

RE: Julie London's biographical information

More and better motion picture roles followed during the 1950's, with *The Fighting Chance* (1955), *Crime Against Joe* (1956), and *The Great Man* starring Jose Ferrer. London was so impressive in the 1956 film she received guest television appearances with such super stars as Dinah Shore, Bob Hope and Steve Allen. She also had a co-starring role on *Playhouse 90* with Ann Sheridan and Errol Flynn. She was the cover story for *Life* Magazine, February 18, 1957. The following year Julie appeared in *Saddle In The Wind*, which brought her more film offers. However, it is as a singer that she is most recalled.

Julie, Herm and Kae Saunders enjoyed visiting a number of Hollywood clubs in 1954. Several of their favorites spots included the Bantam Cock Club & Restaurant and the Celebrity Room on La Brea in Hollywood. There they enjoyed the music of mostly jazz trios and listened to other musicians perform. Several celebrities who were in town included Walter Gross, who wrote *Tenderly*, and Bobby Short. The Encore Club featured the popular singer, composer, and jazz pianist Bobby Troup, who concluded that Julie was the most beautiful woman he had ever seen upon meeting her. He was not reluctant to approach her and introduce himself. It was love at first sight for Bobby. He immediately, and later, realized that with such beauty and talent, London could be a smashing hit; but it required a year-and-a-half for Troup to persuade Julie to audition for him.

Through Bobby's encouragement, London's first professional singing appearance was at Johnny Walsh's chic Los Angeles "881 Club" on La Cienega Boulevard, where she became an immediate success! She eventually signed with the Liberty record label and recorded over thirty albums for the company, which also contracted Troup. Julie did not train with the Big Bands like many other famous vocalists. Instead, she rapidly emerged via the more intimate club circuit, with her "quintessential sexy voice." Her appearance and vocal style were identified as "husky," "over smoked," "sleek and sultry," having a "full lower lip, tawny, and tumbling" hair. As the "consummate cocktail siren," her sensual style was called "smoky," and "furry." But Julie simply described her voice as not being very "big." She had to stand near the microphone for amplification.

This caused many to label her a "breathy" singer, too. However, Julie was emphatic that, "If I have to, I can belt songs out, but I don't like them that way. That's not the natural me."

London's first album was *Julie Is Her Name* and included the selection *Cry Me A River,* which was her greatest hit. The piece was written by her Hollywood Professional School classmate, Arthur Hamilton, who seems to have intended the song for Ella Fitzgerald in Jack's motion picture of *Pete Kelly's Blues.* But when the piece was omitted from the movie, it was suggested that Julie perform it for the Liberty label, and the rest was history. The recording immediately sold 800,000 copies and continued climbing on the charts to pass the one million mark. It remains a standard for singers to emulate today.

Julie credited several people for her successful career. Former classmate and disc jockey Jack Wagner, of Hollywood radio station KHJ was always impressed with her looks and sultry voice. "He, as much as anyone, helped tremendously to promote her albums." Webb wrote the liner notes for Julie's 1957 album, *About The Blues* (Liberty 3043). But it was Bobby Troup who she most credits for advancing her singing career.

RE: Bobby Troup's biographical information
Robert W. Troup, Jr., was born on October 18, 1918, in Harrisburg, Pennsylvania. His father played the piano, and the family owned the "J. A. Troup Music House" in Harrisburg and Lancaster. Bobby was a natural musician who played the piano, violin, trumpet, clarinet, saxophone, bass horn and tuba. But, having been drawn to Count Basie's recordings while attending one of the finest prep schools in the East, the piano became his instrument of choice. He became the youngest member of the Lancaster, Pennsylvania, Musicians' Union.

While Bobby was attending the University of Pennsylvania, he joined the "Mask & Wig" show, which had been a university production and event since 1881. For the 1941 show he wrote the sensational *Daddy,* which became a nationally known popular song. *Daddy* achieved the "Number One" selection on the radio *Hit Parade* for seven weeks, and remained in the top of the charts for seventeen weeks. The song was interpreted by many of the big bands including Sammy Kaye, Harry James' Orchestra, and uncounted female singers including Julie London, film star Betty Grable, the sensuous Eartha Kitt, and so many more.

After graduating with a degree in economics from the University Wharton School of Business, Troup arranged music for Tommy Dorsey's big band into World War II. He served as a Marine Corps officer from 1942-1946 in the Pacific War and as the activity director for World War II black Marines stationed at Montford Point, Camp Lejeune, North Carolina. He remained active with the Montford Point Marine Association's Los Angeles Chapter after the war. In 1946 Bobby and his wife Cynthia drove to Los Angeles in their 1941 Buick convertible with the intention to make their mark in the music business. While dining at a restaurant on the Pennsylvania Turnpike Cynthia, perhaps in jest, suggested that he should write a song about Route 40. Troup dismissed the idea since they were nearing their western highway — Route 66. After departing St. Louis, Cynthia next suggested that he should write a song about Route 66 and cleverly phrased, "Get Your Kicks On Route 66." Bobby instantly realized that Cynthia's wording was natural for a song.

As the couple drove the more than 2,000 miles from Chicago to Los Angeles, they recorded information about the famous highway in song. Their lyrics became a virtual map of Route 66. The primarily blues piece was recorded on March 16, 1946, and when Nat King Cole recorded the song Troup was unquestionably established in the entertainment world. He eventually made eight albums. Other Troup compositions known to the World War II generation include, *Baby, Baby, All The Time,* and *Snooty Little Cutie.* Bobby also contributed to writing the title song for the film *Man Of The West,* which starred Gary Cooper in 1958. Julie appeared in the film, which some consider one of her best. Several songs were especially written by Bobby for Julie and include his *Meaning Of The Blues.* His later musical offerings were, *Lemon Twist, Girl Talk,* and *The Girl Can't Help It.* The latter was the title for a 1956 film which London appeared in.

Girl Talk was a Neil Hefty instrumental that interested Bobby, who approached Hefty abut writing the words to the piece. Neil replied, "Go ahead, write 100 lyrics to it." Troup turned his talents to the music, and while he was driving over to Webb's house, the words to the melody fell into place. At Jack's home, he immediately sat down at the piano and sang his words. Webb recorded a "rough demo" of the song, and the end result was that Bobby, with some small assistance from Jack, had another hit.

Bobby and Cynthia eventually divorced, and Troup and Julie London were wed on December 31, 1959. They built a house in Encino for their instant family that included Jack's two girls, Stacy and Lisa, and Troup's two daughters by his first marriage. Julie and Bobby had a daughter Kelly and twin sons Jody and Reese — "a truly splendid mix of his and her's and theirs."

Although mostly knows as a jazz musician, Troup appeared with Van Johnson in the 1950 film, *Duchess Of Idaho*. He played the part of bandleader Tommy Dorsey (for whom he once worked). Some of his other films include *Bop Girl* (1957), *The High Cost Of Loving* (1958), and *The Five Pennies* (1959). In 1959 Bobby appeared in *The Gene Krupa Story* and later in a number of "Perry Mason" television productions. He was also in the 1966 two-hour pilot that launched the return of *Dragnet 1967*, and he appeared in following episodes. Otherwise he had parts in Webb's *Adam-12*, and both he and Julie, and two daughters from Troup's first marriage appeared in Jack's *Emergency* television series. Troup appeared in the movies again in *First To Fight* (1967), *Number One* (1969), and he was the Jeep driver in the 1970 classic film, *M*A*S*H*.

Being a close friend of the celebrated song writer Johnny Mercer, and a recognized jazz authority, Troup was awarded an Emmy for being the host and narrator on KABC's television series *Stars Of Jazz*, which began in 1957 and ran for several years. He also appeared in television's *Fantasy Island*, *Acapulco* (in which he also wrote the music), and *Musical Chairs*. Troup was proclaimed as "one of the nation's top jazz singers" by the yearly *Downbeat* poll, "right up there with his wife, singer Julie London."

TEN — "MY NAME'S FRIDAY. I'M A COP!"

See Ed Weiner, *The TV Guide: TV Book*. (1992); *Reminisce* Magazine, March/April 1997; Tim Brooks, Earle Marsh, *The Complete Directory To Prime Time Network TV Shows, 1946 - Present*. (1992); *Newsweek*, January 14, 1952. Nolan was unaware of his consideration until later years; see "Jack, Be Nimble," *Time*, March 15, 1954.

The first two Academy Award winning films were *Wings* and *Broadway Melody*. (Ephraim Katz, *The Film Encyclopedia*. (1990). Isabella Taves, "Nobody's Man Friday," *McCall's*, September 1953. John Dunning, *Tune In Yesterday. The Ultimate Encyclopedia Of Old-Time Radio, 1925-1976*. (1976). Donald F.Glut, Jim Harmon, *The Great Television Heroes*. (1975). Thomas Aylesworth, *Television In America — A Pictorial History*. (1986). Rex Miller, "Just The Facts, Ma'am." About Sergeant Friday & Sergeant Preston," *The Antique Trader Weekly*, February 2, 1994.

Vincent Terrace, *The Complete Encyclopedia Of TV, 1947-1979*. (1979). Jay S.Harris, *TV Guide: The First 25-Years*. (1978). For Ben Alexander, see, "Friday's Man Friday," *TV Guide*, April 30 - May 6, 1954. For Marjie Millar, see "Friday's Date, *TV Guide*, January 14-20, 1956. Ray Anthony's recording of *Dragnet's* music appeared on both 78rpm and 45rpm recordings. It ranked number three on the charts in November 1953. The Ames Brothers, *You, You, You*, was number one. Mr. Jerry Haendiges has cataloged Webb's radio appearances, and lists them on the world-wide-web.

Jack's first Cadillac is noted in *Newsweek*, January 14, 1952. The Emmy awards are found in Cobbett Steinberg, *TV Facts*. (1985). His criticism of the Emmy Awards is found in, Dean Jennings, "Facts About Me," *Saturday Evening Post*, September 19, 1959. Also see, "The History Of Emmy's Life And Hard Times," *TV Guide*, May 2, 1959. The Mark VII Limited logo information was reported by Stacy Webb. The lengthy quote was taken from Lewis Grossberger, "Obit Jack Webb," *Rolling Stone*, February 17, 1983. *Jack Webb: The Christmas Story*, RCA Victor LPM 3199 jacket cover. "Can You Guess The Faces, Ma'am?" *TV Guide*, May 11-17, 1968.

Additional awards presented to Webb include "County of Los Angeles — District Attorney — Jack Webb — Honorary Deputy, 1955." The "Torch Bearer" Award. "In Grateful Appreciation For Distinguished Services To The City Of Hope." The "LAPD Award — In Appreciation To Jack Webb June 27, 1956." "To Jack Webb — 'Sgt. Joe Friday' Of Dragnet. In Recognition For Your Outstanding Contribution To The 'Peace Officer' And Betterment Of Law Enforcement, November 27, 1954." "Colgate Achievement Award For Outstanding Dramatic Program 1955 —'Dragnet.'" The *TV Guide* "Gold Medal Award," and the 1972 "Magnetism Award. In Appreciation To Jack Webb — Southern California, Los Angeles." An award from "The Chicago Press Photographers Association," for Webb's film *-30-* which concerned a newsroom. "Annual Award 1952 Forecast — Dragnet." "1952 Dragnet — Personality Poll Award," and more too numerous to list. During his career he belonged to The Screen Actors Guild, Screen Directors Guild, The American Society of Cinematographers, and The American Federation Of Radio Actors. For Bobby Troup see, *Leatherneck* magazine, May 1999, "In Memoriam."

Other famous persons who appeared on *Dragnet* include Lee Marvin, Milburn Stone ("Doc Adams" of *Gunsmoke*), Cliff Arquette (better known on television as "Charlie Weaver"), Leonard Nimoy ("Mr. Spock" on *Star Trek*), Carolyn Jones, and Robert Bray (of *Lassie*)

Bob Leeds recalled that the early *Dragnet* television episodes were so pressed for time that he had to personally deliver the program reels to the Los Angeles airport. One reel was placed on a plane to Chicago and the other on a flight to New York. "That's how tight of a schedule we were on."

The *Dragnet* description was slightly altered over the years from the account, which cites the episode of

"Harold Ruston." Film authorities Leonard Maltin and Ephraim Katz offer the following concerning *Dragnet*'s music and *The Killers*. "Miklos Rozsa's dynamic score features the familiar dum-da-dum-dum theme later utilized by *Dragnet*." Rozsa won Academy Awards for *Spellbound* (1945), *A Double Life* (1947), and *Ben-Hur* (1959). He "wrote full-bodied scores for many major films, and his music was much in demand for psychological dramas of the 40's and later also for historical epics." *The Killers* cast Burt Lancaster, Ava Gardner, and Edmond O'Brien. Several other actors in the film, and who later appeared in Webb productions included Virginia Christine and William Conrad. *The Killers* was released again in 1964, starring Lee Marvin, John Cassavetes, Angie Dickinson, and was Ronald Reagan's last film.

Jean Miles recalled that the construction supervisor was Harold "Hal" Nyby, whose son became a director. Webb's hands were used in later tapes.

ELEVEN — "IT IS THE MOST REALISTIC POLICE PROGRAM ON TELEVISION."

See Jay S. Harris, *TV Guide: The First 25 Years.* (1978); Ed Weiner, *The TV Guide: TV Book.* (1992). The *Dragnet* code as a public service was mostly printed in jest. The dictionary was printed in the *TV Guide* July 3, 1953 edition, and reprinted in *The TV Guide TV Book* (1992). Roy Knight was visiting Jack and Julie when Lisa was born in 1952. Peggy Webber recalled the difficult birth. Moyer interview of Roy Knight. Isabella. Taves, "Nobody's Man Friday," *McCall's*, September 1953. George Eells, "For Dragnet's Jack Webb Crime Pays Off," *Look*, September 8, 1953. Jack reported he shaved once in the morning, but that his beard grew fast and occasionally showed up on TV. Richard Tregaskis, "The Cops' Favorite Make-Believe Cop," *Saturday Evening Post,* September 26, 1953. "Jack, Be Nimble," *Time*, March 15, 1954. For the top-rated listings see, Alex McNeil, *Total Television.* (1996). Letter or fan mail percentages are reported in Helen Gould, "Jack Webb Talks About Women," *TV Star Parade*, August 1954. Jack's other favorite clothing colors were a conservative light gray and black. He enjoyed all sports, including watching bowling on television.

Among the top television programs from 1952-1957, the Number One show and *Dragnet's* yearly ranking are noted. *Dragnet* was unlisted in the 1958 TV top twenty listings and first went off of the air in 1959.

1951-1952	(1) *I Love Lucy.*	(19)	*Dragnet*
1952-1953	(1) *I Love Lucy.*	(4)	*Dragnet*
1953-1954	(1) *I Love Lucy.*	(2)	*Dragnet*
1954-1955	(1) *I Love Lucy.*	(3)	*Dragnet*
1955-1956	(1) *The $64,000 Question*	(8)	*Dragnet*
1956-1957	(1) *I Love Lucy.*	(11)	*Dragnet*

TWELVE — *PETE KELLY'S BLUES* — "THE BEST DAMNED PICTURE I EVER MADE."

Webb did *Medic* on radio with Richard Boone. See: Moyer interview of Peggy Webber; Stacy Webb and Moyer interview of Bob Leeds; "Behind The Scenes With Webb - Jack Webb In 'Pete Kelly's Blues,'" *Screen Stories Magazine*, September 1955; "Jack Webb's 'Blues,'" *TV Guide*, July 23, 1955; "Jack, Be Nimble," *Time*, March 15, 1954; Cobbett Steinberg, *TV Facts.* (1985); Daryl F. Gates, Diane K. Shah, *Chief: My Life In The LAPD* (1992); Donald Glut & Jim Harmon, *The Great Television Heroes* (1975); Richard Levinson & William Link, *Stay Tuned: An Inside Look At The Making Of Prime-Time Television.* (1981); "Jack Of All Trades," *Life*, August 30, 1954; Leonard Maltin, *Movie And Video Guide 1993.* (1992). Maltin awarded *Dragnet* (1954) a respectable three stars, adding it "evokes its era better than almost anything." See, Ephraim Katz, *The Film Encyclopedia.* (1990); "He Taught Hollywood A Lesson," *TV Guide*, July 24-30, 1954.

Janet Leigh was married to film star Tony Curtis. See, Peggy Lee, *Lee: An Autobiography.* (1989); Moyer interview of Herm Saunders. John Dunning wrote that *Dragnet* stereotyped Webb "indelibly into his hardboiled role." A listing of Webb recordings may be found in Jerry Osborne, *Records* (1997). Webb had a great interest in the 1920's He maintained an impressive private collection of phonograph records and photographs, in addition to periodicals and more concerning the 1920's. Webb's secretary Jean Miles provided much of the Dorothy Towne information. Webb stated,"I am not a playboy who plays the field. I can't figure out these fellows who can seem to maneuver a whole string of females. I couldn't stand the intrigue." See, Helen Gould, "Jack Webb Talks About Women," *TV Star Parade*, August 1954; Moyer interviews of Herm Saunders and Dick Turner. The divorce was reported in *Newsweek* magazine, May 27, 1957. Margaret MacGregor recalled seeing Dorothy and Jack on a flight returning from Hawaii in 1954, and was embarrassed by their familiarity in public. Their engagement touched off a bitter feud between Webb and Jack O'Brian, a syndicated television columnist for the *New York Journal-American*. See, Dean Jennings, "Facts About Me," *Saturday Evening Post*, September 19, 1959. Pictures of "The Office That Jack Built" are found in *TV Guide*, February 2-8, 1957. For the Smith & Wesson gift see, "Jack Webb Gets First 9 mm. Smith & Wesson," *Outdoor Life*, June 1955.

THIRTEEN — "THIS MOTION PICTURE WILL BE OF IMMENSE VALUE TO THE MARINE CORPS."
Jean Miles provided the Dorothy Towne information. See Moyer interview of Frank Comstock and Herm Saunders. Bill O'Hallaren, "Let's Try Plasma," *TV Guide*, August 16 - 22, 1975. For the divorce see, *TV Guide* February 2-8, 1963. "How To Live On TV," *Newsweek*, May 27, 1957 is unclear who charged "cruelty." It was common at that time for men to assume blame to obtain a divorce. See: Tim Brooks, Earle Marsh, *The Complete Directory To Prime Time Network TV Shows, 1946 - Present* (1992); Alex McNeil, *Total Television. The Comprehensive Guide To Programming From 1948 To The Present* (1996) lists the *Noah's Ark* dates as September 18, 1956 to February 26 1957. Jack "basically discovered and introduced Paul Burke." See, Moyer interview of Hal Graham. For "Black Cat" see, *Saturday Evening Post*, September 19, 1959. Sources used for *The D.I.* include Ephraim Katz, *The Film Encyclopedia*. (1990); Leonard Maltin, *Movie And Video Guide 1993* (1992); numerous articles from the Stacy Webb collection (undated and untitled); "Sgt. Holmes Recalls Jack Webb," *Huntsville [Alabama] News*, December 24, 1982; "Webb Made To Order For Marine 'D.I.' Role," *Dallas News*, July 29, 1957; TSgt. Robert A. Suhosky, "The D.I.," *Leatherneck* Magazine, June 1957. Former World War II Marine Captain Bobby Troup recalled that Webb "was a Marine buff," who was razzed that he did not go overseas while in the Army Air Corps. See *TV Guide*, August 16, 1975.

See interviews conducted by Moyer and Stacy Webb, with Jackie Loughery [Webb], and Master Gunnery Sergeant Joseph C. Holmes, USMC (Ret.); Alvarez correspondence with Colonel Richard Mample, USMC (Ret.) and Master Gunnery Sergeant Joseph C. Holmes, USMC (Ret.). Mample mentioned that James R."Riff" Rodgers was "Jack's right arm in many areas." Alvarez and Corporal Brown served together as Drill Instructors in Platoon 351, which graduated December 31, 1956, First Recruit Training Battalion, MCRD Parris Island, S.C. The most recent study on the training tragedy is John C. Stevens, *Court-Martial At Parris Island: The Ribbon Creek Incident* (1999). The work discusses *The D.I.*

See, Alvarez correspondence with former Technical Sergeant Charles A. Love; Alvarez, "Parris Island: The Cradle Of The Corps," unpublished manuscript; copy in Marine Corps History Center, Washington, D. C.; J. L. Mueller, U. S. Marine Corps Director Of Information to Com-mandant Of The Marine Corps, November 9, 1956; Donald E. Baruch, Chief, Motion Picture Section, Pictorial Branch, Office Of Public Information, Office Of The Assistant Secretary Of Defense, Washington, D. C. to Mr. George Dorsey, Warner Bros. Pictures, Warner Building, Washington, D. C., November 16, 1956; Jack Webb to Major William McCullough, U. S. Marine Corps Division Of Information, Headquarters U. S. Marine Corps, Washington, D. C., February 8, 1957; Information Section Marine Corps Recruit Depot San Diego, California; Release No. 1357, February 8, 1957. The press release cited the Hollywood establishment as the "Falcon Restaurant." See, Donald E. Baruch, Chief, Motion Picture Section, Pictorial Branch, Office Of Public Information, Office Of The Assistant Secretary Of Defense, Washington, D. C. to Jack Webb, February 14, 1957; Lieutenant Colonel Wyatt B. Carneal, Jr. to Commandant Of The Marine Corps, Code AG, April 2, 1957; Lieutenant Colonel Wyatt B. Carneal, Jr. to Colonel H. D. South, April 2, 1957; Donald E. Baruch, Chief, Motion Picture Section, Pictorial Branch, Office Of Public Information, Office Of The Assistant Secretary Of Defense, Washington, D. C., April 19, 1957. The appearance of the Commandant and Mr. Webb on the Ed Sullivan Show is recorded in undated correspondence from H. D. South, Director Of Information, to the Commandant of the Marine Corps. Shooting Final "The D.I." Mark VII Ltd. for Warner Bros. Release. Judge John C. Stevens III to Alvarez, March 25, 1998. A Lee Marvin biography is by Pamela Marvin, *Lee: A Romance*. (1998).

Webb displayed his Marine Corps baton or "swagger-stick" on the wall of his Radford Avenue apartment adjacent to Jackie Loughery's large "Miss USA" trophy. Jackie recalled, "He loved that baton." Jack was also awarded the Marine Corps rank of "Honorary Sergeant."

FOURTEEN — "I WAS NEVER CAUGHT JAYWALKING AGAIN."
Much of Jackie's biography was offered in correspondence and telephone interviews with Alvarez and Moyer. See Jack Webb, *The Badge* (1958). Captain James Hamilton was for many years a technical adviser for *Dragnet*. Herm Saunders recalled Jack dating Peggy Lee. See "Jackie Loughery: The Gal Who Put The Cuffs On Jack Webb," *Laff* Magazine, May 1959. For television and *Pete Kelly's Blues*, see Jack Webb's Blues," *TV Guide*, May 2-8, 1959. See also Dean Jennings, "The Facts About Me," *The Saturday Evening Post*, September 5, 19, 1959; photographs appear in the article; *TV Guide*, February 2-8, 1963; Donald F. Glut, Jim Harmon, *The Great Television Heroes* (1975); Moyer interview of Jane Gibson; Dean Jennings, "The Facts About Me," *The Saturday Evening Post*, September 5, 19, 1959; *Time*, March 15, 1954. *Hot Rod* magazine January 1955 reported "Dragnet's 'Big Rod.'" See Ed Weiner, "You, Too, Can Speak Dragnet," *The TV Guide: TV Book* (1992); Alex McNeil, *Total Television: The Comprehensive Guide To Programing From 1948 To The Present* (1996); Tim Brooks, Earle Marsh, *The Complete Directory To Prime Time Network TV Shows, 1946 - Present* (1992); Leonard Maltin, *Movie And Video Guide 1993* (1992); Moyer interview of Frank Comstock.

Webb also owned the "Pete Kelly Music" publishing firm. Several examples of published case stories are Richard Deming, *Dragnet*, published in 1957 and in 1970. The books include "The Jewel Robbery Case," "The Diamond Swindle Case," "The Firebug Case," "The Monogrammed Watch Case," "The Strong-Arm Bandit Case," "The Crybaby Case," and "The Hit-And-Run Case." David H. Vowell also wrote *Dragnet* books. When *Dragnet* was taken off the air in 1959, it was opposed by *The Lineup*, which was in Webb's opinion a CBS "direct copy" of *Dragnet*. See Dan Jenkins, "Jack Webb Revisited," *TV Guide*, January 10-16, 1959.

Jackie Loughery appeared in numerous films and television shows which list *The D.I., Prince Of Baghdad, 18 & Anxious, Mississippi Gambler, The Hot Angel, Partners, A Public Affair, Abbott & Costello Go To Mars*, and *The Most Beautiful Girls In the World*. Her more notable TV appearances were in *Judge Roy Bean* (39 episodes), *F Troop, West Point Story, The Millionaire, Kraft Theater, Dragnet, Highway Patrol, Surfside 6, Burke's Law, Roaring 20's, Studio I, Third Man, Divorce Court, Bob Cummings Show, Perry Mason, Wagon Train, Bonanza, Howard Duff, Rick Jason Show*, and *Wanted Dead Or Alive*. She was a guest on the Johnny Carson, Steve Allen, Milton Berle, Red Skelton, Perry Como, Bob Hope, Jack Benny, Jackie Gleason and other shows.

Although little is known about "Maggie," she was unquestionably a character who caused problems for Jack. Several people recall that for "Gram," "Maggie," and Jack, "There was a lot of love in the house." Following Jack's success, neither of the women "wanted for nothing."

Recordings in the 1950's were available in 78 rpm's (revolutions per minute), and 45 and 33rpms. Some were designated EP for "extended play." Tapes and CD's came later.

FIFTEEN — "TO JACK WEBB, THE BEST REEL COP FROM LAPD, THE BEST REAL COPS."
Webb enjoyed narrating *The Commies Are Coming, (Red Nightmare)"* since he was a Rod Serling *Twilight Zone* fan. See Stacy Webb and Moyer interview of Bob Leeds, Herm Saunders, Marion Fitzsimmons and Marco Lopez. Bob Leeds was married to Donna Douglas who played "Elly Mae" of the *Beverly Hillbillies* television program. See Tim Brooks, Earle Marsh, *The Complete Directory To Prime Time Network TV Shows, 1946 - Present* (1992). Stacy recalled that in the 1970's, Webb posted a sign directly above a toilet in his Encino mansion using four letter words of what Jack thought about Communism. Bob Thomas' biography of Jack L. Warner notes when Webb first came to Warner Bros., "he wielded considerable influence on Warner." He convinced Warner to "collaborate on a [Warner] autobiography with Dean Jennings, an able writer for the *Saturday Evening Post*. Jennings moved into a studio office for a five-month assignment. He stayed for a year and a half," publishing *My First Hundred Years In Hollywood*, in 1964. See Michael Freedland, *The Warner Brothers* (1983).

Both *Adam-12* officers were promoted in later episodes. See Vincent Terrace, *Television 1970-1980* (1981); Moyer interview of Bob Forward and Herm Saunders; Leonard Maltin, *Movie And Video Guide 1993* (1992); Alex McNeil, *Total Television: The Comprehensive Guide To Programming From 1948 To The Present* (1996); Lesile Raddatz, "Jack Webb Revisited," *TV Guide*, February 2-8, 1963; Moyer interview of Dan Cooke and Pierce Brooks; Dan Cooke, "Jack Webb Tribute," *The Link*. News Magazine of the Los Angeles Police Historical Society, February 1995. Lieutenant Brooks was listed as a captain on October 26, 1968.

See *Hollywood Reporter*, March 17, 1966; Terrace, Vincent, *The Complete Encyclopedia Of T.V., 1947-1979* (1979). For program time listings, see Jay S. Harris, *TV Guide: The First 25-Years* (1978); Lester L. Brown, *The New York Times Encyclopedia Of Television* (1977); Updated edition by Gale Research Inc., 1992; Fred Goldstein, Stan Goldstein, *Prime Time TV* (1983). Other television shows Warner Bros. wanted Jack to oversee included *Surfside 6*, and *Hawaiian Eye*. For Harry Morgan, see David S. Reiss, *M*A*S*H. The Exclusive, Inside Story Of T.V.'s Most Popular Show* (1983). For information on Martin Milner, see Bill Davidson, "Law And Order's Peter Pan," *TV Guide*, August 4, 1973. Attention is also devoted to Milner's Fallbrook, California, avocado farm. For the LAPD presentation of Badge 714, see Richard Warren Lewis, "Happiness Is A Return To The Good Old Days," *TV Guide*, October 19, 1968. See Dan Cooke, "Jack Webb Tribute," *The Link: News Magazine Of The Los Angeles Police Historical Society*, February 1995. An April 1998 history of *Adam-12* badges appeared on the Internet and follows:

> The "POLICEMAN" badges used in the [Adam-12] television show were real, authentic "Series 6" LAPD Badges. To date, there are some twenty of these badges left and in active use by LA Police Officers. The "744" and "2430" badges disappeared in the late 70's, and their whereabouts are unknown. A LAPD badge is considered by collectors as a premium collectible, and can exceed $1000.00 and over $3000.00 for turn of the century badges. Possession of an LAPD badge is a misdemeanor under local ordinance and state law except for retirees, and those specifically issued by the department.

Jackie recalled that Jack was not a very good father to his daughters in the early years, since he was often away from home. Jackie was partly responsible for Jack and Julie mending their problems for the sake of the children.

Webb was sensitive about criticizing the police. When he was once asked to do an episode about bad police officers he replied, "There's enough bullshit on the air today and I don't want to get into that." Eventually he did several episodes regarding police activities which were utilized as training films and for in service classes for the Police Academy Detective School.

Webb was bitter over the London divorce. However, Stacy on several occasions commented that Jack and Julie still had strong feelings for one another long after their divorce, but that Jackie was "a wonderful mother." Stacy in high school was called by some, "Spacy."

Ben Alexander departed *Dragnet* to sign on with *The Felony Squad* and another network. Webb at this time hired Harry Morgan. See Mike Fessier Jr., "You Ought To See What They've Got Harry Doing Now," *TV Guide*, May 6, 1967. Moyer interview of Stacy Webb concerns many of the children stories. Some of Jack's criticism was in true jest. For example, when Stacy was in her twenties she baked her first loaf of bread, and delivered it to Jack's home for his opinion. He was then speaking with Officer Dave Paulsen of the LAPD, who commented the bread was as hard as a rock. He and Webb played catch with the loaf as if it were a football. "They both teased me about it for the longest time."

Stacy recalled Julie climbing the hospital fire escape.

See Sally Hammond, "Martin Milner And The Realities," *New York Post*, October 26, 1968, Section 3 Television; Leonard Maltin, *Movie And Video Guide 1993* (1992); Les Brown, *The New York Times Encyclopedia Of Television* (1977); August 28, 1968 correspondence of Los Angeles Chief of Police Thomas Reddin to Howard R. Leary, Commissioner of Police, New York, New York. Michael Burns by 1967 had appeared in *The Many Loves Of Dobie Gillis*, and played actor (president) Ronald Reagan's son on the *General Electric Theater*. He was in *The Twilight Zone*, and played "Joey" in a *Lassie* episode. Burns acted in *Wagon Train*, and then in *Dragnet*. See Michael Burns Career File. For McCord's comment on Vietnam, see Burt Prelutsky, "The Making Of A Cop," *TV Guide*, July 5, 1969.

Police Inspector Ed Walker's retirement was reported in *The Eight Ball*, April 1967. Marion Fitzsimmons recalled a Patrol Car 12 in the Los Angeles neighborhood. See Alex McNeil, *Total Television: The Comprehensive Guide To Programming From 1948 To The Present* (1996); *The Link: News Magazine of the Los Angeles Police Historical Society*, February 1995; interviews of Marion Fitzsimmons and Frank Comstock by Stacy Webb and Moyer; Peggy Hudson, *TV 70* (1969). The long quote is by former Police Chief Joseph Paul Kimble, who offers an excellent and realistic appraisal of *Adam-12* in *TV Guide*, June 26, 1971. A book published on the NBC series was by Chris Stratton, *Adam-12*; New York: Popular Library, 1972. See Richard Warren Lewis, "Happiness Is A Return To The Good Old Days," *TV Guide*, October 19, 1968.

Lieutenant Dan Cooke also served as the LAPD spokesman for better than two decades, and briefed the media on such events as the Charles Manson murders, the assassination of Robert F. Kennedy, and the Symbionese Liberation Army "shootout," following Patty Hearst's kidnapping. He died of cancer on April 30, 1999, at the age of 72. See Myrna Oliver, "Obituaries," *Los Angeles Times*, May 5, 1999.

"Kookie" always combed his hair and during the first program, sang a novelty number called *Kookie, Kookie, Lend Me Your Comb*. The song was released as a Connie Stevens and Edd Byrnes duet and became a hit. One person described "Kookie" as a "Fonzie" of the 1950's.

At one time *Dragnet* aired prior to *The Dean Martin Show*. Jack was a Martin fan, and was moved when Dean sent him a message expressing how much he enjoyed *Dragnet* and that its large following placed viewers in line to see his show.

Jack, Bobby and Julie owned The China Trader Restaurant near Toluca Lake, California. Bobby performed there, and Stacy as an adult occasionally sang in the lounge.

Chief Reddin appointed Webb as "The Keeper Of The Badge," and he was the first civilian to receive an actual LAPD shield. Yet, there were actually two Sergeant Badges 714 used in *Dragnet*. The early design showed an eagle insignia along the top, which was later dropped for a redesigned shield displaying an insignia of the Los Angeles City Hall Building. A similar version remains in use today. After Webb's passing, Mrs. Opal Webb presented Lieutenant Dan Cooke with the first version of Badge 714. The City Hall copy of Badge 714 is encased in lucite and is displayed in the historical section of the LAPD. When Sergeant Dan Cooke was promoted to lieutenant on February 22, 1974, he took the single "Lieutenant Friday's" Badge 714 for himself. "Joe Friday" was promoted to lieutenant in the final 1959 episode, but returned to a sergeant's rank in *Dragnet 1966*. Dan Cooke carried a miniature "Retired" Lieutenant Badge 714 until the time of his death in 1999.

SIXTEEN — "WITHOUT EMERGENCY, WHO KNOWS HOW LONG IT WOULD HAVE TAKEN FOR THIS COUNTRY TO REALIZE THE BENEFITS IT DERIVED?"

Stacy Webb recalled that Jack last acted the part of "Sergeant Friday" on the *Jack Benny Farewell Show* in 1974. See Stacy Webb and Moyer interviews of Roy Knight, Bob Leeds, and Bob Forward; Vincent Terrace, *Television 1970-1980* (1981); Leonard Maltin, *Movie And Video Guide 1993* (1992); Alex McNeil, *Total Television: The Comprehensive Guide To Programming From 1948 To The Present* (1996). For the Muhammad Ali story see, Daryl F. Gates with Diane K. Shah, *Chief: My Life In The LAPD* (1992); Moyer interview of Ed Walker; Dick Adler, *TV Guide*, July 22-28, 1972.

See Moyer interview of Bob Forward; Dan Cooke, "Jack Webb Tribute," *The Link: News Magazine Of The Los Angeles Police Historical Society*, February 1995. For information regarding Bobby Troup and Julie London see, Bill O'Hallaren, "Let's Try Plasma," *TV Guide*, August 16 - 22, 1975; "This One's On The House," *TV Guide*, February 11, 1978; "Julie London Stars In 'Emergency," *Los Angeles Herald-Examiner TV Weekly*, June 16, 1974; Ginny Weissman, "It's Randolph Mantooth And Kevin Tighe In An 'Emergency," *Chicago Tribune TV Week*, April 10-16, 1977. A well done sketch of *Emergency* and the paramedic history and the cast is found in a story book, *Emergency*, Vol 1, No. 1, July 1976, published by Charlton Publications, Inc., Derby, Connecticut.

See Richard Warren Lewis, "Saturday Night Celebrity," *TV Guide*, August 3, 1974; Fred Goldstein, Stan Goldstein, *Prime Time TV* (1983); Lester L. Brown, *The New York Times Encyclopedia Of Television* (1977); updated edition by Gale Research Inc., 1992. Tim Brooks, Earle Marsh, *The Complete Directory To Prime Time Network TV Shows, 1946 - Present* (1992), use the title *Emergency + 4*," on NBC from September 1973 to September 1976. No cast is given. See Vincent Terrace, *The Complete Encyclopedia Of T.V., 1947-1979* (1979); Vincent Terrace, *Television 1970-1980* (1981); Chris Stratton, *Emergency*. New York: Popular Library, 1972; Arnold Hano, "She's On Hand To Provide The Basic Femininity," *TV Guide*, June 17, 1972. For *Project UFO* see, Robert MacKenzie, "Review" Of "Project UFO," *TV Guide*, April 15, 1978; Dick Russell, "They Fly In The Face Of Logic," *TV Guide*, June 10, 1978. *TV Guide*, September 19, 1992.

For *Sierra*, see *TV Guide*, September 12, 1974. Much of the *Sam* information was offered during interviews with Len Wayland. See Alex McNeil, *Total Television. The Comprehensive Guide To Programming From 1948 To The Present* (1996). *Hec Ramsey* was narrated by Harry Morgan who was also in the cast and a Director. See Vincent Terrace, *Television 1970-1980* (1981); Tim Brooks, Earle Marsh, *The Complete Directory To Prime Time Network TV Shows, 1946 - Present* (1992). Broadcast dates vary in Tim Brooks, Earle Marsh, *The Complete Directory To Prime Time Network TV Shows, 1946 - Present* (1992).See Vincent Terrace, *The Complete Encyclopedia Of T.V., 1947-1979* (1979). Stacy Webb reported that when Julie first worked on *Emergency*, she came home at night with hives, and had to take Benadryl and special baths to calm her nerves; Moyer interview of Stacy Webb. For Bobby Troup information see, Bill O'Hallaren, "Let's Try Plasma," *TV Guide*, August 16 - 22, 1975. See interview by Stacy Webb and Moyer of Bob Leeds and Billy May; *Hec Ramsey*, *TV Guide*, September 9, 1972; *Mobile One*, *TV Guide*, September 6, 1975. Bob Leeds supplied the information about *Calvin And Clyde*.

See Fred Goldstein, Stan Goldstein, *Prime Time TV* (1983);. Alex McNeil, *Total Television: The Comprehensive Guide To Programing From 1948 To The Present* (1996); Vincent Terrace, *Television 1970-1980* (1981); Moyer interviews of Stacy and Opal Webb; Tim Brooks, Earle Marsh, *The Complete Directory To Prime Time Network TV Shows, 1946 - Present* (1992). It appears that Webb made a guest or other appearance in an episode of *The Partners*, in 1971. The story concerned Los Angeles Police Detectives and cast Don Adams, Rupert Crosse and Dick Van Patten; created by Don Adams.

Only a limited number of *Adam-12* and *Emergency* test market bubble gum cards were released by the Topps Company. Numbers 1-27 were *Adam-12* cards. Numbers 28-55 were *Emergency* cards. They were discontinued by the Topps Company following poor sales. A complete set of the cards today could be worth at least $3,000.00.

1972 was a banner year for Mark VII Limited. The company produced five television programs — *Adam-12*, *Emergency*, *The D.A.*, *O'Hara: U.S. Treasury*, and *Hec Ramsey*.

Jack wrote for *Sam* under the pseudonym of John Randolph. "Randolph" was Webb's middle name, but no origin for the Randolph name was found. Webb's concern was that persons would tire of seeing his name in the credits so much.

During filming, *Sam* wore several collars. One was to alert the dog to look for people, another to search for drugs, and one for explosives. The animal was also a trained attack dog. Webb may have considered reviving *Sam*, as pilot inventories list the program in 1981 and 1982.

SEVENTEEN — "SUCH RECOGNITION AND HONORS FOR JACK WOULD SURELY HAVE BEEN THE CROWNING ACHIEVEMENT OF HIS LIFE."

Webb's opinions are found in Richard Warren Lewis, "Happiness Is A Return To The Good Old Days," *TV Guide*, October 19, 1968. See Moyer interviews of Jackie Loughery [Webb], Stacy Webb, Bob Forward, Peggy Webber, Dick Turner, Dan Cooke, and Opal Webb. Bob Forward earlier suggested a series to be called "The Rangers," and is perhaps due some credit for *Sierra*.

Jack R. Webb's Certificate Of Death, State Of California is #0190-058248. See Eric Malnic, "Jack Webb, Sgt. Friday of TV Dies," *Los Angeles Times*, December 24, 1982; Dan Cooke, "Jack Webb — Just The Facts," *The Link*, The News Magazine of the Los Angeles Police Historical Society, February 1995. For information on Morgan, see David S. Reiss, *M*A*S*H. The Exclusive, Inside Story Of T.V.'s Most Popular Show* (1983); introduction by Alan Alda. See "A Memorial Tribute To Jack Webb," December 30, 1982, Los Angeles Police Academy. Mr. Bob Forward provided much of the information concerning Webb's later projects.

Opal recalled that Jack had only two photographs in their apartment at Doheny and Sunset to show for his remarkable career.

EIGHTEEN—"JACK WEBB: HE TRIED."

The authors are indebted to all who offered their recollections of Jack as a person. Opinions were offered during interviews, by telephone and through correspondence with those listed. James Bacon, "Just The Facts, Only This Time The Truth Hurts," *Los Angeles Herald Examiner*, December 24, 1982. See Moyer interview and correspondence of Dick Turner and Dan Aykroyd; Dick Adler, *TV Guide*, July 22, 1972; "The Actors Move In," *TV Guide*, May 31-June 6, 1958.

Several of Webb's quotations are found in his obituary.

See Tim Brooks, Earle Marsh, *The Complete Directory To Prime Time Network TV Shows, 1946 – Present* (1992); Chris Rodell, "'Dragnet' Widow to Ken Starr: You're No Joe Friday!" *National Enquirer*, May 5, 1998 and *New York Post*, April 25, 1998.

Stacy's death was reported in *The National Enquirer*, November 12, 1996, and was in error on several accounts. E.g., Jack did not die of alcoholism and she was "reconciled" with her father.

For Bobby Troup see, *Leatherneck* magazine, May 1999, "In Memoriam."

Information regarding the Webb funeral arrangements were offered by Dan Moyer. See "Friday's Man Friday," *TV Guide*, April 30-May 6, 1954; *TV Guide*, July 23-29, 1955; Bob Forward and Hal Graham interview by Moyer; *TV Guide*, January 29, 1983; Aaron Spelling with Jefferson Graham, *A Prime-Time Life: An Autobiography* (1996). The lengthy quote regarding the elderly lady is found in Dean Jennings, "The Facts About Me," *Saturday Evening Post*, September 5, 1959.

From Webb's radio, television and personal endorsements, Californians affirmed in 1968 "an otherwise obscure" $25,000,000 bond issue that furnished money for the construction of new police stations, and the repair of older ones.

Bobby Troup also attended school functions with Jack.

Among Jack's pleasures in life were foods, music, and automobiles.

The original *Dragnet* radio scripts were bound in red leather and presented to UCLA.

Bibliography

Books

Alvarez, Eugene, *Parris Island: "The Cradle Of The Corps."* Privately published by the author, 1996.

Aylesworth, Thomas G., *Television In America - A Pictorial History.* New York: Exeter Books, 1986.

Brooks, Tim, Earle Marsh, *The Complete Directory To Prime Time Network TV Shows, 1946 - Present.* New York: Ballantine Books, 1992.

Brown, Lester L., *The New York Times Encyclopedia Of Television.* New York: The New York Times Book Company, Inc., 1977. Updated edition by Gale Research Inc., 1992.

Campbell, Robert, *The Golden Years Of Broadcasting.* New York: Charles Scribner's Sons, 1976.

Candee, Marjorie Dent, *Current Biography Yearbook 1955.* New York: The H. W. Wilson Company, 1955.

Crump, Spencer, *Route 66 — America's First Main Street.* Corona del Mar, California: Zeta Publishers Company, 1995.

Deming, Richard, *Dragnet. Case Histories From The Popular Television Series.* Racine, Wisconsin: Whitman & Western Publishing Companies, 1957, 1970.

Dunning, John, *Tune In Yesterday. The Ultimate Encyclopedia Of Old-Time Radio, 1925-1976.* Englewood Cliffs, New Jersey: Prentice-Hall, 1976.

Eliot, Marc, *Walt Disney: Hollywood's Dark Prince.* New York: A Birch Lane Press Book, 1993.

Freedland, Michael, *The Warner Brothers.* New York: The St. Martin's Press, 1983.

Gates, Daryl F., Diane K. Shah, *Chief: My Life In The LAPD.* New York: Bantam Books, 1992.

Glut, Donald F., Jim Harmon, *The Great Television Heroes.* New York: Doubleday & Company, Inc., 1975.

Goldstein, Fred, Stan Goldstein, *Prime Time TV.* New York: Crown Publishers, Inc., 1983.

Harris, Jay S., *TV Guide: The First 25-Years.* New York: Simon & Schuster, 1978.

Hudson, Peggy, *TV 70.* New York: Scholastic Book Services, 1969.

Kaplan, Mike, *Variety: International Show Business Reference.* New York: Garland Publishing, Inc., 1981.

Katz, Ephraim, *The Film Encyclopedia.* New York: Harper & Row, 1990.

Lackman, Ron, *Same Time. Same Station: An A-Z Guide To Radio From Jack Benny To Howard Stern.* New York: Facts On File, Inc., 1996.

Lanza, Joseph, *The Cocktail: The Influence Of Spirits On The American Psyche.* New York: St. Martin's Press, 1995.

Lee, Peggy, *Lee: An Autobiography.* New York: Donald I. Fine, Inc., 1989.

Levinson, Richard, William Link, *Stay Tuned: An Inside Look At The Making Of Prime-Time Television.* New York: St. Martin's Press, 1981.

Maltin, Leonard, *Movie And Video Guide 1993.* New York: Signet Books, 1992.

Marvin, Pamela, *Lee: A Romance.* New York: Faber and Faber Limited, 1998.

McNeil, Alex, *Total Television. The Comprehensive Guide To Programming From 1948 To The Present.* New York: Penguin Books, 1996.

Osborne, Jerry, *Records.* New York: House Of Collectibles, 1997. Distributed by Ballantine Books.

Reagan, Maureen, *First Father, First Daughter. A Memoir.* Boston: Little Brown & Company Publishing, 1989.

Reiss, David S., *M*A*S*H. The Exclusive, Inside Story Of T.V.'s Most Popular Show.* New York: The Bobbs-Merrill Company, Inc., 1983.

Rouse, Sarah, Katharine Loughney, *Three Decades Of Television, 1949-1979.* Washington: Library Of Congress, 1989.

Santangelo, John, Jr., *Emergency.* Derby, Connecticut: Charlton Publications, Inc., 1976.

Slate, Sam J. and Joe Cook, *It Sounds Impossible: The Hilarious Story Of Radio Broadcasting From The Beginning To The Future.* New York: The Macmillan Company, 1963.

Spelling, Aaron with Jefferson Graham, *A Prime-Time Life: An Autobiography*. New York: St. Martin's Press, 1996.

Steinberg, Cobbett, *TV Facts*. New York: Facts On File Publications, 1985.

Stevens, John C., *Court-Martial At Parris Island: The Ribbon Creek Incident*. Annapolis, Maryland: Naval Institute Press, 1999.

Stratton, Chris, *Adam-12*. New York: Popular Library, 1972.

Stratton, Chris, *Emergency*. New York: Popular Library, 1972.

Terrace, Vincent, *The Complete Encyclopedia Of T.V., 1947-1979*. Cranbury, New Jersey: A. S. Barnes, Inc., 1979.

Terrace, Vincent, *Television 1970-1980*. New York: A. S. Barnes & Company, Inc., 1981.

Thomas, Bob, *Clown Prince Of Hollywood: The Antic Life And Times Of Jack L. Warner*. New York: McGraw-Hill Publishing Company, 1990.

Waide, Douglas L., *How The United States Won World War II In Spite Of Douglas L. Waide*. Long Beach, California. Privately Published, 1997.

Webb, Jack, *The Badge*. Englewood Cliffs, New Jersey: Prentice Hall, 1958.

Weiner, Ed, *The T V Guide: TV Book*. New York: HarperCollins Publishers, 1992.

Wetterau, Bruce, *The New York Public Library Book Of Chronologies*. New York: Prentice Hall Press, 1990.

Winship, Michael, *Television*. New York: Random House Publishing, 1988.

Magazines
(Arranged alphabetically by publication)

"The Jack Webb Story," *Cosmopolitan*, May 1954.

Bob Greene, "The Big Rod," *Hot Rod*, January 1955.

"Jackie Loughery: The Gal Who Put The Cuffs On Jack Webb," *Laff* Magazine, May 1959.

TSgt. Robert A. Suhosky, "The D.I.," *Leatherneck*, June 1957.

"In Memoriam, Robert W. Troup Jr.," *Leatherneck*, May 1999.

"Jack Of All Trades," *Life*, August 30, 1954.

"A Small Voice Makes Big Stir. Julie London Gets Back To Movies," *Life*, February 18, 1957.

Dan Cooke, "Jack Webb Tribute," *The Link*. News Magazine of the Los Angeles Police Historical Society, February 1995.

George Eells, "For Dragnet's Jack Webb Crime Pays Off," *Look*, September 8, 1953.

Newsweek, January 14, 1952.

"How To Live On TV," *Newsweek*, May 27, 1957.

Isabella Taves, "Nobody's Man Friday, *McCall's*, September 1953.

"Jack Webb Gets First 9 mm. Smith & Wesson," *Outdoor Life*, June 1955.

Charles B. Block, "A Talk With Jack Webb," *Popular Photography*, October 1955.

"Television," *Reminisce*, March/April, 1997.

Lewis Grossberger, "Obit Jack Webb," *Rolling Stone*, February 17, 1983.

Richard Tregaskis, "The Cops' Favorite Make-Believe Cop," *Saturday Evening Post*, September 26, 1953.

Pete Martin, "I Call On Julie London," *Saturday Evening Post*, August 17,1957.

Dean Jennings, "Facts About Me," *Saturday Evening Post*, September 5, 12, 19, 1959.

Dean Jennings, "Portrait Of A Police Chief," *Saturday Evening Post*, May 7, 1960.

"Behind The Scenes With Webb - 'Pete Kelly's Blues,'" *Screen Stories*, September 1955.

"Jack, Be Nimble," *Time*, March 15, 1954. Cover story.

"Is Jack Webb Quitting TV?" *TV*, November 1954.

John C. Johnson, "The Riddle Of Jack Webb," *TV And Movie Starland*, May 1954.

"Jack Webb — Purely Personal," *TV Annual 1955*.

Connie Bates, "Jack Webb – Now He Wants To Be A Cowboy," *TV Fan*, December 1954.

"The Loves In Their Lives," *TV Fan*, January 1955.

TV Guide
(Listed chronologically)

"Dragnet Catches 38 Million Viewers," April 10, 1953. "Friday's Man Friday," April 30-May 6, 1954. "What Jack Webb Taught Hollywood," July 24-30, 1954. "Jack Webb's 'Blues,'" July 23, 1955. "Friday's Date," January 14-20, 1956. "The Office That Jack Built," February 2-8, 1957. "The Actors Move In," May 31 - June 6, 1958. Dan Jenkins, "Jack Webb Revisited," January 10-16, 1959. "The History Of Emmy's Life And Hard Times," May 2 - 8, 1959. Lesile Raddatz, "Jack Webb Revisited," February 2-8, 1963. Mike Fessier Jr., "You Ought To See What They've Got Harry Doing Now," May 6, 1967. Richard Warren Lewis, "Happiness Is A Return To The Good Old Days," October 19, 1968. "Can You Guess The Faces, Ma'am?" May 11, 1968. Also, see, Richard Warren Lewis, October 19, 1968. Burt Prelutsky, "The Making Of A Cop," July 5, 1969. Also, see, Burt Prelutsky, *Ibid.*, September 20, 1969. Joseph Paul Kimble, "The Good Cop," June 26, 1971. Arnold Hano, "She's On Hand To Provide The Basic Femininity," June 17, 1972. Dick Adler article, July 22, 1972. Hec Ramsey, *TV Guide*, September 9, 1972. Bill Davidson, "Law And Order's Peter Pan," August 4, 1973. Richard Warren Lewis, "Saturday Night Celebrity," August 3 - 9, 1974. "Sierra," September 12, 1974. Bill O'Hallaren, "Let's Try Plasma," August 16 - 22, 1975. "Mobile One," *TV Guide*, September 6, 1975. "This One's On The House," February 11, 1978. Robert MacKenzie, "Review" Of "Project UFO," April 15, 1978. Dick Russell, "They Fly In The Face Of Logic," June 10, 1978. Copy of September 19, 1992.

"Genius At Work — Jack Webb," *TV Illustrated*, March 1956.

"Super - Sleuth," *TV Star Parade*, March 1953.

Helen Gould, "Jack Webb Talks About Women," *TV Star Parade*, August 1954.

.

Newspapers, Yearbooks, Etc.
(Listed chronologically)

"High Rating Wins Coveted Scholastic Distinction," *Los Angeles Times*, December 22, 1937.

Belmont Life, January 1938.

Belmont Sentinel, November 25, 1936, February 25, 1938. March 11, 1938.

New York Herald, June 13, 1949.

George Pollard, *Jack Webb's Safety Squad Coloring Book*. Kenosha, Wisconsin: Abbott Publishing Company, 1955.

TSgt. Robert A. Suhosky, "The D.I.," *Leatherneck* Magazine, June 1957.

Made To Order For Marine 'D.I.' Role," *Dallas News*, July 29, 1957.

Los Angeles Herald-Examiner, Pictorial Living, Week of January 27, 1963.

Don Page, "Dragnet 66 To Be More Than 'Just The Facts, Ma'am.'" *Los Angeles Times*, March 1966.

Hollywood Reporter, March 17, 1966.

Richard C. Neuweiler, *New York Times,* January 8, 1967.

Sally Hammond, "Martin Milner And The Realities," *New York Post*, October 26, 1968, Section 3 Television.

Morton Moss, "Julie London Stars In Emergency, *Los Angeles Herald Examiner TV Weekly*, June 16, 1974.

"People," *New York Daily News*, May 11, 1976.

Ginny Weissman, "It's Randolph Mantooth and Kevin Tighe In An 'Emergency,'" *Chicago Tribune TV Week*, April 10-16, 1977.

"Sgt. Holmes Recalls Jack Webb," *Huntsville [Alabama] News*, December 24, 1982.

Eric Malnic, "Jack Webb, Sgt. Friday Of TV Dies," *Los Angeles Times*, December 24, 1982.

Jack Hawn, "Jack Webb. An Original," *Los Angeles Times*, December 28, 1982.

Rex Miller, "Just The Facts,

Ma'am." About Sergeant Friday & Sergeant Preston," *The Antique Trader Weekly*, February 2, 1994.

National Enquirer, November 12, 1996.

"The 4th Annual Jack Webb Awards," *Beverly Hills Courier*, October 17, 1997.

Chris Rodell, "'Dragnet' Widow to Ken Starr: You're No Joe Friday!" *National Enquirer*, May 5, 1998.

Myrna Oliver, "Obituaries," *Los Angeles Times*, May 5, 1999. Lieutenant Dan Cooke.

Miscellany

Roster And Detachment Order Number 229. Headquarters Aviation Cadet Detachment, 4th AAF Flying Training Detachment Office Of The Commandant Of Cadets. Tulare, California, November 1, 1943.

Correspondence with the Los Angeles Unified School District, January 5, 1996.

Military discharge of Private Jack R. Webb, Army of the United States. National Personnel Records Center, St. Louis, Missouri, September 5, 1995.

"Rank'n File." Published in the Interest of the Aviation Cadets, Rankin Aeronautical Academy, Tulare, California. No date.

"The Hall Of Fame" — Academy Of Television Arts & Sciences Hall Of Fame Magazine. Published by Hank Rieger, 1993. A publication only available to those attending the Hall Of Fame induction ceremonies, Disney World, Florida.

"Los Angeles Police Beat," April 1967.

"Hundreds Honor Police Inspector Ed Walker At PC Dinner," *The Eight Ball*, April 1967.

Correspondence of Los Angeles Chief of Police Thomas Reddin to Howard R. Leary, Commissioner of Police, New York, New York, August 28, 1968.

Correspondence of Jack Webb to Peggy Webber, September 12, 1951.

Information Section Marine Corps Recruit Depot, San Diego 40, California, Release Number 1357, February 8, 1957.

From Director of Information to Commandant of the Marine Corps, "The D.I.," Office Memorandum, November 9, 1956.

Shooting Final "The D.I." Mark VII Ltd. for Warner Brothers Release, February 4, 1957.

Correspondence of Donald E. Baruch, Chief, Motion Picture Section, Office of the Assistant Secretary of Defense, Department of Defense, to Mr. Jack Webb, February 14, 1957. Approval of "The D.I." script. *Ibid.*, February 14, 1957. *Ibid.*, April 19, 1957, the U. S. Marine Corps approves of release of "The D.I."

Correspondence of Mr. Donald E. Baruch, Chief, Motion Picture Section, Office of the Assistant Secretary of Defense, Department of Defense,to Mr. George Dorsey, Warner Brothers Pictures, November 16, 1956. Approval of "The Death Of A Sand Flea" production.

Jack Webb correspondence to Major William McCullough, U. S. Marine Corps Division of Information, headquarters U. S. Marine Corps, Washington, D. C., February 8, 1957. Submission of final "The D.I." script to the Marine Corps.

Report of Lieutenant Colonel Wyatt B. Carneal, USMC to Colonel H. D. South, Headquarters Marine Corps, April 2, 1957. Production of "The D.I." *Ibid.* to Commandant of the Marine Corps, April 2, 1957. Regards history of the Marine participation in filming "The D.I."

August 28, 1968 correspondence of Los Angeles Chief of Police Thomas Reddin to Howard R. Leary, Commissioner of Police, New York, New York, concerning visit of *Adam-12* stars Martin Milner and Kent McCord.

Jack Webb: The Christmas Story, RCA Victor LPM 3199 jacket cover.

Michael Burns Career File.

Charlton Comics *Emergency!* June 1, 1976. First issue.

A Memorial Tribute To Jack Webb, December 30, 1982, Los Angeles Police Academy.

Patrick Lucanio, Sperdvac Radiogram, (June 1999).

INDEX

The Authors

DAN MOYER has devoted many years researching Jack Webb's life. He and Stacy Webb pursued their extensive research together and remained best friends, until an automobile accident tragically claimed Stacy's life. Moyer is also a musician and singer who portrays John Lennon in an authentic recreation of "The Beatles," called "Backbeat ... A Tribute." He enjoys acting, filmmaking, and songwriting. He holds an Engineering degree.

EUGENE ALVAREZ, PH.D., received his doctorate from the University of Georgia and retired Professor Emeritus from Macon State College, University System of Georgia. The former Marine Korean War veteran, and Parris Island Drill Instructor, has published several books and numerous magazine and journal articles. Gene currently lives in Georgia, where he pursues his writing and research.